Gay Affirmative Therapy
for the Straight Clinician

Gay Affirmative Therapy for the Straight Clinician

The Essential Guide

Joe Kort

W. W. Norton & Company, Inc.
New York • London

For information about permission to reproduce selections from this book, write to
Permissions, W. W. Norton & Company, Inc., 500 Fifth Avenue, New York, NY 10110

For information about special discounts for bulk purchases, please contact
W. W. Norton Special Sales at specialsales@wwnorton.com or 800-233-4830.

Manufacturing by Courier Westford
Production Manger: Devon Zahn

Library of Congress Cataloging-in-Publication Data

Kort, Joe.
Gay affirmative therapy for the straight clinician : the essential guide / Joe Kort.—1st ed.
p. ; cm.
"A Norton Professional Book."
Includes bibliographical references and index.
ISBN 978-0-393-70497-6 (hardcover)
1. Gays—Mental health. 2. Lesbians—Mental health. 3. Homosexuality—
Psychological aspects. 4. Psychotherapy. I. Title. [DNLM: 1. Homosexuality—psychology. 2.
Psychotherapy—methods. 3. Professional-Patient Relations. WM 420 K85g 2008]

RC451.4.G39K67 2008
616.890086'64—dc22
2007029106

W. W. Norton & Company, Inc., 500 Fifth Avenue, New York, N.Y. 10110
www.wwnorton.com

W. W. Norton & Company Ltd., Castle House, 75/76 Wells St., London W1T 3QT

1 3 5 7 9 8 6 4 2 0

This book is dedicated to the memory of my dog, Maud (1995–2007), who taught me to rest, play, and especially, to become more alpha!

Contents

Acknowledgments

First and foremost I want to thank my partner of 15 years, Mike Cramer. You are my good luck charm. Ever since we met my life has totally changed for the better and has continued to get better ever since. You encouraged me to write and follow my dreams. I cannot imagine any other partner being as supportive as you have been of a partner like me who is so driven to get the words and message out about the lives of gays and lesbians. I appreciate your encouragement, support, and love for my dreams—without them I am not sure I could have done as much. I love you.

Next, I don't know where I would be without the mutual love and respect of my sister and best friend Lisa Kort-Jaisinghani, her husband Raj, and their children Jacob, Zack, Noah, and Zoe. I never knew how much better the world looks through the eyes of a child. Thank you for gifting me with them and giving me the opportunity to have them so close to me in my life. Your children help me remember my life as a child and all that I missed. They are showing me that it is never too late to have a happy childhood as I go through theirs with them. I love you all!

To Lynn Grodzki, MSW, my private practice and business coach, who has believed in me and my words and helped me maintain my private practice and write at the same time. You have been very meaningful to me as a coach and human being.

To Barb Shumard, MSW, who has been both a supervisor and therapist to me, guiding me to the highest integrity in working with all my clients.

To Tam Mossman, Roberta Israeloff, and Casey Ruble, who worked with me so hard and diligently to help me edit and organize each chapter every step of the way. All of you helped keep my voice, tone, and manner in my written words. Thank you for helping take care of my words and seeing the importance of this book.

To Deborah Malmud and the W. W. Norton staff for accepting the idea of a book like this for straight clinicians and seeing the need for them to have this as a reference when working with lesbians and gays.

To all the clients I have worked with, who have touched my life professionally and personally. You have made me a better therapist as I have learned from each and every one of you.

To every straight therapist who took my trainings and classes and encouraged me to write a book for them. Your support and encouragement of my work is invaluable.

For more information about my workshops, therapy, trainings, supervision, and coaching services, go to www.joekort.com, which provides regular updates and online newsletters.

Gay Affirmative Therapy
for the Straight Clinician

CHAPTER 1

Psychotherapy for Lesbians and Gays: Setting the Gay Record—Straight!

Q: *How many therapists does it take*
   to change a light bulb?
A: *Only one. But the light bulb has to*
   want to change!

Historically, lesbians and gays were told that their only salvation was to seek good psychotherapy and that they really had to *want* to change. If they weren't highly motivated, they were told, psychotherapy would fail, condemning them to a life plagued by depression that would ultimately end in suicide.

Modern attitudes toward homosexuality, including those in psychotherapy, have religious, legal, and medical underpinnings, and prejudice and misinformation have prevailed over accurate information (Ritter & Terndrup, 2002). The past offers a sad litany of ineffective, wrong-headed treatment for homosexuality, right up to the present-day reparative therapy and sexual reorientation camps. Every such "cure" is based on some faulty etiology, yet the debate of nature versus nurture still rages with regard to the "origins" of homosexuality.

Given this history of pathologizing homosexuality, lesbian and gay clients are often understandably wary of psychotherapy and fear hiring a therapist who won't be objective about their gayness. Many seek out lesbian or gay therapists, but this isn't necessarily the best step. It's no guarantee that they won't still receive doses of homophobia and heterosexism, as lesbian or gay therapists can harbor negative thoughts about gay culture in general, even when they are comfortable with being gay themselves. It is therefore crucial that straight clinicians know and understand the history of psychotherapy for lesbians and gays. It is also important to remember that, like other clients, most lesbian and gay clients seek therapy for help in dealing with their presenting problems—they don't want to be bothered with what you might do or feel about their homosexuality.

Even young lesbian and gay clients who have not been directly exposed to the harmful effects of psychotherapeutic treatment for homosexuality are still well aware of the historical record. Furthermore, because of societal homophobia, straight therapists may receive negative transference just for being straight. It was, after all, heterosexist straight therapists who pathologized homosexuality as an alternative negative lifestyle.

Although the psychotherapy field has changed dramatically in its attitudes toward homosexuality over the past 50 years, homophobic therapists are still around, often treating patients while keeping their homophobia closeted. Many of these therapists are involved in "reparative" therapy—also known as "sexual reorientation" therapy. This chapter is geared toward helping straight clinicians treat clients who have directly experienced homophobia from psychotherapists who still use outdated modes of psychotherapy. The more you know and can show you know about gay history and gay affirmative therapy (GAT), as well as gay affirmative living, the more you will gain the trust of your lesbian and gay clients and be able to help them effectively.

Nature or Nurture?

To date, there is no scientific evidence suggesting that homosexuality is either innate or learned. However, science seems to be on the side of biology, where it is probable that hormones and genes play a large role.

Research has indicated that sexual orientation may be related to maternal stress during pregnancy, to high or low prenatal sex hormone levels (either estrogen or testosterone), to an extra gene, to a smaller or larger hypothalamus, and even to different sizes of various sections of the brain (Wilson & Rahman, 2005). There is also growing evidence that the more male children a woman has, the higher the likelihood she will have a gay son. This is attributed to hormones. The best books on this topic are *Born Gay: The Psychobiology of Sex Orientation* (Wilson & Rahman, 2005) and *Gay, Straight, and In-Between* (Money, 1988). Clearly, more research is needed if we are to fully understand the impact of biology on sexual orientation.

Traditionally, psychology viewed homosexuality as a "stage" toward the natural, eventual goal of heterosexuality. There is still a widely held belief among psychologists, social workers, and counselors that homosexuality is just "straight gone bad" and that it is a behavior rather than a true orientation. The belief is that gay individuals didn't make it out of childhood or adolescence successfully. They are developmentally stalled and somehow damaged, like a moth whose wings did not open fully when it emerged from its cocoon. This theory leads many psychotherapists to believe that in adolescence, young men and women get a second chance to "repair" their homosexuality. But trying to "repair" something that is not broken does an untold amount of damage to these young people's lives.

During one's teen years, experimenting with homosexual (and heterosexual) behavior is commonplace. Boys may engage in "circle jerks" or perform fellatio on one another, and girls may digitally masturbate each other or kiss. Gay and lesbian teens experiment both homosexually and heterosexually as well. This is where some of the controversy lies.

The heterosexist perspective viewed homosexual behavior as simply experimentation, because heterosexuality was seen as the natural ending for everyone. Thus, lesbians and gays were viewed as being developmentally stunted at the experimental stage and were accused of being confused, misguided heterosexuals acting out homosexually. Gay affirmative therapy, on the other hand, views homosexuality as the *natural culmination* of a sexual identity—a sexual and romantic development—not as experimentation only.

Psychologists also used to believe that overprotective mothers and absent, distant fathers "made" their sons gay. But these parental attitudes are a reaction rather than a cause. If a mother senses that her infant is "different," she might react by being more protective of him, whereas the father may distance himself from his gay son. A similar impulse to blame the parents occurred with early hypotheses about the causes of schizophrenia. Mothers of schizophrenic adolescents and young adults typically showed little or no signs of attachment, leading psychologists to assume that these "refrigerator moms" were the root of the problem. Subsequent neurobiological research, of course, vindicated these mothers, who were simply reacting to their children's inability to bond with them.

Now that we are more than certain that family constellations do not make a child gay or lesbian, we must begin the task of cleaning up the mess that therapy has left. The psychotherapy ghosts of the past still haunt the therapy sessions of today, and clients can be equally vulnerable to archaic thinking and outdated myths that may keep them closeted.

The Case of Ellen

When 16-year-old Ellen came out to her parents, they made an appointment with a straight therapist, Sarah, to discuss ways of helping Ellen to be heterosexual. Ellen's parents did not believe that their daughter could know that she was a lesbian at such a young age, and they felt guilty that their parenting had somehow made her think she was a lesbian. Ellen's parents were in their late forties and had heard that it was the parents that caused the child to be homosexual. Their church had reaffirmed this belief and had told them to pray for their daughter and try to persuade her to seek reparative therapy.

Sarah explained to the parents that current information showed that family constellations do not make a child gay or lesbian, but the parents were not convinced. They still believed it was something they did, and they insisted that Ellen was too young to know whether she was a lesbian.

Sarah could see the problem. If Ellen's mother and father believed that homosexuality was caused by parenting, accepting Ellen's sexual orientation would automatically make them "bad parents." Sarah suggested that if their daughter said she was lesbian, it was to their advantage to take her word for it. She explained that their feelings of accountability made sense given what they had been told throughout their lives, but she also gently told them that the problem was not with Sarah but rather with *them* and their unwillingness to accept their daughter. She followed this by giving them the titles of several current books and referred them to organizations where families of lesbians and gays meet and support one another.

My Own Therapy

As a 15-year-old in 1978, I met with a psychoanalytic therapist who strongly believed that "homosexual tendencies" resulted from a dominant, smothering mother and a distant, mostly absent father. His theory (shared by most others at the time) was that poor parenting structure could vandalize a young heterosexual toddler and that if homosexuality was not corrected there, it could be corrected during adolescence.

We always argued about whether I was gay. He believed it wasn't my true orientation; I knew it was—and that I could not change, try as I might. To me, however, he was a "doctor," an authority figure. So I tried dating a girl named Laurie. While she taught me to French kiss, I fantasized that she was Billy, a boy in my class whom I was in love with.

I did everything my therapist asked. I tried to establish a stronger relationship with my father. I made efforts to distance myself from my mother. The truth was that my mother had already been doing this for me throughout my life by putting me in situations with other males—mostly through sports—to make a "man" out of me. However, I hated it all. It was not the type of male I knew I was.

Although my therapist's efforts did not make me heterosexual, his encouragement of my being open and frank about my homosexuality helped me grow more comfortable talking about it—and for that I'm grateful. He'd ask me for details of my sexual and romantic interest in boys, and I'd talk to him about it—twice a week, for 3 years. Without his insistence that I talk candidly about my homosexuality and my persistence in getting what I want out of life, I couldn't have come out at as young an age as I did.

Pathologizing Homosexuality: An Overview

The pathologizing of homosexuality in psychiatry and psychology can be traced back to religious edicts and beliefs, which were eventually incorporated into legal sanctions, including stiff criminal penalties for sodomy (Silverstein, 1991). Before the 19th century, neither medicine nor psychiatry universally viewed homosexuality as pathology, but by the end of the 1800s, these disciplines were effectively competing with religion and the law for jurisdiction over sexuality (Herek, 2006a). As a consequence, discourse about homosexuality expanded from the realms of sin and crime to include that of pathology.

Many people believe that it was Freud who related homosexuality with psychopathology. This is not true. It was Freud's followers who interpreted his studies of homosexuality as indicating pathology. I first learned about this in Kenneth Lewes's (1988) *The Psychoanalytic Theory of Male Homosexuality*. Lewes wrote that Freud seemed to have been undecided on the relationship between homosexuality and psychopathology and that much of what is attributed to Freud's thinking is taken out of context. Lewes found in his research that " . . . Freud's own attitude toward homosexuality included a profound respect for the achievements of homosexuals as well as an interest in the way homosexuality threw a new light on more usual behaviors and orientations taken for granted" (p. 34).

Dr. Gregory Herek, a professor of psychology at the University of California at Davis and an authority on prejudice against lesbians and gay men, hate crimes and antigay violence, and AIDS-related stigma, wrote that Freud's basic theory of human sexuality was that all human beings are innately bisexual, and that they become heterosexual or homosexual as a result of their experiences with parents and others (Herek, 2006a). Unlike many who tout the "nurture" explanation of homosexuality, however, Freud believed that a homosexual orientation should not be viewed as a form of pathology. In a now-famous letter to an American mother in 1935, Freud wrote:

> Homosexuality is assuredly no advantage, but it is nothing to be ashamed of, no vice, no degradation, it cannot be classified as an illness; we con-

sider it to be a variation of the sexual function produced by a certain arrest of sexual development. Many highly respectable individuals of ancient and modern times have been homosexuals, several of the greatest men among them (Plato, Michelangelo, Leonardo da Vinci, etc.). It is a great injustice to persecute homosexuality as a crime, and cruelty too. . . .

If [your son] is unhappy, neurotic, torn by conflicts, inhibited in his social life, analysis may bring him harmony, peace of mind, full efficiency whether he remains a homosexual or gets changed. (Jones, 1957, pp. 208–209)

"Advances" in Psychotherapy

It was Freud's psychoanalytic followers, not Freud himself, who expounded on the homonegativity they interpreted from his writings (Lewes, 1988). Some analysts argued that homosexuality resulted from pathological family relationships during the oedipal period (around 4 to 5 years of age) and claimed that they observed these patterns in their homosexual patients. Dr. Bieber (Bieber et al., 1962) is known for contributing to the myth that male homosexuals are a result of "detached fathers and close binding, intimate mothers." In a 1962 research study, he used a 500-item questionnaire to query 106 male homosexuals, with a comparison group of 100 male heterosexuals (Bieber et al., 1962). He believed the outcome proved that family constellation caused homosexuality.

In the documentary film *One Nation Under God* (Maniaci & Rzeznik, 2004), there is a black-and-white clip of the antigay Dr. Bieber talking to a class of psychiatry students in the 1960s. A student asks him if there is such a thing as a "happy homosexual." The good doctor responds by saying, "An *obligatory* homosexual can never be happy, so there is no such thing as a 'happy homosexual.'"

Another analyst practicing during the 1960s, Charles Socarides, speculated that the etiology of homosexuality was preoedipal and, therefore, even more pathological than had been supposed by earlier analysts (Drescher, 1996). Socarides also espoused the notion that family-of-origin dynamics produced homosexuality, as he noted in his 1968 book *The Overt Homosexual*: "The family of the homosexual is usually a female-dominated environment wherein the father was absent, weak, detached or sadistic. This furthers feminine identification. The father's inaccessibility to the boy contributed to the difficulty in making a masculine identification" (quoted in Drescher, 1996, pp. 158–159; Socarides, 1968, p. 38). (In an interesting, later turn of events, Charles Socarides's son became an openly gay activist in gay and lesbian rights. I wonder what kind of father Socarides would now portray himself as!)

Another contributing factor to the pathologizing of homosexuality was that psychological studies only examined homosexuals who were *already* under psychiatric care. Patients, however, are not necessarily representative of well-adjusted individuals in the general population. Just as it would be inappropriate to draw conclusions about all heterosexuals based only on data from heterosexual psychiatric patients, we cannot generalize from observations of homosexual patients to the entire population of gay men and lesbians.

It is also important to note that although psychoanalytic theories of homosexuality have had considerable influence in psychiatry and in the larger culture, they have not been subjected to rigorous empirical testing (Herek, 2006a). Instead, they have been based on analysts' clinical observations of patients already known by them to be homosexual. Overall, it seems that the negative framing of homosexuality by the mental health field has been the result of theoretical orientations, expectations, and personal attitudes that biased clinicians' observations of gay and lesbian clients (Gould, 1995).

Given the homophobia and prejudice throughout the 20th century, it is not surprising that gay and lesbian professionals in social work, psychology, psychiatry, and other mental health fields worried about exposure and losing their jobs. Many who were closeted stayed away from out lesbian and gay professionals, who were growing in numbers by the late 1960s. As Silverstein (1991) noted in *Gays, Lesbians, and Their Therapists*, a handful of brave gay and lesbian psychotherapists were essentially banned from employment and psychoanalytic training. Many of these clinicians applied to and were accepted by programs in Gestalt training, which was a more radical approach for therapy at the time and more liberal in admitting therapists (Silverstein, 1991).

Historic Treatment of Homosexuality

Historically, the most common treatments for homosexuality were aversion therapies such as electroshock treatments (ECT), castration, hysterectomy, clitoridectomy, lobotomy, and various drug and hormone therapies (especially on women). Sometimes drugs were used to induce vomiting while patients were shown images of members of the same sex in various states of disrobement. Other treatments involved showing pictures of partly unclothed individuals of both sexes and applying shock therapy when the patient chose the "wrong" picture (i.e., that of the individual of the same gender as the patient). The aim was to get asexual or heterosexual orientation as a means to relieve the homosexual orientation.

These are just a few examples of the brutality of the various treatments employed to cure homosexuality. For a more in-depth look at these treatments, see Martin

Duberman's *Cures: A Gay Man's Odyssey* (Duberman, 1991) and the previously mentioned documentary *One Nation Under God.*

Changing Views

A few people and events have been responsible for the changing views in the field of mental health as it relates to homosexuality. Those individuals who made the most change did not have a bias but more of a heuristic approach to understanding homosexuality. Perhaps the biggest force for change toward viewing homosexuality as a healthy lifestyle came from lesbians and gays themselves, who broke the silence and began sharing their lives and pointing out that most were not in therapy and had developed happy, healthy lives, adjusting well to their sexual and romantic orientation.

Alfred Kinsey

Dr. Alfred C. Kinsey, a pioneering researcher on sexual orientation, originator of the "Kinsey Scale," and subject of the 2004 film *Kinsey*, suggested that most people's sexual behavior exists on a continuum from heterosexuality to homosexuality. Up to the time of his research in the late 1940s, much of the antigay prejudice and misinformation was targeted against males. Kinsey's books, on the other hand, included information about females (Kinsey, Pomeroy, Martin, & Gebhard, 1953). Kinsey and his colleagues reported that 10% of the males in their sample and 2 to 6% of the females (depending on marital status) had been more or less exclusively homosexual in their behavior for at least 3 years between the ages of 16 and 55 (Kinsey, Pomery, & Martin, 1948). This research situated sexuality on a more normative level and helped pave the way for dismantling myths about homosexuality.

Evelyn Hooker

Evelyn Hooker's well-known 1957 study suggested that homosexuality as a clinical entity does not exist and that homosexuality is not inherently associated with psychopathology (Hooker, 1957). Rather than simply accepting the predominant view of homosexuality as pathology, Hooker posed the question of whether homosexuals and heterosexuals differed in their psychological adjustment. She recruited a sample of homosexual men who were functioning normally in society rather than studying psychiatric patients, and she employed a procedure that asked experts to rate the adjustment of men without prior knowledge of their sexual orientation.

This method addressed an important source of bias that had vitiated many previous studies of homosexuality. Hooker ultimately found that, in terms of psychological adjustment, you could not tell the difference between men who were homosexual and men who were heterosexual.

Stonewall

Another important development contributing to the depathologizing of homosexuality was the event known as Stonewall. Stonewall was a gay bar in New York City's Greenwich Village. Like many other gay bars across the United States, Stonewall was frequently raided by police, who arrested and accused patrons of lewd conduct. These bars would be shut down for serving alcohol without a liquor license. But one night in 1969 during a routine raid, the patrons of Stonewall rioted against the police, protesting their being arrested for doing nothing wrong. There are many stories and fables about what happened that night at Stonewall, and it has continued as an enduring marker of advances in gay and lesbian civil rights. (The best overview and compilation of accounts from sources who were there is the 1993 book *Stonewall* by Martin Duberman.) Much of gay and lesbian life is talked about in terms of "before" and "after" Stonewall. It remains a landmark symbolizing the point at which gays and lesbians declared, "We are not going to take it anymore!"

The DSM and Homosexuality

In 1973, the weight of empirical data, coupled by changing social norms, led the board of directors of the American Psychiatric Association to remove homosexuality from the *Diagnostic and Statistical Manual of Mental Disorders* (*DSM*). In 1980, in the third edition of the *DSM*, the term *ego-dystonic homosexual* was created to describe clients who are uncomfortable or in conflict with their homosexuality and want to change their orientation (*DSM-III*, 1980). Typically, the client would report that homosexual urges were interfering with his or her life and that a lack of heterosexual arousal interfered with the client's desired lifestyle. The opposite term, *ego-syntonic homosexuality*, was used to acknowledge the significant numbers of gays and lesbians who were quite satisfied with their sexual and romantic orientation and showed no signs of psychopathology.

Ego-dystonic homosexuality remained in the *DSM-III* until 1987, when the manual was revised as *DSM III-R*. The board concluded that *all* gays and lesbians start out as ego-dystonic (that is, uncomfortable with their orientation), but upon fully coming out, they become ego-syntonic. The APA thus voted "to urge its members to stop using the '302.00 Ego-dystonic homosexuality' diagnosis in the current *DSM-III* or future editions of either document" (*DSM-III-R*, 1987).

The present *DSM-IV* (1994) doesn't include homosexuality as a disorder but still permits a diagnosis of "Sexual Disorder, Not Otherwise Specified" for anyone with "persistent and marked distress about sexual orientation"—the same diagnosis used for sexual addiction and compulsivity.

As a social worker and a gay man I knew that in 1973 homosexuality was removed as a disorder from the *DSM*. What I did not know was that gay political pressure did *not* play a role in the APA's decision to have it removed, a myth that was popularized by antigay therapists Irving Bieber and Charles Socarides. In reality the decision was "influenced by the weight of scientific studies" and put into effect by a vote by the APA board of trustees with two abstentions (Drescher & Merlino, 2007).

Today's Psychoanalysts

Psychoanalysts today have changed a great deal. Author and psychiatrist Richard Isay helped make it possible in 1991 for openly gay men and women to be accepted into analytic institutes (Drescher & Merlino, 2007). Isay's books, *Becoming Gay* and *Being Homosexual,* had a profound effect in advancing analytic circles to embrace gay and lesbian analysts and clients.

The approach to treating lesbian and gay clients has changed as well. I have noticed over the past few years an outreach from the psychoanalytic community to show gays and lesbians that they no longer consider homosexuality a disorder. It may take a while to get the message out, as much suffering and anger still persists from the damage done to victims of psychoanalytic training. Many who felt abused by psychoanalysis went to other, more accepting therapeutic approaches such as gestalt and humanistic therapies. Some, however, did not, as in the case of Rob.

The Case of Rob

Rob, a heterosexually married, 55-year-old schoolteacher with four children, spent 20 years with an orthodox psychoanalyst. During sessions, Rob laid on a couch behind his analyst, who worked to help him not give in to his "pathologic" homosexual tendencies. Rob was closeted to everyone but himself—and his analyst.

Rob terminated his psychoanalysis and met with a new, humanistic therapist,

Sally, shortly after a session in which the psychoanalyst made a startling comment. "After 20 years," Rob told Sally, "my analyst turns around and we face each other. With grief in his eyes and sadness on his face, my analyst has the nerve to say to me, 'I am sorry, Rob. I have been wrong. You are gay and I have done you a disservice trying to make you straight. You are not heterosexual. I believe you are gay.'"

"What was I supposed to do with that?!" Rob asked Sally, with anger in his voice. "I knew he couldn't change me—I told him that the day we met! But I wanted to believe him and I wanted to be changed."

The following few months of therapy with Sally were difficult for Rob. He missed the language and free-associating of psychoanalysis, and he was not used to being directed or coached by a therapist. When Rob began criticizing Sally, she responded by defending her approach and trying to educate him on humanistic psychotherapy, but this just made him even angrier.

Rob then began criticizing Sally about not being lesbian. "I think I need a gay therapist, but are they any good?" he asked. "How are they trained? Are there any analysts who can help me come out and not fight me on who I am?" Clearly Rob was angry, grieving, and placing negative transference onto Sally.

Sally contacted me for a referral and told me Rob had been difficult. She thought he might have borderline personality disorder because of his continuous anger and criticism of her and her work. I agreed to evaluate the client to see if I could work with him, but when Sally presented this option to Rob, he said he did not want to leave Sally completely. Instead, he agreed to attend my gay men's group therapy and continue to see Sally for individual therapy.

I set up an initial evaluation with Rob to make an assessment about a possible borderline diagnosis as I do not place personality disordered individuals in group therapy. Immediately upon sitting down in my office, Rob said to me, "You are 20 years younger than I am and look at you! You are an out gay man, you have a partner, a successful practice, and pride in who you are. I am older, closeted, and spent the best parts of my life—and a lot of money—trying to change who I am." He said he was not mad at Sally or me—he was mad at his analyst and angry about his lost years. He talked about his analyst's trying to be the "good father" but letting down just like his birth father had done. He wondered now if I was going to let him down too.

It was obvious that Rob had a tremendous amount of negative and positive transference toward me, but he did not seem to have any characterological disorders. We all agreed it was a good move to put him in the gay men's group and continue his seeing Sally. Sally and I both knew that his decision to continue seeing her was a way of keeping his foot in the door to heterosexuality, but neither of us acknowledged that to him, as we wanted to allow him to have that insight for himself.

Rob: Clinical Interpretation and Treatment

I quickly normalized Rob's anger about the lost years spent in analysis regarding his homosexuality. He was right that he could have been an out gay man much earlier had he not been in psychoanalysis. Although he was close to his four children and was grateful for them, he was not particularly fond of his wife.

He talked for months about nothing else but his past therapy and how he felt betrayed, misled, and manipulated. I helped the group relate to the homophobia and the trust they put in the hands of other professionals—and family—who wanted them to be gay. It took Rob a year before he felt that he could trust anyone in the group or even me. It took another year before he felt like he finally belonged.

Group therapy for Rob was about calling into question everything he learned in psychoanalysis and identifying what parts were good and helpful and what parts were not. This questioning caused much stress and duress for him. Rob also role played talking to his former therapist and telling him how angry he was. This took a while to get him to do; he minimized the efficacy of role playing as he had never done this before in therapy and saw it as contrary to therapy norms. Although the group and I encouraged him go back to his former therapist to talk to him face to face, Rob saw this as too tall a task. His anger and depression worsened as he thought about how he should come out and what it would do to his wife and now adult children.

I encouraged Rob to talk about how his family of origin had let him down as well. He talked about how his father made fun of him for being a "sissy" and a "mama's boy." For years, he had thought that this was what had made him gay, but he was beginning to realize that this was not true.

Rob began stating his jealousy, envy, and anger toward other group members, saying things like, "At least you have someone and a supportive family" and "Why are you complaining? You are young and have all this time to change your life!" I interpreted these comments for Rob as negative transference and helped him reflect back to himself what the comments meant. I created a safe place for the group to hear him and for him to be able to speak openly and honestly about the loss of time, opportunities, and experiences that he could have had as a younger gay man. His projections were that everyone's lives were better than his and he spent much of the time staying in the victim role.

Over time, however, Rob was able to get past his victimhood. He came to realize that he could come out and move forward in the time he had left. It was not easy, but he eventually told his wife he was gay and started his coming out process socially.

Today's Antigay Therapists and Therapies

There are still therapists today who view being gay as a disorder that needs to be changed or cured via so-called reparative therapy. Even though *all* the major mental health professions—the American Counseling Association, the American Psychiatric Association, the American Psychological Association, and the National Association of Social Workers—have gone on record that reparative therapy is unethical and should never be implemented, it is still being done.

Too many gay men and lesbians find themselves drawn to "reparative" therapies that supposedly will readmit them to heterosexuality, with all its privileges and status. Reparative therapies assume that gay men and lesbians aren't fully developed, that there's some inherent flaw in being gay. In my judgment, this is abuse—specifically covert cultural sexual abuse, a subject I address in Chapter 4.

Reparative therapy was developed in 1991 by Dr. Joseph Nicolosi, who still seeks to help clients change their sexual orientation. Nicolosi and his followers theorize that a "failure to fully gender-identify" with members of the same gender leads to a "deficit in sense of personal power, causing a homosexual identity (Nicolosi, 1997). Because reparative therapy views homosexuals as "sexually broken," Nicolosi purposefully avoids using affirmative words like *gay* and *lesbian*, which don't reflect the negative connotation that *homosexual* does.

The National Association for Research and Therapy of Homosexuality (NARTH), formed in 1992, claims considerable success in changing homosexual clients' orientation. NARTH's primary goal is to provide psychological therapy to all gay men and women who seek change (www.narth.com). Furthermore, they wish to open for public discussion all issues relating to homosexuality.

Those who go through these types of therapies and programs call themselves "ex-gays." In his book *Anything But Straight,* author Wayne Besen explained the histories of—and differences between—ex-gay groups like "Exodus," "Courage," and "Homosexuals Anonymous" (Besen, 2003). Each of these groups, along with reparative therapy, use religion as a primary form of healing. Exodus professes to "cure" homosexuals' broken sexuality and to help them become more male or female. Courage gives "the gift of chastity," according to Besen, and was founded by the Catholic Church. Homosexuals Anonymous (HA) was begun by a man named Colin Cook, who was inappropriately sexual with multiple participants of HA according to the members who attended his meetings. Colin was forced to leave his position. Today, Exodus and HA are the largest ex-gay groups in existence.

Reparative therapies hinge on several basic concepts, among them "same-sex ambivalence" and "gender rejection." Coined by reparative therapists, this terminology is "a veil that thinly disguises their contempt for same sex relationships" (Drescher, 1998, p. 170). "Same-sex ambivalence" is based on the erroneous belief that two people of the same gender are "looking for parenting through each other, yet they cannot provide parenting to each other, as they are both damaged" (Besen, 2003, p. 102). "Gender rejection" is about "defensive detachment" from one's gender, where "boys will avoid sports and girls will shun their femininity and embrace more masculine endeavors, such as fixing cars" (Besen, 2003, pp. 101–102).

Today's reparative therapists are getting savvier about what they call their work and the words they use to describe it. They are aware that the public is catching onto the fact that their work is disrespectful toward gays and lesbians. They now use terms like *sexual reorientation* or *same-sex attractions* rather than *ex-gays*. Some Christian psychotherapists, like Mark Yarhouse and Warren Throckmorton, have developed websites, created institutes, and written papers stating that psychotherapists have "an ethical responsibility to allow individuals to pursue treatment aimed at curbing experiences of same-sex attraction or modifying same-sex behaviors" (Yarhouse, 1998, pp. 248–259).

I actually don't totally disagree with Drs. Yarhouse and Throckmorton. You will read about cases in this book where gay and lesbian clients cannot adopt an affirmative gay or lesbian identity and do not choose or wish to live that way. I have helped many men and women who have a "homosexual" orientation but do not wish to adopt a gay or lesbian identity or lifestyle to live a heterosexual or asexual lifestyle. For them, coming out as lesbian or gay would mean more trauma. However, I do not believe that these individuals can—or do—change their innate sexual and romantic orientation. They simply change how they live and whom they love, just like a heterosexual could do if he or she so chose.

This is, of course, a complex and hotly debated issue, with people at one extreme declaring that there is no such thing as a "happy homosexual" and people at the other extreme insisting that homosexuality is the *only* right choice for gays and lesbians. I believe, however, that there are many shades of gray between these polarized views, which I hope this book illuminates.

Top 10 Myths About Lesbians and Gays

It is important to debunk the myths about what homosexuality is and is not so that you are aware of them and do not allow them to get in your way of your work with this population. Making the myths overt can help clinicians challenge personal beliefs that stem from what they learned early in their careers and even from childhood.

Myth #1. Being gay or lesbian results from stunted, immature sexuality. Any stunting that occurs in relation to being homosexual results from a lack of permission to explore and express one's true orientation. Beginning in childhood, the sexual development of lesbians and gays is neglected, and gay and lesbian children (and adults) receive numerous developmental insults (see Chapter 6). They are shamed for being what they are. What GAT asks is what is *wrong* with a boy's being effeminate or a girl's being tomboyish? Certain actions or appearances do not define masculinity or femininity. Also, this concept fails to take into account the fact that there are many heterosexuals who *are* sexually immature or stunted in their gender development.

Myth #2. Homosexuality is caused by a smothering, overprotective mother and an absent, emotionally distant father. As I noted earlier, a mother can tell very early on that there's something different about her child. She may become more protective of him to prevent any teasing and playground abuse. The father, sensing that his son might be gay, will distance himself, seldom knowing exactly how to react. One day, I believe, we will learn that children are biologically gay or lesbian and that a parent can only react to that sexual orientation, not create it.

Myth #3. Acquainting children with gays and lesbians and teaching them about homosexuality can make them gay. Perhaps one of the biggest myths is that a child can be swayed by a homosexual "role model." The main argument behind this myth is that gays and lesbians should not raise children, who will perhaps be influenced and "choose" a gay lifestyle.

Arguments to the contrary say that heterosexuality is not that fragile, and that children can handle knowledge and exposure to gays and lesbians. In fact, studies show that children of openly gay parents grow up more tolerant and accepting of differences. These children do experiment more with same-sex behaviors than those raised by heterosexual parents do, but their orientation remains stable in terms of what they are innately. The truth is that all children should be able to grow up exploring their own sexuality and learn for themselves what their sexual/romantic orientation is.

Myth #4. Being sexually abused in childhood can turn a person gay. Early sexual abuse can't shape orientation, but it can shape *behavior* and confuse individuals as to their real orientation. Adult males who abuse boys can cause so-called homosexual imprinting: When the boy grows up, he may reenact his own abuse by seeking out sex with other men. This is not innate homosexuality, as it is based only on behavior.

Women sexually abused at an early age by male perpetrators might seek out women for romantic and sexual relationships to avoid reexperiencing the trauma that was originally perpetrated onto them by men. For lesbians, this can spark an earlier awareness of an innate lesbian orientation, but it does not *create* that orientation: These women would be lesbian even if they had not been abused. Innately heterosexual women who were abused and later partner with women eventually return to relationships with men. There is a link between early sexual trauma and later sexual acting out, which can include same-sex behavior, but it has nothing to do with orientation. After psychotherapy helps clear away the trauma, the imprinted sexual behavior often subsides and the client's true orientation—gay or straight—can surface.

Myth #5. Homosexuality can be prevented or cured. No matter how gentle or loving a parent may be, trying to prevent or forestall homosexuality inevitably winds up harming a child, causing gender confusion or low self-esteem. In my office, countless gay men and lesbians have shed tears as they recalled how a parent took away their "inappropriate" toys or imposed stereotypical gender behaviors. As adults, lesbians and gays who engage in "reparative therapies" experience high rates of relapse and suffer a considerable amount of trauma due to these therapeutic approaches.

Fundamentalists and reparative therapists assert that no one is born homosexual. Heterosexism teaches that everyone is or should be heterosexual. GAT, on the other hand, assumes that we are all born with a certain sexual/romantic orientation, just as we are born with a given temperament. The truth is that everyone is born *sexual*, and what that means is discovered over time for each particular individual.

Myth #6. People can choose to change their orientation. People *can* choose to live as they wish, but orientation, like temperament, is stable. Children are born with a temperament and personality traits that can alter somewhat as they grow into adulthood. They can learn to modify and adapt to their environments, but their core temperament and personality stays largely within the same range.

The same is true of sexuality. People can mimic a heterosexual lifestyle, but they cannot change their true orientation. Study after study shows that for those who do try to change, the relapse rate is very high. Those who "succeeded" at changing were *not* essentially homosexual to begin with, but rather were either acting out past sexual abuse or were bisexual, tending more toward heterosexuality than homosexuality. Their basic orientation did not change.

This myth arises because of the seeming suddenness of the lesbian or gay individual's coming out of the closet. For the gay or lesbian, of course, making the decision to come out can take months or years, but to those who are hearing about their friend or family member's homosexuality for the first time, it seems like the person was straight one day and gay the next. Others then assume that people can change their orientation consciously. But if young people felt free to explore sexual and romantic orientations (which today's teenagers and young adults in college often do), they would not need to suppress their innate sexuality and could come out earlier rather than later.

Myth #7. Adolescence offers a "second chance" at heterosexuality. Many teens experiment during adolescence: Straight kids try out same-sex relationships, and gay kids try out the opposite sex. This is a normal part of the developmental process. But this investigation doesn't prove that teens are interested in converting to a new orientation. Each teenager ultimately discovers his or her true orientation if allowed to do so, no matter how much experimenting and exploring is done. Again, orientation is predetermined.

Myth #8. Homosexuality is merely sexual behavior. Being gay or lesbian is not limited simply to sexual behaviors. It is also about attraction and attachment—psychological, emotional, mental, and spiritual—to a member of one's own gender. For gay and straight alike, behavior follows from one's sexual and romantic orientation, which is based on emotions.

Myth #9. Homosexuality is an "alternative lifestyle." Calling homosexuality an "alternative" implies that being straight is standard for everyone. Since childhood, we are taught the negative belief that being gay is a more difficult way to live. But for gays and lesbians, pretending to be heterosexual is actually more difficult and can lead to depression and self-defeating or even self-destructive behavior.

Myth #10. Lesbian and gay relationships don't last. Gay and lesbian relationships do last and can endure—just like their heterosexual counterparts. There is less support for these relationships in terms of the law, religion, and sometimes family, which puts the relationships at risk. But just like healthy heterosexual relationships, healthy lesbian and gay relationships that are based on good communication, validation of the other, and respect for each other's differences can and do survive.

CHAPTER 2

What Is Gay Affirmative Therapy?

It is prejudice to be only gay friendly. You must be gay informed.
—Joe Kort

Many straight therapists who say they are "gay affirmative" mean that they are gay *positive* or gay *friendly*. They tell lesbian and gay clients things like, "I'm open-minded" and "People are people." These well-intentioned therapists are, indeed, accepting and pro-gay—but they're also uniformed. Even lesbian and gay therapists may be uninformed (Kort, 2004). Over the years, I've known well-meaning gay and lesbian colleagues and students who were unaware of the specific issues that gays and lesbians face. They've said they didn't realize there were stages to coming out, or that there were differences between gay and straight couples.

To be uninformed is a form of prejudice by omission. Having a healing, affirmative stance in the therapy room does help relieve some of the distorted thinking that most clients bring in, but having an affirmative stance *without* being informed about the specific issues that lesbians and gays experience limits your clinical effectiveness.

The first time the term *gay affirmative* was used was in an article by Alan Malyon (1982) in which he described the most complete definition of "gay affirmative therapy":

> Gay affirmative psychotherapy is not an independent system of psychotherapy. Rather, it represents a special range of psychological knowledge which challenges the traditional view that homosexual desire and fixed homosexual orientations are pathological. . . . This approach regards homophobia, as

opposed to homosexuality, as a major pathological variable in the development of certain symptomatic conditions. (pp. 68–69)

In essence, Malyon coined the term by giving a name to a concept already used in journals and books when explaining how to use psychotherapy techniques with lesbians and gays without stigmatizing them. The two books which were already published at the time were *Loving Someone Gay* by Donald Clark (2004) and Betty Berzon's *Positively Gay* (2001). These books advocated improving the lives of lesbians and gay men without regarding homosexuality as pathological. These two books were the first to advocate GAT for gays and lesbians without actually using the term.

GAT takes the position that there is nothing inherently wrong with being gay or lesbian. What's wrong is what is *done* to gay men and lesbians by a homophobic, homo-ignorant society and heterosexist therapy. Living in a shame-based culture creates a variety of behavioral and psychological disorders. GAT focuses on repairing the harm done to these clients, helping them move from shame to pride. GAT does not in itself constitute a specific system of psychotherapy but rather is meant to provide a framework that informs psychotherapeutic work with lesbian and gay clients (Downey & Friedman, 2002).

In and of itself, a homosexual orientation does not *create* disorders. Religions condemn gays and lesbians with no hope for salvation. Imagine believing your Higher Power is against you simply for being who you are at your core. Although it doesn't attack homosexuality overtly, the educational system remains silent on the topic, doing little to help gay and lesbian students who are picked on, bullied, and ignored. It is only by looking at the trauma done to them and by addressing the specific problems and post-traumatic stress they face that individuals can fully achieve a healthy self-esteem.

Gays and lesbians themselves often do not know the issues and facts, and you, as a therapist, need to inform them of the issues related to their being gay. Begin by dispelling the top ten most common myths about homosexuality outlined in Chapter 1.

The Fundamentals of Gay Affirmative Therapy

Providing clients with a corrective emotional experience is of utmost importance while examining the roots of issues that arise for gays and lesbians. Specifically, in many cases, their sexual identity development has been suppressed, and therapists need to know the negative psychological consequences of this.

As you do GAT, some fundamental principles operate. Many of the terms used here have political connotations, but the psychological consequences of these politics affect the work of the gay affirmative therapist.

Understanding and Combating Heterosexism

The concept of heterosexism is usually explored from political, social, and legal perspectives. It is the assumption that all people are (or should be) heterosexual—the belief that heterosexual is superior and homosexuality is inferior. Rights and privileges automatically granted to heterosexuals are denied to lesbians, bisexuals, and gays. The most egregious examples of heterosexism are that gays and lesbians cannot be legally married in most states, can be evicted from housing, can be legally terminated from their jobs, and cannot serve in the military.

The bias that everyone is heterosexual does psychological harm to the development of a gay or lesbian child (Rich, 1980). This book will not be looking at the politics of heterosexism as much as at the psychological consequences of heterosexism on lesbians and gays. This is explored further in Chapters 3 through 6.

Understanding Heterosexual Privilege

Heterosexism breeds heterosexual privilege, which—like any other unearned privilege—seems to operate largely unconsciously, with no malice. With heterosexual privilege come institutional, legal, and societal freedoms that are granted automatically.

- *Institutional freedoms.* Heterosexuals can be employed and housed without fearing termination or eviction because of their orientation. They are able to serve in the military and adopt children, and they are accepted in religious practices.
- *Legal freedoms.* Heterosexuals have the right to marry, which entails monetary advantages and federal protections such as tax breaks, the freedom to visit hospitalized spouses, and the right to claim custody of children after divorce.
- *Societal freedoms.* Heterosexuals can hold hands and kiss the ones they love without concerns for their physical safety or fear of harassment or negative judgments.

Heterosexual privilege teaches lesbians and gays that misleading others into thinking they are straight is the standard—indeed, the only—way to live. Honesty brings the threat of rejection, isolation, and even punishment. Your clients may experience some degree of grief from losing heterosexual privilege, and their expression of this grief can range from adjustment disorders to dysthymia to major depression.

The Case of Vicky

Vicky, a 35-year-old school counselor, entered therapy after she discovered she was lesbian, 6 months after having sexual feelings for—and then sex with—another woman. Vicky and her husband had three children under the age of 10, and prior to meeting this woman at her job, she had no idea that she was anything but straight, although her husband's "aggressive sexual urges" had always turned her off. She was married to her high school sweetheart, whom she loved with all her heart, and lived a mainstream life in a Detroit suburb. She considered her husband her best friend and enjoyed being a wife and mother, loved coaching her son and daughters in sports, and enjoyed the company of her neighbors. Devastated by the thought of losing all this, she entered therapy to fight her "urges" and return to the life that she'd enjoyed.

Vicky's first therapist could not understand why Vicky's depression kept worsening. She affirmed Vicky's sexuality and applauded her for coming out and finally grasping the true nature of her sexuality. Her husband was supportive, as were her family and friends. The therapist told Vicky that all the literature suggested that her staying closeted was the root of her depression. But this did not help Vicky's affect, and she continued spiraling down into an ever-deeper depression. The therapist put Vicky on antidepressant medication and sent her to support groups for coming out, but neither approach helped.

When the therapist came to me for supervision, I told her that Vicky was grieving the loss of the heterosexual privilege she had worked hard to establish. Vicky had achieved the straight woman's ideal—staying married to the first man she fell in love with. She still loved her husband, and everything was good except for the fact that she now knew she wasn't heterosexual.

Because Vicky didn't want to change anything in her life, she viewed her lesbianism as more of a problem than a positive discovery. She did not want to leave her family and lose everything. But Vicky was no longer able to be sexual with her husband, who had decided he couldn't stay married to a woman who was not able to be there for him "a hundred percent." Vicky also was worried about how she would be judged as a mother, and that the courts might not let her keep her children. Her husband reassured her that he would not do anything to stop the children from seeing her. But the worries kept piling up: Would she be fired from her job if the school discovered her sexual orientation? What would it be like to live with another woman? How would she be perceived by the other parents to whom she'd grown so close?

Her grieving process triggered depression and high levels of anxiety. It also activated post-traumatic stress disorder (PTSD), caused by Vicky's suppressing the conflict of growing up lesbian and hiding her same-sex attraction from everyone, including herself—a subject I address in Chapter 5.

Vicky's therapeutic work was to grieve the loss of what she and most everyone else take for granted—heterosexual privilege. Embracing her lesbianism was bittersweet, as it was a welcome piece of integrity to align who she was on the inside with who she was becoming on the outside. However, she loved her life and everything and everyone in it, and having to end the very things she worked so hard to nurture and love made her feel threatened and anxious.

Vicky's emotional response was realistic and she needed to be supported. Coming out of the closet was not enough for Vicky to feel better. Inside that closet were other closet doors that still needed to be opened.

Affirmation Versus Alienation

Marcia, a clinical therapist, received a phone call from Pam, a potential client, who identified herself as a lesbian. Pam wanted to come in concerning problems with her partner, Susan. But before she agreed to make an initial appointment, Pam asked Marcia about her own sexual orientation.

Marcia replied that she saw Pam's question as "a treatment issue," and that her own "sexual preferences" should not affect the sessions. She told Pam that if she came in, they could discuss it during the session. "I've worked with many homosexuals in the past," Marcia added. "To me, a couple is a couple." Pam reluctantly agreed to meet with her.

During the initial individual intake, Marcia referred to Pam as "gay" and asked her how long she and Susan had been "lovers." Pam replied, "Twenty years—much longer than most gay and lesbian relationships." Marcia commended her, agreeing. When Marcia inquired about Pam's sex life with Susan, she asked how often they had "intercourse." When Pam replied, "Never—I think we have Lesbian Bed Death," Marcia didn't know what the phrase meant, but she did feel that their lack of intercourse indicated a stunted and immature form of sexually relating to each other.

Later in the session, Pam asked if Marcia knew of any lesbian support groups for couples. Marcia responded that she did not provide resources to her clients and urged the two to seek out what they felt they needed. Most of her responses to Pam were deliberately reflective and mirroring, not offering much in an attempt to let Pam come to her own conclusions. This was Marcia's therapeutic style.

Over the next two sessions, while taking Pam's history from childhood, Marcia asked when Pam came out to her parents, but did not ask about Pam's childhood as a lesbian little girl. Pam recalled having crushes on other girls in first grade, but Marcia dismissed this as normal and natural, saying that "Children that young cannot know. They were most likely just feelings of closeness."

Pam had questions for Marcia as well: How long had she been in practice? How much of her caseload had been working with gays and lesbians? What was her approach in working with clients? Marcia did not respond to any of these questions, considering them in terms of therapeutic transference. She again placed the emphasis back on Pam: "What does it mean to you to know this?"

Pam thought that Marcia was being homophobic and heterosexist in her questions about her sexuality, and she confronted Marcia with this. "I am not antigay," Marcia responded. "I feel comfortable with gays and lesbians and am very gay friendly." She added that for Pam, this was a transference issue.

After four sessions Pam terminated therapy without explaining why. Marcia followed up with phone calls and a letter, but Pam did not respond.

As you can see, much is wrong with this scenario. Marcia meant well and was using much of psychodynamic theory and practice, but she made ten common errors in her therapeutic responses and orientation. These errors effectively alienated her client.

Error #1. Not disclosing your own sexual orientation when asked. A gay or lesbian client calling for an initial appointment may ask about your sexual and romantic orientation. Many therapists do not answer, believing that's a therapeutic question best left to the consulting room. It's true that this may be a therapeutic issue, but clients "shopping" with initial calls still want to know whom they're entering treatment with. Most gays and lesbians are well aware of the history of psychotherapeutic treatment for their sexual orientation, and they're sensitive not just to homophobia but also to ignorance and insensitivity. If you're not open about your own orientation, you may lose the referral.

Error #2. Denying your own homophobia and heterosexism. Marcia wasn't even willing to consider that she harbored any level of heterosexism, even covert, and dismissed Pam's concern as transference. Many therapists who genuinely like working with gays and lesbians still do not see their own homophobic countertransference simply because they feel so accepting of the population.

From childhood, we are all imprinted to be heterosexist, and denying this is a form of covert homophobia. If you don't check your countertransference when working with gays and lesbians, you will inadvertently collude with *their* internalized homophobia. For example, when Pam said that the number of years they'd been together was uncommon within the gay community, Marcia agreed, inadvertently supporting Pam's internalized homophobic belief that gay and lesbian partnerships do not last.

Asking if the women had "intercourse" was also a form of heterosexism. As I explain later, many gay and lesbian couples do not have intercourse, yet still consider themselves sexual and satisfied. Penetration is a heterosexist, patriarchal construct to which many couples—lesbians particularly—do not always aspire. On the other hand, to assume that two women only snuggle and never engage in intercourse is erroneous as well.

Error #3. Not offering resources for clients. Marcia admitted she did not know of any resources, locally or otherwise. Some therapists believe in keeping the therapy room completely neutral by not suggesting resources to clients. However, clients who have suffered prejudice and discrimination are at the mercy of what the popular media says about them. Often they feel isolated and need good, correct information about the challenges they need to face.

For these clients, one of the most important tasks is what I call *homosocialization*. The job of any gay affirmative therapist is to inform clients of the kind of resources that heterosexuals automatically know about through churches, schools, families, and the media. You might need to contact the local gay community center or go online to research what newsletters and gay newspapers are available in your area. And why not subscribe to a couple of them to offer to your clients?

Error #4. Using the wrong terminology. Terms like *sexual preference* and *alternative lifestyle* are no longer considered appropriate. *Preference* implies that sexuality is a choice—which it's not—and for gays and lesbians, heterosexuality is the "alternative" lifestyle. The correct term is *sexual and romantic orientation*.

Although the term *homosexuality* is still used, describing gays and lesbians as "homosexuals" is as offensive today as the words *Negro*, *colored*, or *crippled*. The correct words are *gays* and *lesbians* or the *GLBT (gay, lesbian, bisexual, and transgender) community*.

It's also vital that you ask how clients self-identify. Marcia referred to the couple as "gay," but some lesbians do not like to be referred to as gay—they prefer lesbian.

Error #5. Using heterosexist paperwork and intake forms. Your intake form should ask about sexual and romantic identity, and include *partner* and *significant other* in addition to *married* and *spouse*. Your new client paperwork should ask, "How do you self-identify?" for sexual/romantic orientation. Options should let the client self-identify as "heterosexual," "bisexual," "gay," "lesbian," "transgendered," or "questioning." In place of "marital status," ask whether the client has a partner and if so, ask the partner's first name. (This is also a good measure for being inclusive of straight couples living together.) If you are concerned that some straight clients might have a negative reaction to this, check out your own heterosexist attitudes and homophobia.

Error #6. Adopting a blank screen as a therapeutic style. In an attempt to stay neutral and not self-disclose, many therapists do not share personal information about themselves, but this is not helpful to gay and lesbian clients. In their daily life, these clients feel disconnected and are treated as outsiders. Being a neutral mirror to these clients can make them feel even more excluded and disenfranchised. In therapy, lesbian and gay clients who feel shut out by others need relational models. Appropriate self-disclosure by the therapist is not just therapeutic—it is essential.

Marcia could have easily revealed her sexual and romantic orientation and then explored whether there was a therapeutic issue behind the question, keeping in mind that there might not have been. She could have confirmed information about herself that her client had already gathered. These kinds of disclosures do not need to involve divulging extremely personal issues but rather can be limited to sharing understandings she might have arrived at as a woman and as a marriage partner. Such sharing would have helped Pam view her own relationship to Marcia in a more useful, authentic way.

A therapist's self-disclosure helps clients view the therapist "as a fellow human" (Zur, 2007). Citing research, Zur stated: "Self-disclosure that is in tune with clients' needs and personalities also reduces clients' sense of alienation" (p. 158). He reinforced that it is therapeutic to self-disclose with members of minority groups as well as those who are trauma survivors and suffering PTSD—all of which applies to gays and lesbians (see Chapters 4 and 5). This is why it is essential to offer some elements of self-disclosure to your gay and lesbian clients.

Error #7. Neglecting to recognize that your gay/lesbian clients were gay/lesbian since childhood. Your lesbian and gay clients were once gay and lesbian children. This insight makes most people (including clinicians)—uncomfortable: They do not like to think of children as being sexual. However, being gay does not equate to sexual behavior alone. Heterosexual adults were once heterosexual children. Although most gays and lesbians did not self-identify as such as children, they will tell you as adults that they knew they were different. How did they know? What made them feel different? Their answers are important in helping them in the consulting room.

Error #8. A waiting room devoid of gay and lesbian literature. Your waiting room says a lot about you as a therapist and how you treat clients. I have had therapists tell me that they want to keep their waiting rooms "neutral" and still keep magazines such as *Time* and *Newsweek* around. But the absence of gay-oriented magazines mirrors the neglect that your gay and lesbian clients have felt before walking in your door. Having literature, magazines, and newspapers aimed only at heterosexuals communicates the impression that you don't acknowledge—or at least don't welcome—any other clients. *The Advocate*, which is the *Time* and *Newsweek* for the gay culture, is a good publication to include in the waiting room. At the very least, have flyers for local gay-community and health-oriented services on your waiting room bulletin board to offer an immediate welcome.

Error #9. Believing that a "couple is a couple." I often hear well-intended therapists say that "a couple is a couple" in an effort to show that they are nonjudgmental. But gay and lesbian couples are very different from straight couples, with very different dynamics. The "doubling" factor—which you will read about in Chapter 10—intensifies the traditional gender role conditioning of both partners. Male couples are often disengaged, magnifying conflicts around restricted emotional expression, achievement, competitiveness, and sexual expression. Female couples are typically too engaged: They struggle with enmeshment, lack of differentiation, and sexual expression.

Error #10. Failing to assess your clients' stage of coming out and asking about their coming out process. Without knowing the stages of gay and lesbian identity development (see Chapter 7), clinicians can misunderstand certain thoughts and behaviors. For example, stage 5 (identity pride) resembles an adolescent stage of development—meaning that short-term relationships with some sexual promiscuity are to be expected and are developmentally appropriate. In stages 1 and 2, clients prefer to be identified as "homosexual," not as gay or lesbian. In GAT, the Cass Model of coming out is the most widely used (Cass, 1979). Asking clients how their coming out process went or is currently going will tell you where their strengths and weaknesses are developmentally. This is discussed further in Chapter 7.

Homophobia: The Client's and Yours

In the late 1960s, George Weinberg coined the term *homophobia* for "the feeling(s) of fear, hatred, disgust about attraction or love for members of one's own sex and therefore the hatred of those feelings in others" (Lorde, 1984, p. 45). The word first appeared in print in 1969 (Weinberg, 1983). Then, as now, many people, especially straight men, fear associating with lesbians and gays—physically, mentally, and emotionally—lest they be perceived as "one of them." Fears of venturing beyond accepted gender-roles can afflict even lesbians and gays.

Today, *homophobia* does not apply as it was originally defined, as it does not fit the definition of a true phobia: an uncontrollable, irrational, persistent fear of a specific object, situation, or activity. Use of the terms is more important today as a way to track in your clients and yourself attitudes that are homonegative, homoprejudiced, and homo-ignorant (Morrow, 2000). Ignorance is usually the most common of the three.

Homophobia, for example, can manifest for a straight therapist in the form of worry that potential and existing straight clients might perceive you as gay or lesbian yourself simply because you have gay clients or keep gay resource materials in your office.

I've seen such reactions firsthand. Several years ago, I decided to advertise my group therapy and weekend workshops for gay men by doing an unsolicited advertising mailing. Scanning phonebooks and newsletters, I compiled a list of about 500 local listings of gay and likely gay friendly businesses. I printed up a batch of one-page flyers, tri-folded them, and affixed a sticker to make sure they'd stay shut after I mailed them. I figured that if recipients were not interested, would simply toss the flyer or, at best, pass it along to a friend. Having been open and out for 12 years myself, I'd grown quite distant from the kind of reactions I was about to encounter.

I received several heartening calls from men in the Detroit area, eager to join a gay men's group. To their knowledge, if anything like this existed, it hadn't been advertised—until now. But other callers were outraged! "How dare you send me this mailing about a gay group with no envelope?" Some feared that a family member or someone they lived with—to whom they were not out—would notice my flyer and connect the dots. Still others were annoyed at my presuming that they were gay.

My next mailing was in a sealed, opaque envelope, but even these provoked outrage. One man called me to heatedly demand that I take him off my mailing list. "I ain't gay!" he insisted. "Never been gay! Just because I slept with a guy once, that don't make me gay!" A woman left a voice message saying that she was "*not* gay" but "a *good* Christian woman" and how dare I send her a piece of mail regarding homosexuality? She then swore at me, before leaving her name so that I could take it off my list.

For most of those who overreact this way, my mailings simply rekindle their own inner conflicts. I could stop my mailings, but I won't let homophobic reactions keep me from advertising effective, supportive therapy for my gay brothers and sisters.

Homo-Avoidance

The vast majority of people—clients and therapists alike—are *homo-avoidant*, not knowing how to react to someone's being gay. Many therapists tell me they suspect a client might be gay, but fear to ask. Conversely, some lesbians and gays get upset because their therapists, after learning that they're gay, never ask follow-up questions or initiate any discussion.

The homo-avoidant often fear assigning "negative" labels, lest they be wrong in thinking the client is gay. For instance, many therapists avoid asking clients—particularly adolescents—if they are gay or lesbian. "I don't want them to think I assumed they were." "What if they get offended or self-conscious?" "What if they think my question is homophobic or ignorant?"

My answer is that the client's reaction then becomes diagnostic and therapeutic. Either way, it can be of help to the client. If they are struggling with homosexuality, the door is open. If they are not gay and have a strong reaction to your question, that can become part of their work in therapy.

Still other therapists are gay and lesbian themselves but avoid telling their gay and lesbian clients, believing that it would be inappropriate. "If the client were to ask I would tell but otherwise I let them transfer onto me whatever comes from them." Although this can be a very effective form of helping someone through transference, it can also be a way for the gay therapist to avoid being out. Ultimately, such a decision serves the therapist's needs rather than those of the clients, who need to have a role model and ally during the times they feel alone and isolated. It also further discourages clients from revealing their concerns to you.

Gay and lesbian clients often express their own homo-avoidance by claiming that if someone else doesn't broach the issue of their being gay, the individual doesn't want to talk about it, is homophobic, or simply is not interested. After clients come out, you'll hear these type of remarks:

"I told my family, but they never brought it up again."

"My friend asked, and I told her, but she never asked me any further questions."

"My children know. But they never ask, so I can tell they don't want to talk about it."

These excuses and reasons may—or may not—be true. But the only way for clients to discover whether their own beliefs are accurate is to *keep* talking about it themselves. After clients announce themselves as gay, I encourage them not to wait for others to keep the conversation going, but rather to bring up the subject whenever appropriate and to keep informing friends and family about their lives. I remind them that other people may not want to seem *too* interested—or disinterested. With any troubling issue, most people's default solution is avoidance: "Don't ask, don't tell."

Clients should be coached on how to ask others how they are dealing with the information. Encourage them to stop "editing" and to keep bringing up subjects in their lives that involve being gay. Have them tell friends, coworkers, and family members, "If you have any questions, go ahead and ask."

If others complain that clients are "talking too much about being gay," encourage clients to ask them what they mean by that. Remind them that they have a right to talk about their relational lives, just as straight people do.

Internalized Homophobia

All clients, gay or straight, have experienced some form of oppression related to their sexuality—directly or indirectly. You as a GAT therapist must bring their subjective reaction into consciousness so that you both can work with it and remove it. For lesbians and gays, this subjective reaction is called *internalized homophobia*.

Gays and lesbians don't normally walk in stating, "I have internalized homophobia," or "I'm grieving the loss of heterosexual privileges." Typically, clients are depressed, anxious, and troubled about issues that don't *seem* to arise from being gay or lesbian. It's your job to rule out any problems resulting from internalized homophobia and poor self-esteem due to being lesbian and gay.

Internalized homophobia is a national, if not international, experience among gay men and lesbians. I especially realized this after wrting my first book. I'd written the book because I felt confident that I had something to tell gay men locally and in Midwestern states about the internalized homophobia that comes from living in these more repressed regions. But I never imagined that gay men in San Francisco, New York, Chicago, and Los Angeles would benefit as much as they did. At a book reading and signing in San Francisco, I asked the men attending why they thought my book was so well-received there. One said, "Joe, you have to remember we are not from here originally. We fled here from places like where you grew up." They said that reading my book reminded them of the unfinished work on internalized homophobia they had yet to do. It still haunted them, even while living on the West Coast.

Internalized homophobia is really internalized shame about being gay or lesbian—an internalization of the very thing you have been taught to despise and consider evil. Authors Barbara Buloff and Marie Osterman explained it eloquently in Iasenza and Glassgold's (1995) *Lesbians and Psychoanalysis: Revolutions in Theory and Practice*:

> In her search to find mirrors that reflect her emerging self, a lesbian enters a veritable Coney Island Hall of Mirrors. She sees queer reflections. Mirrored back to her are grotesque and distorted image [*sic*] reflected back in words

like: perverse, sinful, immoral, infantile, arrested, inadequate, or she sees no reflection at all—a peculiar silence—invisibility. (p. 95)

Unconscious internalized homophobia manifests in negative imagery that becomes the lens through which gays and lesbians see each other and themselves. Learning to recognize subtle forms of unconscious internalized homophobia—even in gay and lesbian clients who are out and open—takes experience and skill. This is why it's vital to be aware of your own covert homophobia, or you might collude with your client's internalized version, with your countertransference adding to their problems.

Signs of internalized homophobia include women who put down "chapstick lesbians" and men who look for "straight-acting" gays. They are just as biased as Jewish males looking for gentile females or African-American women seeking "white-acting" men. Other symptoms of internalized homophobia include:

- Discomfort with obvious "fags" or "dykes"
- Denigration of gay ghettos by asking, "Why do gays and lesbians all have to live in the same area?"
- Fear of being found out, even when there is no danger
- Romantic attractions to only unavailable targets—particularly heterosexuals
- Passing as straight even when it is safe to be openly gay/lesbian
- Making comments like "I don't have to tell others what I do in bed; I don't want to know what they do!"
- Commenting that a person or establishment is "too gay"
- Looking for straight-acting boyfriends or girlfriends

Shame

Our American culture does not have the ability to admit that shame even exists, let alone have a language for how to talk about the experience of it (Kaufman & Raphael, 1996). This silence is deafening and creates toxic shame for gay and lesbian individuals. In *Coming Out of Shame: Transforming Gay and Lesbian Lives*, authors Kaufman and Raphael (1996) wrote:

How does that silence originate? Shame itself is the source. What cannot be openly expressed is perceived as too shameful to speak about. It is shame that bars the tongue from speaking. When parents either fail or refuse to speak openly about some subject, whether sexuality or a family secret, shame forges the chains of their silence. When a culture's media, churches and synagogues, as well as its schools all fail to engage in frank discourse about homosexuality, that deafening silence only strengthens and validates shame. (p. 10)

Tracking the manifestations of shame and internalized homophobia in your clients is imperative. As a gay affirmative therapist, you must know what to look for and how to help clients understand that it exists within them.

What Gay Affirmative Therapy Is Not

In general, GAT explores the trauma, shame, alienation, isolation, and neglect that occur to lesbians and gays as children. Although this is important, it has the potential of going too far and eclipsing other issues that your clients face. Because of the historical pattern of pathologizing homosexuality (discussed in Chapter 1), GAT has tended to deemphasize emotional disorders and not examine *any* pathology. GAT is not supposed to explain all the problems facing gays and lesbians—rather, it is supposed to be an essential inclusion.

In an effort to avoid pathologizing the gay or lesbian client, therapists may blame homophobia for too much and overlook mental and emotional problems. As a gay affirmative therapist, being affirming and supportive is only part of your work. The other part is looking for other issues that could—or might not—result from the client's homophobia and heterosexism. Some emotional and personality disorders, I believe, result from a lifetime of closeted dissociation, adapting to the sexual/romantic orientation that others expect.

Historically, gay-negative therapists jumped to conclusions and applied homophobic and heterosexist trauma models and theories, when in fact gay clients exhibit *other* individual problems. For example, a gay male who appears promiscuous and in stage 5 of the coming out process could actually be a suffering from bipolar disorder or sexual addiction. The closeted lesbian complaining of low libido may not be repressed but rather have suffered sexual abuse in her childhood. That said, don't be afraid to diagnose and pathologize gay-specific problems if need be just because homosexuality itself has been overdiagnosed and pathologized.

If this seems confusing, you're on the right track! As therapists, our responsibility is to be armed with all the up-to-date information. If you know all the ways problems *can* arise, you can then assess—with the client's help—what applies and what doesn't.

Homo-Work for the Straight Therapist

Just as you strive to have clients do their "homo-work," so should you examine your own imprinted heterosexism and develop comfortable, appreciative feelings about homosexuality. As a clinician, it is important to examine yourself for any covert and overt bias that hampers your effectiveness. It can also be helpful to explore any homosexual impulses, homoerotic interests, or tendencies that you may have.

Targeting Your Countertransference

Imagine yourself going to your local bookstore, choosing gay and lesbian books and magazines like Signorelli's *Outing Yourself*, Tracey and Pokorny's *So You Want To Be A Lesbian*, Isay's *Becoming Gay*, or *The Advocate* and letting customers and cashiers clearly see what you're buying, believing the books are for you and that you are lesbian or gay. Or imagine yourself reading these books openly on a plane, at the park, or at the beach. Consider putting McNaught's *Now That I'm Out, What Do I Do?* on your coffee table at home where visitors can see it. Although these examples may seem extreme, they can be a good litmus test to see what level of shame and homophobia lives in you.

To check yourself for heterosexist/homophobic countertransference, ask yourself the following questions:

- Do I question the origins of my clients' gayness—if not aloud, then to myself?
- Do I assume that same-sex attractions have a pathological origin? Do I infer etiology rather than developmental identity formation?
- Do I align with my client's reluctance to admit being gay or lesbian?
- Do I think gays and lesbians should not tell others they are gay unless they are asked?
- How do I really feel about legal and religious marriage for gays and lesbians?
- How do I feel about gays and lesbians parenting children?
- Do I agree with complaints from gay and lesbian clients that the gay community is immature and too focused on sex and politics?
- How comfortable am I talking to 10- to 15-year-olds about the possibility they are gay or lesbian? Do I assume they can't really know their sexual orientation at that age?

Having screened yourself for covert homophobia, you can more easily spot it in your clients—and especially in other therapists who believe that reminding lesbian and gay clients of their "choices" when they are struggling with gay life is helpful. These same therapists would not give a heterosexual struggling with straight life choices about gay or lesbian living. Such people typically believe their own biases to be irrelevant or nonexistent.

CHAPTER 3

Growing Up Lesbian or Gay

When I told my parents I was gay, they said, "Let's see how the second grade goes first, dear."

—Carson Kressley, of the TV show *Queer Eye for the Straight Guy*, to Oprah Winfrey

This epigraph—although funny—is based on the reality that lesbian and gay children know from a very young age that they are different. They may not know exactly *how* they're different or what to call themselves, because there is little to no permission to explore anything other than heterosexuality, but they still know they aren't like most other children. GAT acknowledges that homosexuality in children exists—from birth. To deny this would be to believe that homosexuality comes from life experiences that change an innate heterosexual orientation.

Many lesbians and gays aren't able to identify what makes them different until adolescence. As children, they received messages—verbal and nonverbal—about how to sit, walk, dress, talk, and so on. One client told me he hadn't danced for 30 years because he thought being a good dancer would out him as gay. Another man told me that since his teens, he'd been careful about how he dressed because the clothes he felt drawn to were ones his peers saw as "gay." A lesbian client said that she wore dresses, grew her nails long, and used nail polish even though she felt uncomfortable doing so—just to pass as heterosexual.

Clients also talk about playground prejudice they encountered, and how it was typically discounted. Adults assume that if heterosexual children hurl "That is so gay!" slurs and chortle over homophobic jokes, no harm is being done. But gay and lesbian children pay attention to what other kids are saying and doing—and to what the teachers are allowing. They get the message that it's okay to demean others by calling them "fags" or "dykes."

I don't mean to imply that there is only one type of gay boy or lesbian girl, or one way of growing up homosexual. However, there is little discussion, let alone research, that focuses on the traumatic experience and shame of growing up gay and lesbian. One excellent book that does tackle this subject is Jean M. Baker's (2002) *How Homophobia Hurts Children*. In it she talks about how not anticipating or knowing your child might be or is gay can have a negative effect on the child.

Given all of this, it doesn't matter how functional one's family of origin is—a gay or lesbian child can inadvertently experience trauma both within the family and outside of it. Remembering that your clients were once gay children who endured trauma while growing up will help you better understand them and how to work with them.

From the Beginning: Gays and Lesbians as Children

When I talk about gay and lesbian children, the one question I'm commonly asked is "How can you tell if a child or teenager is gay or lesbian?" I don't have an answer for that, and I haven't found any scientific literature that claims to, either. There are anecdotal writings from mothers and fathers who, looking back, recall signs that their children might be gay. One thing I *do* stress is that, as I mentioned earlier, every lesbian or gay adult was once a gay or lesbian child.

However, many people—including too many psychotherapists—do not believe this. They cannot imagine that a child before the age of 12 (or even an adolescent) can be born with and have a fixed homosexual sexual/romantic identity. They can imagine the child being born with and having a fixed *heterosexual* identity, however, as all children (and adults, for that matter) must be heterosexual unless proven otherwise. When I ask therapists about this they often say they don't even think of children and teenagers as gay or straight. However, they will ask their young clients if they have romantic interests in the opposite sex and assume they are heterosexual. This is their covert homophobia in their countertransference. When I teach and lecture about GAT to therapists, usually half the audience believes that one is born gay or lesbian and the other half believes that one becomes gay through learning and from environmental factors. It makes straight individuals, even therapists, uncomfortable and anxious to consider a child gay or lesbian. Their anxiety results from their belief that homosexuality is an adult, primarily sexual experience. However, being gay is about having an identity, just as being straight is. In other words, sex and sexuality are present in both orientations. But homosexuality is overly sexualized by others, an important point that is discussed in more depth in Chapter 4.

Children and teenagers *can* handle a lesbian or gay orientation within themselves. What they cannot handle is the trauma of concealing it, not being able to express it or talk about it, and the negativity surrounding it by others around them.

The Case of Jake

Thirteen-year-old Jake told his mother he was gay. Surprised and concerned, she offered to take him to therapy. He agreed to go, but not for the reasons she assumed.

Jake's mother believed that no boy could know what his orientation was at such a young age—but Jake did. His Unitarian church had offered a human sexuality course, and when they reached homosexuality and bisexuality, Jake recognized himself as a gay male on the cusp of becoming a teenager.

He'd thought he could handle hearing other kids saying, "That's so gay"; in fact, he had even said it himself. But now that he was accepting himself as gay, hearing it was making him feel isolated from his peers. Being self-aware at such an early age, he figured he needed therapy.

My work with Jake was to build up his confidence enough that he could tell his peers that he didn't appreciate their "humor." We worked together on ways he could invite the teachers he felt safe with to help him, as well as his mother, who wanted to help him feel secure in school.

Jake is an excellent example of how young teens and even children can—if given permission to explore their own sexuality—have some awareness of their sexual and romantic orientation. His case also illustrates the fact that young people can handle the development of their core identity—gay or straight and everything in between.

Fortunately, Jake was spared the severity of trauma that you will see in many of your gay and lesbian clients.

The Oedipus and Electra Complexes

Homosexuality was long considered as "Oedipus gone wrong" or "Electra gone badly," wherein children failed to achieve an alternative "healthy" heterosexual identity. Heterosexuality was seen as nature's default. Therapists typically misunderstood, underreported, dismissed, or ignored the messages found in the developmental narratives of gay men and lesbians. And, of course, their theories reflected the values of the culture in which they practiced.

More contemporary psychotherapists and gay theorists, including Lewes (1988), Drescher (1998), and Isay (1994), have added to this oedipal discussion of how gay boys develop. All agree that oedipal feelings exist, but they add that from these oedipal feelings arise other issues that are *not* about homosexuality but instead revolve around the lack of acknowledgment of *normal* homosexual development. They surmise that gay boys naturally yearn to get physically close to their fathers, and so fall in love with them—which usually leads to rejection and a source of wounding that never gets resolved.

Working psychodynamically involves understanding the developmental oedipal or electra complex (as developed by Freud), and how our clients negotiate this as small children in their families. In thinking of children as being gay or lesbian, it makes sense to consider *both* complexes. When a young boy announces that he plans to grow up and marry his mother, he'll probably be told that he cannot marry his mother, but he may be told that when he grows up he can marry a woman *like* her. Likewise, when a young girl announces that she plans to grow up and marry her father, she'll probably be told that she when she grows up, she can marry a man just like him. This is the positive resolution of the oedipal complex and is seen as the standard of a healthy heterosexual male and female identity.

But what of the girl who wants to marry her mother, or the boy who expresses a desire to marry his father? Gay boys learn that they not only can't marry their fathers, but also can't marry other boys. Little lesbian girls learn there is no hope for them either, and they must face the loss of their mothers and any other women for their future. So these little gay children not only get rejected by their parents, but also never receive a promise that someday they will meet someone to care for.

I spend a great deal of time with my sister's four children. They understand that I am married to my partner, Mike; when they were toddlers, the oldest two attended our wedding. When one of my nephews was age 6, he asked me why I'm not married to a woman. I told him that I love Mike, so I married him.

"Boys can't marry other boys," he told me.

"You can marry anyone you fall in love with," I said, "as long as you're both adults."

My nephew then said, "Then when I grow up, I want to marry you!"

My answer to my nephew—"You can marry anyone you fall in love with"—kept the door open for him, as he probably did not know his sexuality, nor did we. This is why I recommend that parents and caretakers keep their responses gender-neutral. This is the best way not harm a gay or lesbian child.

Neglect of Gay and Lesbian Children

Therapists know that clients coming from neglectful families are harder to treat and often remain in therapy longer because of what *didn't* happen or what *wasn't* said. Overt abuse is often easier to treat, even when clients are in denial, because what *was* done or said to the client can be pinpointed and addressed. Passive forms of abuse are harder to spot. For example, if a client says she was loved and attended to, and you ask, "How so?" she may tell you how well fed, clothed, and housed she was. You would then ask, "But how did they show their affection for you?" Clients who say, "It wasn't shown, I just knew I was loved," have a harder time understanding that what *didn't* occur was itself neglect and, therefore, a form of abuse. Custodial care is what foster care can offer. Providing love by overt forms of affection—mirroring children and highlighting the special talents they bring to the family—honors children as individuals and gives them a sense of belonging.

Lesbian and gay children have an additional layer to the lack of attunement from their early primary caretakers—no one was tracking or attending to the homosexual side of their core selves. No matter how attuned gay and lesbian children may be, they may still feel lost because of the neglect and silence surrounding their homosexuality.

As children, gays and lesbians are not offered the same sense of belonging by their families, schools, or religious institutions. Media and books offer few, if any, gay and lesbian characters that are out and proud. Parents who hope that their children are not gay or lesbian simply do not talk about it. Schools for the most part hardly acknowledge the presence of gay and lesbian students. Churches, synagogues, and other religious institutions condemn homosexuality by denying the gay and lesbian members of their audiences. Essentially, GAT examines the negative psychological effects on gays and lesbians. Splitting of their sexual and authentic selves and repressing their sexuality from childhood on dishonors and ignores the reality that gay adults were once gay children.

Looking at how our society handles cartoon characters created *for* children sheds light on what is done *to* children. Bert and Ernie, from *Sesame Street*, minded their own business for years, singing show tunes together, taking baths together, and sleeping next to each other in twin beds. But in 1990, a North Carolina minister, Joseph Chambers, pronounced Bert and Ernie a gay couple. "They're two grown men sharing a house—and a bedroom!" bellowed Chambers, whose radio ministry is broadcast in four Southern states. "They share clothes. They eat and cook together. They vacation together and have effeminate characteristics. In one show Bert teaches Ernie how to sew. In another, they tend plants together. If this isn't meant to represent a homosexual union, I can't imagine what it's supposed to represent."

Although the Children's Television Workshop and *Sesame Street* both issued a statement defending the characters, the pair's behavior changed: They no longer took baths together, for example. Clearly, the message was sent and received that it's bad and wrong for children to be exposed to a couple who might or could be gay.

An equally ridiculous outing of a cartoon character occurred in 1999, when Reverend Jerry Falwell outed Tinky-Winky, a purple Teletubby who carried a magic bag and spoke in a high voice. While this controversy was unfolding, I spoke to a class at a nursing school. One of the nurses told me that on the children's ward where she worked, Tinky-Winky had been banished. What a cruel metaphor it was—for this is what happens to gay boys: They are made to feel as if they are not wanted and as if they certainly can't be around other children. A few years later, James Dobson, the founder of Focus on the Family, accused SpongeBob Squarepants and his creators of "promoting the gay agenda."

Interestingly, female cartoon characters are never outed. Peppermint Patty from the *Peanuts* comic strip, clearly a lesbian, is obviously in romantic love with Lucy, always following her around. Patty's friend Marcie, who is clearly a lesbian, even calls Patty "sir"! Some lesbians say that Velma from *Scooby-Doo* is a lesbian because her hairstyle is very butch and she always wears sensible clothes and shoes.

Author and psychotherapist Terrance Real (1997) accurately summarized why males are punished for engaging in nontraditional male behavior:

> Boys and men are granted privilege and special status, but only on the condition that they turn their backs on vulnerability and connection to join in the fray. Those who resist, like unconventional men or gay men, are punished for it. Those who lose or cannot compete, like boys and men with disabilities, or of the wrong class or color, are marginalized and rendered all but invisible. . . . The exclusion, isolation, of a failed winner is so great, it is as if he never existed at all. (p. 180)

Not standing up to denounce homophobic slurs is another form of neglect. To a gay or lesbian child, or to any abused child, the fact that she wasn't protected is sometimes more of an insult and an assault than the initial abuse itself. These children internalize the message that they are not worthy of being protected and that no one will come to their defense. This neglect manifests in gay and lesbian children's feeling invisible, as if they have no right to exist.

Trauma

All gays and lesbians are touched to one degree or another by neglect stemming from the invisibility of their homosexuality. This can be traumatic. How they are affected and how it manifests depends on the individual, his or her personality, and the family of origin. When working with gays and lesbians, it is important to assess and treat them through the lens of the effects of the trauma of homophobia and heterosexism.

My working definition of trauma is an event or episode, acute or chronic, that causes overstimulation without an outlet or release for that overstimulation. This leaves individuals feeling helpless and overwhelmed. According to this definition, any seemingly harmless event or situation can be *subjectively* traumatic when it leaves an individual feeling unable to cope, or fearing some ongoing threat.

You've heard many clients recount traumatic experiences—typically abrupt, dramatic, and therefore memorable. You've also probably seen victims of long-term verbal abuse from a spouse or parent. These clients grow accustomed to chronic insults and habitual belittling that, if it were to come all at once from a stranger, would feel intolerable and would spark a normal fight-or-flight reaction.

Growing up gay or lesbian is similarly incrementally traumatic. Slights happen over a period of many years, and children learn to internalize them, all the while struggling to cope with being alone and in secrecy. For those for whom heterosexuality is the "alternative lifestyle," trying to develop an identity while role playing (or, as one of my clients calls it, "doing straight drag") is chronically painful. And it sets the stage for awkward identity development and difficult future functioning.

As Bessel A. van der Kolk (1996) warned in his book *Traumatic Stress: The Effects of Overwhelming Experience on Mind, Body, and Society*:

> . . . if clinicians fail to pay attention to the contribution of past trauma to the current problems in patients with these diagnoses, they may fail to see that they seem to organize much of their lives around repetitive patterns of reliving and warding off traumatic memories, reminders, and affects. (p. 183)

According to van der Kolk, therapists' attitudes toward the traumatic symptoms will determine their approach to treating their clients. This is why it's crucial to understand the trauma that has overwhelmed your lesbian and gay clients, whether or not they report it. Most won't view it as trauma at all and if they do, they believe it is all "done and gone"—in the past. But if left unresolved, the effects of trauma repeat themselves. Keeping a discerning eye for this likelihood is the best way to help your gay and lesbian clients.

Religious and Spiritual Abuse

Another place—and perhaps the worst—where there is a break in a sense of belonging is religion. Because of the damage so many religions have done to the developing self of gays and lesbians, these individuals cannot seek spiritual counseling and guidance. They not only are isolated from others but also feel isolated from their higher power and anyone in a religious or spiritual capacity. So they turn to psychotherapy and often ask the therapist to give them spiritual guidance and counseling.

In my practice, I've had gay men and lesbians who called themselves "recovering Catholics." They'd spent years in therapy trying to undo the damage of hearing, throughout their lives, that gay sex is an "abomination" and that they'd go to hell if they "practiced" it.

Joe Amico, an ordained minister, licensed substance abuse counselor, and president of the National Association of Lesbian and Gay Addiction Professionals wrote an article titled "Healing from 'Spiritual Abuse': Assisting Gay and Lesbian Clients." In it, he addressed the difference between religion and spirituality. At his talks, for example, he asks people to shout out what comes to their minds about religion. They say things like "rituals, money, rules, the Pope, priests, nuns, ministers, rabbis, confirmation, confession, abuse, obligation, and homophobia." When he asks them about spirituality, they yell out things such as peace, serenity, nature, hope, trust, acceptance, unconditional love, and individual and personal fulfillment (Amico, 2003). Amico wrote that "at his talks everyone usually agrees that the words on the spirituality side are more positive than those on the religion side" (p. 18). Many lesbians and gays agree that religion does not feel accepting for them and that spirituality does. They wish to stay with their own religion but feel rejected and out of place. Amico has said: "To ignore spiritual abuse is the same as ignoring sexual, physical, or emotional abuse as a part of the healing process" (p. 18). The case of Cindy is a good example of what he means.

The Case of Cindy

Cindy was a 53-year-old woman who came to treatment after her diagnosis of breast cancer. She needed guidance as to whether to undergo a recommended double mastectomy or to begin other treatment. She wanted to receive spiritual guidance, but she hadn't attended her Catholic church in a decade—she'd vowed to never return after she came out at the age of 42. Although she turned to other religious institutions for spiritual direction, she never connected successfully to any of them. Seriously depressed and estranged from her religion, she entered therapy.

Like with many gay and lesbian individuals, Cindy's self-awareness and eventual coming out were delayed by her strict Catholic upbringing. Her religious family was rigid when it came to rules and gender roles. Determined to please her devout family, Cindy became rule-oriented and believed—as they taught her—that the Church's teachings were law.

When Cindy turned 18, the Church changed its stand on a number of teachings. Eating meat on Fridays was now acceptable. Mass was done in English, a change that disillusioned Cindy, but she still subscribed to the Church's teachings and remained a good Catholic girl in terms of sexuality.

In her twenties and thirties, Cindy completely repressed her awareness that she was a lesbian. She married and had two children. She prided herself on living out her childhood mission of being a "good little Catholic girl" and felt that if it were not for her homosexuality she could have maintained the life "she was meant to have with her husband and children."

At the age of 42, when her children reached adolescence, Cindy became a teacher and fell in love with the principal of her school. She divorced her husband and began a relationship with the woman, with whom she had stayed ever since.

In therapy Cindy expressed anger at herself and worried that she was being punished for having come out and not "doing God's work"—that is, staying closeted as a lesbian. She cried often, remembering the comfort the church teachings had once offered her.

In Cindy's 6 months of treatment with me, she became angry about minor inconsistencies she noticed in my therapeutic interventions. She remembered details of things I had said and would directly confront me if she witnessed anything that resembled a contradiction. She became exquisitely sensitive to the words I chose. But the issue she had the most trouble with was when she was charged for an appointment she missed without giving me sufficient notice. This upset her greatly. She acknowledged that she'd signed consent forms agreeing to my rules about missed appointments, and she knew that this was standard practice in the mental health field. When I became ill, however, and had to cancel her appointment with less than 24 hours' notice, she claimed that this was unfair. She felt that because I did not give her enough notice, she should get a free session. This became such a central issue for her that she almost terminated, claiming that therapy was no different than the Church: Both had unfair rules. She accused me of "changing the rules" at my own whim.

Cindy: Clinical Interpretation and Treatment

Cindy could easily be characterized as difficult; some might assess her as borderline. She could also have been diagnosed as having an adjustment disorder with depressed mood over the news of her breast cancer. However, knowing about her feelings about the Church and listening to how she suppressed her anger toward them and directed it toward herself, I interpreted her anger as more of negative transference.

Cindy's negative transference toward me arose from the feelings she had repressed about the Catholic Church. She focused on a perceived inconsistent "rule"—like the inconsistent Church rules—that allowed her to express her anger in a "safe" way that didn't contradict her childhood imprint to stay neutral toward the Church. I taught Cindy about negative transference and pointed out to her that it was positive that she finally was directing her anger away from herself. I assured her that I could handle her anger. She struggled with this for 3 months and ultimately was able to see that her anger was, in fact, motivated by the hypocrisy of the Catholic Church. Over time she was able to retrieve her anger toward the Church. As she said, "changing rigid rules at their own whim" conflicted with their teachings that once God spoke, His words could not be changed. After this realization, she began conversations with prominent people in her church about why they did not change their "archaic" beliefs about homosexuality.

During therapy, she expressed her sadness that the Church's teachings had affected her to the point of suppressing her true lesbian orientation for all the years she lived heterosexually. In adapting to her religious and rigid family, she had put her own needs last.

Week after week, we reviewed Cindy's memories of being best in school, perfect in church attendance, best employee, top athlete, and ideal wife. The goal had been to distract everyone, including herself, from seeing that inside, she was an ashamed, self-loathing, anxious young girl—mostly because of what she learned in church.

Now our work was uncovering the trauma that was preventing her from finding spiritual direction. She knew about Dignity—the unauthorized version of Catholicism for gay and lesbian Catholics. She had stayed away from this organization, believing that because the Catholic Church did not recognize it, it was like "playing house" and not real. However, now that she was aware of the trauma she suffered, she was freed to make a decision for herself. Attending Dignity, she found it to be of great help to her as she decided what direction to take to fight her cancer.

Applying the model of abuse to what gay and lesbian children and teenagers learn at church and calling it "spiritual abuse" helps clinicians understand the trauma their clients have experienced. Giving a name to what they are going through helps them get in touch with their anger and direct it where it belongs—at the religious institution and not at themselves.

Integrity and the Divided Self

Integrity is a lifestyle of congruency; it means outwardly being who you are on the inside. Lesbian and gay children quickly learn that being out and open means ridicule, negative judgments, and lack of emotional and physical safety. So the most formative years are spent learning to live out of integrity—in relationship to themselves and others.

Of course, gay men and lesbians don't corner the market on living out of integrity. Heterosexuals get through childhood by burying and disowning parts of themselves that are not acceptable to their families or cultures. Gay and straight alike, we must all come back into integrity—which is often what a midlife crisis is all about. This is why most of our clients enter therapy—they are out of integrity with themselves or someone else. They arrive in our offices in order to find out who they really are and move toward it.

For children of any orientation, integrating all the parts of oneself is impossible. Family rules as well as socialization norms call for children to disown aspects of themselves. For gay and lesbian children, an additional part gets disowned—their gayness—and this corruption happens very early. The cost is a lost self and a damaged core that leaves its victims with many mental health problems, addictions, and characterological profiles. The process of coming out—which is about integration, or becoming congruent with oneself and with others—can be a very difficult task, prompting its own set of maladaptive behaviors. Gay and lesbian clients may present as personality disordered or mentally ill when the real cause of symptoms is the difficulty of growing up gay and the coming out process.

Restrictive Socialization Messages

All kids get *some* social limitations from their families, schools, and communities. Many of these messages are important; they teach children how to behave appropriately in order to be accepted. But the problem with restrictive messages like "don't think," "don't act," "don't feel," and "don't touch" is that they limit children and cause their core selves to remain underground. If, for example, an innately playful child is taught to curtail her playfulness, she is being forced to deny that part of herself.

And so the false self begins. Gay and lesbian children learn to split off important parts of their core identities. This causes them to lose their sense of self early on. We therapists can help clients resurrect their "buried treasures," as I call these lost parts of the self, to discover their authentic identity.

Disowning Aspects of the Self

Cutting off romantic and sexual urges becomes habitual for lesbians and gays. The individual's sense of identity becomes fugitive, and she tends to misinterpret who she really is—not only in relation to sexuality but also in relation to her social sense of self in terms of how to act, feel, think, and experience body sensations. Straight children may disown *parts* of themselves that shape their identity, but gay children suppress much more of their identities.

When gay and lesbian children cut off and disown parts of themselves, they go underground. They still, however, repeatedly seek conscious expression, if only in excessive denial. But such an attempt at camouflage—being the *exact opposite* of what the individual hopes to hide—is often laughably recognizable.

Pretending That Nothing's Wrong

Early on in life, almost everyone learns to present his best face to his peers and classmates—and, conversely, to minimize or deny anything that might subject him to judgments and ridicule. Many gay and lesbian children and teenagers hope that someone will see through their pretending to be straight. They long for someone to say, "I can see something is wrong; let me help you." The "something is wrong" is not their homosexuality but that they are pretending to be someone whom they are not. Unfortunately, this rarely if ever happens.

Becoming a Master of Pretense

Just because a client comes out and seeks to integrate his sexual and romantic orientation doesn't mean he's vowed to embrace integrity in every other aspect of life. Becoming a master of pretense and living out of integrity is the consequence of suppressing homosexuality. Displaying a false self as a heterosexual to others—and oneself—becomes a way of life. This may explain why many gay men and lesbians don't stop pretending and hiding even after they come out. Pretending has become a way of life, manifesting in other ways that need to be addressed. They often do not even realize they are continuing with this defense in relationships.

For example, I spent over a year with a client in group therapy helping him come out to his family and friends. During the second year he revealed he had a boyfriend for the last six months and they were planning their first vacation. He had not told me or the group about this. When group members became angry with him about this, he was stunned and innocently replied, "It didn't even occur to me to talk about it." This client had learned to compartmentalize his life through hiding to the extent that he wasn't even able to allow himself to enjoy the positive accolades he would have received from the beginning of his relationship.

Helping Clients Overcome Humiliation, Shame, and Victimization

Overall, clinicians can see from this chapter that it is humiliating and victimizing to be treated as inferior or invisible simply for being different. As I have already emphasized, most gay and lesbian adults knew as children that something was different about them. Feeling different often gets worse as adolescence approaches.

Freud envisioned trauma as "a breech in the protective barrier against (over)stimulation leading to feelings of overwhelming helplessness" (Levine, 2006, p. 197). It is this sense of helplessness children experience that is humiliating and victimizing. Gay and lesbian children are overwhelmed with heterosexuality, knowing that something inside is not aligned with the way the world wants them to be.

Being seen in contempt by others for being different and being taught that you are not okay is shaming, as it is out of your control as a gay child. In addition, the type of gender bashing that occurs toward male and female children who do not conform to rigid, stereotypical gender behavior further degrades and humiliates these children.

Gay and lesbian children often grow up to be codependent—that is, they subordinate their needs to others and conform to what is expected of them. Gay children often seek to win approval by following the rules "religiously." This is a way of compensating for their own diminished self-worth. Ultimately, of course, it is exactly their self-worth that ends up taking the greatest hit.

Therapeutic Tools For Psychosocial Information Gathering and Treatment Planning

As a clinician it is important to know the right questions to ask and terminology to use to obtain the best possible assessment and decide what direction to head in for treatment. As a straight clinician you need to watch for the negative transference of your clients, who, as you ask these questions, may feel you are coming from a patho-logical stance about homosexuality.

I would suggest that as you do the initial intake, you tell your clients that the questions you ask are those you ask in most every session about growing up in a minority status. Assure lesbian and gay clients that you do not believe in the pathogenic models of homosexuality. Reassure them that you want to obtain the best information to help them and that knowing about their gay and lesbian childhoods—even if they did not know they were gay or lesbian as children—is important to helping them understand the type of adult they have become.

You can tell clients that you do not want to create a victim mentality by asking these questions but that you *do* need to understand their experiences in order to be able to know who and what is accountable for their not having permission to explore their homosexuality. Explain that this is an important part of understanding their adult functioning as gay men and lesbians.

Following are some suggestions of what to ask your clients:

- When do you recall knowing that something about you was different from other children of the same gender—even if you did not call it gay or lesbian?
- When did you discover your gayness or lesbianism?
- Did you feel different from your peers—particularly those of the same gender?
- Did others—adults or peers—notice you were different and shame or bully you for it? If so, how?
- Were you consciously making decisions to hide or pretend to be like everyone else?
- Even if you don't recall overt forms of abuse for being gay or lesbian as a child, what about the covert abuse, which includes the absence of permission to explore your homosexuality or the lack of role models? How do you feel about that?
- Do you think that not being acknowledged by yourself or others as a gay or lesbian child affects your adult life today in terms of self-esteem and relationships?
- Why do you think you did not tell anyone when you were young?

As a psychotherapist, your goal is to teach gay men and lesbians that they're not responsible for any of the abuse they received as children and teenagers. Account-ability rests on the guilty shoulders of those who did the abuse. Having strong and healthy therapeutic attachments helps gay men and lesbians recover the birthright of their sexuality and heal the effects of covert cultural sexual abuse.

CHAPTER 4

Covert Cultural Sexual Abuse

Only by dealing with Gay Shame will we ever get to a
definition of Gay Pride.

—Andrew Holleran

As I described in Chapter 3, the trauma lesbian and gay children experience growing up is pervasive. However, this trauma goes even deeper than that described in the
previous chapter, and it often falls under the radar of therapists and even gays and
lesbians themselves. The trauma I'm referring to is a *sexual* trauma.

The assault on gays' and lesbians' sexuality is profound and becomes worse as they
enter adolescence and adulthood. The trauma not only affects their psychological
identity but also negatively influences their psychosexual formation and identity.
The psychological consequences of homophobia and heterosexism parallel those of
sexual abuse.

The fact is that most children—gay and straight—learn they have to hide and
modify sexual parts of themselves that are discouraged. This hiding modifies, van-
dalizes, and compromises their identities. The sexual oppression and terrorism experienced by those who grow up gay and lesbian—particularly during the adolescent
years when sexuality and intimacy development is at a crucial stage—is profound.

For years, psychological researchers and clinicians believed that those with a
homosexual orientation were unable to form close attachments, maintain relationships, and have healthy self-esteem. In other words, it was thought that these negative characteristics were innate to homosexuality. The truth is that they are the *result*
of what is done to gays and lesbians. The effects of covert cultural sexual abuse persist
into adulthood and are just as pernicious as those of sexual abuse.

This chapter will demonstrate how the trauma is sexualized, how it manifests, how to identify it for your clients, and how to help them heal from it.

Defining Covert Cultural Sexual Abuse

Covert cultural sexual abuse is the foundation for many (if not most) problems for gays and lesbians. And most therapists working with gays and lesbians miss this phenomenon. It's not enough to simply say that gays and lesbians were permanently scarred by the homophobia and heterosexism they experienced growing up. Homophobia and heterosexism are *inherent* to covert cultural sexual abuse and have devastating, complicated psychological and psychosexual consequences, causing guilt and shame to run as deep as in those who have been sexually abused (Kort, 2005b).

I define covert cultural sexual abuse as chronic verbal, emotional, psychological, and sometimes sexual assaults against an individual's gender expression, sexual feelings, and behaviors. Conceptually, it is similar to sexual harassment in that it interferes with a person's ability to function socially, psychologically, romantically, affectionally, and sexually. Its effects persist into adulthood and wreak havoc in people's lives—as does sexual harassment.

My working definition of sexual abuse (both covert and overt) comes from Wendy Maltz's *The Sexual Healing Journey: A Guide for Survivors of Sexual Abuse*. She stated: "Sexual abuse occurs whenever one person dominates and exploits another using sexual feelings and behavior to hurt, misuse, degrade, humiliate, or control another. The abuse comes from a person who violates a position of trust, power, and protection of the child" (Maltz, 2001, p. 31). In other words, sex is simply a tool with which to exert power, dominance, and influence—just as in rape.

Overt sexual abuse involves direct touching, fondling, and intercourse with another person against that person's will. *Covert* sexual abuse is subtle and indirect. It includes inappropriate behaviors such as sexual hugs, sexual stares, or inappropriate comments about one's buttocks or genitals, as well as verbal assaults and denigration, such as punishing a child for not being the "right type" of male or female and homophobic name-calling.

Covert *cultural* sexual abuse involves bullying through humiliation, offensive language, sexual jokes (of antigay nature), and obscenities. These attacks can be directed at the gay or lesbian person directly or indirectly. In other words, what I define as covert cultural sexual abuse is the expression of heterosexism, a belief in mainstream society that demands that all people be—or pretend to be—heterosexual. Heterosexism uses homophobia to exploit the sexual feelings and behaviors of those who are not heterosexual. In other words, heterosexism perpetrates and violates the trust that gay and lesbian children have in those in who are in positions of trust, power, and protection of them.

To be clear, I am *not* saying that gays and lesbians are sexually abused. Nor am I diminishing the profound negative effects of overt sexual abuse. What I am trying to help clinicians understand is that many of the deep-seated problems gays and lesbians have come from covert cultural sexual abuse.

Others have also noticed how the results of sexual abuse parallel the experience of growing up gay. In 1993, Joseph H. Neisen wrote an article in which he explored the parallels of heterosexism and sexual abuse. He wrote of heterosexism as being "a form of cultural victimization that oppresses gay/lesbian/bisexual persons" (Neisen, 1993, p. 55). Niesen's article points to the cultural victimization as an abuse that causes painful effects similar to those of sexual/physical abuse. The cultural victimization of heterosexism, he added, stymies individual growth and development just as it does in individuals who have been sexually or physically abused. I don't believe Neisen takes this far enough. What he called "cultural victimization," I would call "covert cultural sexual abuse."

Don Wright has also compared the effects of homophobia to those of sexual abuse (Wright, 2000). He talked about homophobia as a "sexuality abuse" with "deep lasting effects on a bisexual or gay male, undermining his sense of self as a male, and tainting what for him is a natural attraction to his own gender" (p. 122). He paralleled the resulting shame and guilt with the shame and guilt experienced by those who have been sexually abused.

Children (and adults) are bombarded by messages—from the church, from politicians, from their schools, from their peers and their family—that being gay is morally wrong, sinful, and forbidden, and they internalize these message on some level. The shame and guilt become profound and part of their identity.

Here are some other examples of covert cultural sexual abuse:

When I was in sixth grade, I had a best friend named Max. We'd go everywhere together; looking back I can see that I was in love with him. But I did not know that at the time. One day we were late for gym class, and when we entered the gym at the same time, everyone—including the physical education teacher—laughed at us. Later we learned that the teacher predicted out loud to the class that Max and I would arrive late together because we were "fags together." Of course the implication was that we were sexual with each other. This became a running joke not only for the rest of the school year but also for the remainder of middle school. Imagine how humiliated we felt, especially because we had no one to talk to about how we were being treated. And imagine how other gay and lesbian children in my school felt, hearing my gym teacher call us "fags" and worrying that they'd be next.

Another example: When I was 12, my mother told me I was going to be showering with other boys in gym class. My sexuality had already surfaced and my fantasies were of other boys, so this information left me very stimulated and titillated. I fantasized about it for weeks, thinking how much fun it would be to see my classmates naked. Soon, however, I realized the negative consequences of staring too long—showing an obvious erection.

These memories are quite vivid for me. Many of my gay clients recall similar types of things happening for them. Gay men remember how much they hated gym class and how they did anything they could to avoid participating. Some gay and lesbian teenagers dissociated more than I did and were not conscious of why certain environments were difficult and provocative for them. They were not aware of their homoerotic impulses other than being uncomfortable.

How Covert Cultural Sexual Abuse Operates

Heterosexism is the umbrella for the cultural victimization that gays and lesbians suffer. Most understand heterosexism in terms of politics and how it denies rights to lesbians and gays on a social level. The sexual abuse is overshadowed by the politics and the inhumanity that most people focus on when seeing the effects of heterosexism on lesbians and gays.

As clinicians it is your job to help clients see that what occurred to them during their growing up years was a covert form of sexual abuse. But you can only do this by being convinced and educated yourself that this is a phenomenon for lesbian and gay children. Not all will suffer the negative consequences of covert cultural sexual abuse. We know that even some children of overt sexual abuse do not have the symptomology that most survivors have. However, it is imperative that the clinician rule covert cultural sexual abuse in or out in assessing a client and their presenting problems.

Believing That Lesbianism and Gayness Equal Adult Sex

Because people typically associate gay and lesbian *identity* with adult sexual behavior, thinking that children might be gay superimposes adult sexuality onto them—which is certainly inappropriate. But considering a child to be gay is not more (or less) sexually suggestive than assuming he is straight.

Savin-Williams (2005) stated that the reluctance to perceive children as gay is rooted in the belief that children are asexual. Few are willing to identify prepubertal gay children, assuming that gayness "arrives" only with adolescence or the onset of puberty (Savin-Williams, 2005).

Some (perhaps to avoid accusations of pedophilia) argue that they don't think of children as sexual at all. But as the popularity of Hummel figurines attests, we do think of children as *romantic*—holding hands, even kissing. We don't sexualize grade-school crushes, but justify them as healthy "practice" for teenage dating and adult marriage. We often ask little girls if they have crushes on their male teachers, or a little boy if he "has a girlfriend yet." As early as kindergarten, teachers have students send each other valentines—albeit on a round-robin basis. Later on, we tolerate little girls having crushes on other girls without labeling them lesbians. No one flinches if first- and second-grade boys hold hands. None of this is considered sexualization because we insist that children can't be sexual.

But the underlying assumption in all of these cases is that the child will grow up to be straight, and encouraging or allowing these childhood behaviors is considered acceptable because everyone recognizes that heterosexuality involves more than just adult sexual behavior—it also involves romance. Gayness, on the other hand, is typically seen as purely sexual behavior rather than as a multifaceted *identity* that involves affection, romance, and sex, just like heterosexuality. So if a child or adolescent *does* express romantic feelings toward someone of the same gender or actually embraces a gay identity, we immediately react by sexualizing him or her.

The ramifications of sexualizing same-sex attraction among children do the same damage that would occur to any child who is oversexualized. These children are not developmentally ready to handle adult sexual overtones of any kind. We know as clinicians that early imprinting is most profound and that the earlier the abuse, the more severe the consequences suffered will be.

The negative effects on the child exposed to this early sexual abuse—whether overt or covert—will be feelings of shame, a belief that it is their fault, self-destructive behavior, depression, low self-esteem, anger directed at the self or others, and an inability to trust others.

The Case of John

John, a 43-year-old executive, was experiencing depression, not sleeping well, and becoming easily agitated after his partner of 11 years left him. John had strong negative feelings about the gay community and repeatedly said that no one would want him as a partner because he was monogamous and didn't enjoy "kinky gay sex."

John confided that in all the 11 years he and his partner were together, he never told anyone except his close friends that they were a couple. He was not officially out to coworkers or friends outside his social circle. At family events, he referred to his partner as "my friend." His partner finally grew frustrated at not being included and ultimately left. Though upset by the breakup, John blamed it on his partner and didn't see how his refusal to publicly recognize the relationship negatively affected it. He repeatedly said in sessions, "I don't want to flaunt my sex life," which he felt being out to friends, coworkers, and family meant.

John stated that he knew it was safe to be out to his family and they would have embraced his partner as family but he just felt it would have been inappropriate to announce that "this is my sex partner." "Straight people don't have to do this, and nor should I!" he said.

This comment was a big red flag for me. I recognized that John was buying into the concept that gayness equals adult sex, and that being an out gay man was like telling people about his sex life. This had already cost him his relationship. When I questioned him about this, he became defensive: "Why should I have to tell them? They don't tell me what they do in bed nor do I want to know."

"Telling them you are gay isn't telling them what you do sexually in bed," I quickly replied. "It is about honoring the love you had for your partner and ensuring that your family and friends honored and treated you as a couple." He strongly disagreed and told me how ridiculous I sounded. He had normalized his way of living and accused me of being an "activist gay therapist" who wanted him to wave a rainbow flag. This, of course, was negative transference, and it revealed more about him and his internalized homophobia. John said he purposely stayed away from the gay community because it was too "sexual and immature."

"Why tell them only to have them think of me and my partner being sexual? It is better they not have that image or discomfort," he replied.

I responded to John by telling him that his concern about how people react is also a form of internalized homophobia and that his decision not to tell had more to do with what other people thought than what he actually thought.

"Do you think that your relationship with your partner is solely based on sex?"

"No," he responded.

"Then I am saying it is your opportunity and responsibility to educate your family for your benefit, your relationship's benefit, and your family's benefit. You lost your relationship over this. Imagine the detriment of a heterosexual man not telling his family and friends that his significant other was his wife?"

"This is different—when you tell someone that you are gay, they immediately think of sex!" he argued.

"But your job to heal and grow as a gay male and have successful relationships is to get past this yourself," I responded. "I don't even think about what others think any longer. If they imagine my partner and me being sexual or even just me, that is their issue, not mine. It does not dictate who I tell. As a Jewish man, I don't refrain from sharing I am Jewish just because others might stereotype me. The same needs to hold true about your being gay."

This was the place where John needed to do his work in therapy. He was suffering from covert cultural sexual abuse.

John: Clinical Interpretation and Treatment

Protecting his family was another form of internalized homophobia, as was John's denial that he equated homosexuality with adult sex. Gays and lesbians must detach from the reactions of others, unless they are in danger of physical violence, losing their job or housing, or being rejected by their family when they are dependent on the family financially or otherwise. For John, none of these factors applied: It was safe to tell others. The trouble was that he did not feel safe inside himself. He wanted to protect his family, and I interpreted him as saying unconsciously, "I interpret my gayness as sexual given that I have reduced myself to only that—not only in the eyes of other but also in my own." To me, John was struggling with the effects of covert cultural sexual abuse, which manifested in internalized homophobia. Recovery would be intolerance of not letting others know his authentic self. Moreover, recovery would entail being out everywhere it was safe to be out. Ultimately John's work was detaching from others' false assumptions that his gayness was purely sexual, "sick," or negative in any other way.

Uninformed therapists may overlook signs of internalized homophobia and unintentionally align with a client's reasoning that, for example, the gay culture is "overly sexual" and that it isn't important to come out to people you speak to or exchange cards with once a year. Even if they do catch the internalized homophobia, they may treat *it* and not address the covert cultural sexual abuse. The informed gay affirmative therapist, however, will catch these forms of internalized homophobia and covert cultural sexual abuse and help clients identify and heal from them.

Gender Bashing

Gender bashing is one of the predominant forms of covert cultural sexual abuse on all children but especially gay and lesbian children. As I have already mentioned, many of my gay and lesbian clients—males more than females—recall being "different" in a negative way from an early age but didn't know exactly what that difference was. The reason males notice their difference earlier than females is often because of their desire to play with opposite-gender toys—such as Barbie dolls rather than GI Joes—which they were shamed for. Many admit that if others had granted them permission, they could have discovered why they were different. Instead, they compartmentalized, or even demonized, this major part of their identity.

For example, one of my male clients played mostly with the girls as a child—they dressed up and played house. He was gentle, soft-spoken, and poor at sports. He was teased in school and bullied by being pushed, slapped, spit at, and verbally abused. He still experiences the effects of this trauma. The shame he felt for being the "wrong" kind of boy penetrated his core identity.

A lesbian client of mine was a tomboy as a little girl, excelling at sports and dressing in male-identified clothing. She was then forced to wear dresses by her mother and to "act more like a lady." She was shamed for being the type of female her mother did *not* want her to be.

Children and adolescents may be overly stimulated by the opposite-gender behaviors they wish to engage in. They may even notice something about the same sex that is attractive in a romantic or sexual way but have no one with whom to share this. If they do share, they are often met with contempt or denial. They are titillated by the overwhelming feelings of romance and sexuality and have no positive outlet for these powerful feelings. For these individuals, PTSD symptoms result from having to keep such important and highly emotionally charged information inside. In addition, our patriarchal society punishes gays and lesbians from the start for not complying with rigid gender roles that mandate that only the opposite sex can be your object of passion and desire sexually and romantically.

Overall, little boys tend to be shamed and degraded more often than girls for not being gender conforming. Being male is a privileged status, and anything else is viewed as inferior. Little girls are even rewarded for engaging in opposite-gender behaviors and interests. For example, it's okay for girls to be tomboys for period of time but there is no acceptable time frame for boys to be sissies.

However, this isn't always the case, as the film *Fried Green Tomatoes* illustrates. Although the theme of lesbianism is played down in this movie, it is apparent that the lead character, Idgie, is lesbian. One flashback recalling her younger life shows Idgie as a little girl—a tomboy with scorn for wearing dresses—being coerced to wear one to her sister's wedding. For Idgie, this is humiliating and out of synch with who she naturally is. When her younger brother makes fun of her discomfort, she climbs up to her tree house and flings the dress down to the ground.

But the next scene portrays something that most gay and lesbian children lack—a family member who validates who she is. Idgie's older brother Buddy accepts her being "different." While she's still half-naked and humiliated, he climbs up to the tree house and tells her about "all the millions of oysters . . . at the bottom of the ocean. And then one day God comes along and sees one and says, 'I'm going to make that one different.' . . . He puts a little piece of sand in it [so that particular oyster] can make a beautiful pearl."

"What if God made a mistake?" Idgie asks.

"The way I figure it, He doesn't make mistakes."

The next scene shows her in church wearing a suit and tie—and looking proud, in integrity with herself once again.

As this film shows, the extent of the trauma from growing up gay and lesbian would be reduced tremendously—or even avoided altogether—if every lesbian and gay child had a "Buddy" in their lives.

Forced Gender Identity Confusion

Unlike people who suffer from true gender identity confusion, such as some trans-gendered individuals, gay and lesbian children have no innate confusion regarding their maleness or femaleness. Little girls such as Idgie are *not* confused. They know the type of female they are. It is *others* who are uncomfortable, not them. The confusion and problems come from outside themselves, as others try to mold them into the type of male or female they are "supposed to be." This is counter to the idea that gender confusion causes homosexuality—a belief espoused by the reparative thera-pies discussed in Chapter 1.

Reparative therapy asserts that gay men weren't adequately taught how to behave as boys, and lesbians weren't taught how to be girls. It holds that gay individuals can be "changed" to become straight by eliminating homosexual desires. The male and female ideals touted by these therapies are sexist and outdated. Making people with homosexual desires ashamed for being the "kind" of male or female they are is a form of covert sexual abuse. Your gay and lesbian clients may be suspicious of any therapy at all, thanks to the harmful practices of reparative therapy. Watching for this transference is imperative and assuring clients that you are not in favor of reparative therapy in any form is important.

Probably the most abusive book toward gays and lesbians is *A Parent's Guide to Preventing Homosexuality* by Joseph Nicolosi and his wife, Linda Ames Nicolosi (Nicolosi & Nicolosi, 2002). In a veiled way, this book evades the American Psycho-logical Association's warning that trying to "help" gay people suppress their sexual and romantic desires may lead to a lifetime of depression. Nicolosi's book on prevent-ing "homosexual" orientation in the first place is nothing more than child abuse.

Nicolosi and others in his "extreme makeover" camp have gotten wise to the criticism of their approach and thus have disguised it. They've softened their terminology, telling parents to correct children but not shame them for playing with opposite-gender toys. If your son plays with a doll, they advise taking it away and telling him you're giving it to a little girl who needs it. To me, this is abominable. They want men to be good fathers, but stop them from playing with dolls—which is one way to learn how to parent. Removing toys, whether you do it nicely or in a shaming way, will only wound a child's self-esteem.

Furthermore, playing with dolls does not *make* a boy homosexual or lead to orientation problems. In *The "Sissy Boy Syndrome" and the Development of Homosexuality*, Richard Green reported a study in which 75% of the boys who played with girls' toys and identified with girls grew up to be gay (Green, 1987). Green speculated that playing with feminine toys won't *make* a boy gay, but that it is one possible indicator that he *already* is (Green, 1987).

A Parent's Guide to Preventing Homosexuality tells mothers to "back off" and turn away from their sons, giving the example of a mother who was "disgusted" by her son's asking to use her makeup. The only good advice they give is for fathers to get more involved. I couldn't agree more: Fathers abandoning their sons, gay and straight alike, has caused much of the anxiety and depression in men today. More involved fathers can help their sons grow into more mature men, but they cannot make them straight or gay.

Although most of the literature on this subject tends to focus on male homosexuality, this isn't a phenomenon specific only to males. Females also experience coercion to act like traditional girls.

The Case of Kim

Kim, age 40, came to see me after the loss of a third relationship with a woman whom she had been with for 5 years. Kim was starting to wonder whether or not she was a lesbian. She'd already consulted a therapist who convinced her that her childhood contributed to her lesbian identity and that her relationships failed because she was living the wrong sexual identity.

Kim was the younger of two siblings; her brother, Tom, was 2 years older. Kim recalled having a distant relationship with her mother early on. Her mother wanted her to wear nail polish and dresses and keep her hair long. However, Kim did not like that from a very young age. If her mother put her in dresses she would change into pants and get punished by her mother. If her mother polished her fingernails she would chew them off by the end of the day. Kim's mother even forced her to get her ears pierced, trying to bribe her with diamond earrings. When Kim "lost" the earrings, her mother became very angry.

Kim's mother repeatedly shamed her, asking her why she "did not want to be a girl." But Kim recalled wanting to be a girl even from a very young age—just not the type of girl her mother thought she should be. Kim was labeled a tomboy and her mother ultimately distanced herself from her in frustration.

As a child, Kim was jealous of her brother, who went to baseball games with her father—trips on which she was not included. Her father had been a star athlete in high school and hoped for Tom to follow in his footsteps. Although Kim played baseball in second grade and hoped her father would attend and possibly coach, he was coaching Tom's team instead.

When Kim complained to her father, he would side with her mother, telling Kim to go along with what her mother wanted. "Little girls must be pretty and soft for their boyfriends," he would say to her. She felt rejected and alone.

By fifth grade, however, Kim began to excel at baseball, and by sixth grade, she was the star jock of her school baseball team. Her father began taking a stronger interest in her baseball events and eventually began coaching her. Eventually her father mostly abandoned Tom, as his playing was below average and paled in comparison to Kim's. Kim recalled hearing her mother fighting with her father over this, and said that over time her mother distanced herself from Kim and became closer to Tom.

In high school, Tom complained that he was referred to as the "brother of the best baseball player in their school" and was unhappy about being in Kim's shadow. Kim grew closer and closer to her father, and although she enjoyed her relationship with him, she felt badly for her brother.

Kim also felt responsible for her parents' fighting and for how her father treated Tom. She would hear her mother expressing contempt for Kim and wondering if she was the type of girl who really wanted to be a boy. Her father finally stood up to his wife, stating that all that mattered was she was good at something and he was proud. The truth of the matter, according to Kim, was that he was invested in a child who could play baseball well and it happened to be her. She knew both her parents would have preferred her to be more feminine.

By the time she came to see me, Kim was a physical therapist for sport injuries and a coach for several girl baseball teams; she'd built her entire identity around sports. She had a distant relationship with both her mother and brother and had difficulties in her relationships with women as well. All three of her partners told her she was emotionally distant and did not offer enough closeness and dependency. After seeing the last therapist, Kim wondered now if she might have been attracted to women because of her distant relationship with her mother. She worried that the therapist was correct—that perhaps she turned away from men out of fear of being "smothered" and engulfed by her mother and her attempts to make Kim more feminine.

Perhaps, she wondered, she was looking toward women in an effort to meet her "mother hunger" needs.

Kim: Clinical Interpretation and Treatment

Staying in the model of GAT, I told Kim that how one is raised cannot create homosexuality. Kim did not have any attraction to men in any way and knew inside that she was romantically and sexually attracted to other women and always had been. She acknowledged that this was true, and admitted that this realization had led to her change therapists.

I explained to her that she had taken on the problems in her family, making them her "fault" for how things turned out. I normalized how children blame themselves and have magical thinking about controlling the way things occur in their families. We worked together on understanding that her father was playing out his dream of having a star athlete for a child. That she was naturally athletic, unlike her brother, was not something she made happen.

In terms of her relationships with women, it made more sense that her distant mother created a childhood imprint and that this was why Kim distanced herself from her partners, which led to failed relationships. I explained to her that her mother's discomfort with the kind of female Kim was as a child was her mother's issue, not hers. This had caused a distance between Kim and her mother, which became her love map in terms of keeping a distance from the women with whom she had relationships. In other words, her relationship with her mother caused problems in her relationships; it did not *create* her sexual orientation. This helped Kim direct her attention away from "what made her gay" to the real question of what was causing her relationships to fail.

Linking Homosexuality With Pedophilia

One of the most damaging myths is that homosexuality and pedophilia are linked. This is by far one of the worst forms of covert cultural sexual abuse that children (particularly boys) are taught—to beware of homosexuals who might prey on them. Many of the people who link pedophilia with homosexuality are those who equate gay men with members of NAMBLA, the North American Man-Boy Love Association—which has everything to do with pedophilia and nothing to do with homosexuality.

Many of my male clients were taught as children that pedophilia and ebophilia are forms of homosexuality. (An adult attracted to a preteen is a "pedophile"; an adult attracted to a post-teen is an "ebophile.") This link obviously scares young gay boys, but it can have an even more negative effect as well, as the following story illustrates.

The Case of Mike

Mike was a 54-year-old teacher, still closeted, never married, who paid male prostitutes for sex. When he was a child his parents taught him that he needed to stay away from the man at the end of the block because he was dangerous. The entire neighborhood knew this man was a *homosexual* and tried to be sexual with little boys.

At the age of 13, Mike became titillated by this information. He did not know where to find other males like him interested in being sexual with one another. He reported in therapy that approaching another boy in school would never be acceptable and he was isolated and alone, wanting connection with someone like him.

Over the summer he began going over to the man's house and they became "friends." Nothing sexual happened initially, and Mike believed the man really liked him. Then, one summer night at dusk, he went over the man's house and, sure enough, the man began a sexual relationship with him. The man was in his thirties and although Mike knew it was wrong and shameful, he felt compelled to continue seeing this man, whom he described as loving and nurturing.

One day while Mike was at the man's house, another 12-year-old boy came over, and the man forced the two boys to be sexual. The other boy did not want to, but the man forced him, telling both boys that if they told anyone he would kill their families. The man took pictures of the boys masturbating and fellating one another.

Horrified, Mike went home afterward trembling and frightened. When he returned the next week the man told him to never come back. Mike never saw the man again. He felt betrayed and abandoned—but most importantly, he felt that this man had "loved" him and then "rejected" him.

Mike: Clinical Interpretation and Treatment

Mike lived with this secret all of his life until stepping into my office. He had equated homosexuality with pedophilia. Even though as an adult he knew this wasn't true, he could not break the link. He blamed himself for what happened as all sexual abuse survivors do.

My first step in Mike's treatment was to educate him about sexual abuse. I told him that a sexual advance from an adult to a child is always sexual abuse. The adult is in a position of power and the child is not. Sexual abuse confuses individuals in terms of understanding their true sexual and romantic orientation and causes them to sexually act out promiscuously.

"But I asked for it. He was my first love," Mike told me vehemently. "Sexual abuse is something that happens involuntarily without love—I signed up for what happened!"

I told him that was not possible as a child. He was a gay teenage boy looking for love and attention and a sexual experience. Not knowing where else to go he sought out the pedophile in the neighborhood, whom he was told was a "homosexual." I explained that as a gay adolescent not knowing of any other resources, it made sense that he sought out this man. I also emphasized that this experience should *not* have happened, as the man took advantage of him.

"But I loved this man too and thought he loved me," Mike told me. I told him this relationship was not about love but about power and abuse, and that it had nothing to do with homosexuality and everything to do with trauma and rape.

This made sense to Mike. Weeping, he told me that he felt he was dangerous and had worried throughout his life that he, too, would become a child molester. As an adult, he had compulsive sexual behaviors; he was driven to meet male hustlers and pay them for sexual connection. I interpreted this as his PTSD: Mike felt that he was "a danger" to others the same way the man down the street was identified as dangerous. Paying male hustlers for sex was his way of avoiding feeling dangerous. However, I pointed out, and he agreed, that he often put himself at risk again by finding these male hustlers in dangerous ways and not knowing them very well. Indeed, Mike had been not only robbed by some of these men but also blackmailed—they had threatened to out him if he did not pay them off.

Mike's work in therapy was to understand that he was not at fault for what happened to him or for being a gay little boy who was overstimulated by being told that the molester down the street was a homosexual. It made sense that he went to meet this man, as he had felt so alone and isolated.

With today's access to the Internet, gay children can even more easily make contact with pedophiles and other dangerous characters. If children are overstimulated by having to suppress their innate sexual and romantic feelings as well as their core identity, they will absolutely find places to express themselves that could prove dangerous or even deadly.

In her book *Predators, Pedophiles, Rapists and Other Sex Offenders*, Anna C. Salter (2004), a leader in the field of pedophilia, pointed out that when a man molests little girls, we call him a "pedophile," not a "heterosexual." Research psychologist Gregory Herek defined pedophilia as "*a psychosexual disorder characterized by a preference for prepubescent children as sexual partners, which may or may not be acted upon*" (Herek, 2006b). He added that because of our society's aversion to male homosexuality, and the attempts made by some to represent gay men as a danger to "family values," many in our society immediately think of male-male molestation as homosexuality. He compares this with the time when African Americans were falsely accused of raping white women, and when medieval Jews were accused of murdering Christian babies in ritual sacrifices. Both are examples of how mainstream society eagerly jumped to conclusions that justified discrimination and violence against these minorities. Today, gays face the same kind of prejudice. Most recently, we've seen gay men unfairly turned out of the Boy Scouts of America on the basis of this myth that gay men are likely to be child molesters. But keeping gays out of scouting won't protect boys from pedophiles.

Of importance here is that pedophilia should be viewed as a kind of sexual fetish, wherein the person requires a child or the mental image of a child to achieve sexual gratification. Rarely does a pedophile experience sexual desire for adults of either gender. They usually don't identify as homosexual—the majority identify as heterosexual, even those who abuse children of the same gender. They are sexually aroused by youth, not by gender.

In fact, some research shows that for pedophiles, the gender of the child is immaterial. Accessibility is the more important factor. This may explain the high incidence of children molested in church communities and fraternal organizations; in these venues, pedophiles easily have access to children. In these situations, an adult male is trusted by those around him, including children and their families. Males are often given access to boys to mentor, teach, coach, and advise.

Your gay and lesbian clients have had to live with this false link from childhood. If they have children, want to have children, or want to work with children, it is important that you explore with them whether or not they hold this erroneous belief.

Childhood Origins of Covert Cultural Sexual Abuse

Since childhood, your lesbian and gay clients have been taught—if only implicitly—that they're largely responsible for whatever abuse and neglect they've suffered. Thus they're often wary of demonstrating affection or warmth for anyone of the same gender. Especially if they've sought to "pass" in straight society, gays and lesbians feel lonely and alienated, which only contributes to their emotional isolation and repression.

When therapists treat teenagers who are straight and are dating heterosexual partners, they never say to their clients, "You don't know what you are yet. Keep an open mind, and date someone of the same gender." But when young clients express an interest in romance with their own gender, a well-intended therapist often warns them not to commit to a lesbian or gay orientation—giving the message that hetero-sexuality is still an option and to grab it if they can.

Sexual Anorexia and Aversion

At the core of covert cultural sexual abuse is the teaching of sexual aversion to gay and lesbian children and particularly to gay and lesbian teenagers. All children are taught to suppress, repress, and feel disdain for any sexual or romantic feelings for the same gender that would indicate anything that resembles homosexuality. This leaves gay and lesbian children and teenagers devoid of any opportunities to feel and experience their own authentic homosexual feelings.

This condition is called "sexual aversion disorder" and is listed in the *DSM-IV* for purposes of diagnosis (Carnes, 1997). The *DSM-IV* (1994) defines sexual aver-sion as:

> The individual reports anxiety, fear, or disgust when confronted by a sexual opportunity with a partner. The aversion to genital contact may be focused on a particular aspect of sexual experience. . . . Some individuals experi-ence generalized revulsion to all sexual stimuli, including kissing and touch-ing. The intensity of the individual's reaction when exposed to the aversive stimulus may range from moderate anxiety and lack of pleasure to extreme psychological distress. (p. 499)

Patrick Carnes, who coined the term *sexual addiction*, takes sexual aversion fur-ther and calls it "sexual anorexia." Sexual anorexia is "a disorder that parallels sexual addiction and compulsivity, based on childhood sexual trauma. . . . [It is] an obses-sive state in which the physical, mental, and emotional task of avoiding sex domi-nates one's life" (Carnes, 1997, p. 1). The sufferer of this "obsessive state" finds sex repulsive—quite different from having a low libido or being simply disinterested. The anorexic's primary goal is finding ways to divorce intimacy from sex.

In the movie *Ace Ventura*, Jim Carrey's character discovers that a woman he's been making love with was once a man. The next scenes show the horrified look on his face. With the theme song of the movie *The Crying Game* on the soundtrack, he burns his clothes, scrubs himself in the shower, and even applies a plunger to his mouth to induce vomiting. The audience I saw it with (many of them children) roared with laughter. What movies like this are teaching children (and reinforcing for adults) is that gay sex is revolting and grotesque.

Early on, lesbians and gays learn that if they want to be accepted by their families, peers, and society, they'd better deaden all their homoerotic impulses and feelings. These children are taught to deny anything that seems innately natural for them. When they reach adolescence and find their sexual thoughts and desires directed at the same gender, they buy into the long-standing position that such thoughts and feelings are something to deny.

Sufferers of sexual anorexia experience a typical set of characteristics that parallel those of gays and lesbians, as Table 4.1 shows.

Table 4.1

Characteristics of Sexual Anorexia and Growing Up Gay or Lesbian

Sexual Anorexia	Growing Up Gay or Lesbian
A pattern of resistance to anything sexual	A pattern of resistance to any same-sex attractions
Continuing that pattern of avoidance, even though they may know it's self-destructive (e.g., may harm a marriage, prevent relationships)	Continuing that pattern of avoiding homosexuality even though they may know it's self-destructive (suicide, depression)
Going to great lengths to avoid sexual contact or attention	Going to great lengths to avoid homosexual contact or attention
Rigid or judgmental attitudes toward sexuality—their own and others	Rigid or judgmental attitudes toward homosexuality—that of others and especially their own
Resistance and avoidance of deeper, more painful life issues	Resistance and avoidance of exploring deeper, more painful life issues (which would promote a coming out process)
Extreme shame and self-loathing about their bodies, sexual attributes, and experiences	Extreme shame and internalized homophobia about their own bodies, sexual attributes, and experiences toward the same sex
Obsessing about sex and how to avoid it, to a point where it interferes with normal living	Obsessing about homosexual sex and how to avoid it, to a point where it interferes with normal living

Sexual Anorexia	Growing Up Gay or Lesbian
Possible episodes of sexual bingeing or periods of sexual compulsivity	Possible episodes of homosexual bingeing or periods of sexual compulsivity with same-sex experiences, thoughts, or looking at pornography

The Case of Frank

Frank, a 37-year-old postal worker, came to see me because he was having trouble accepting his homosexuality. He was in a 5-year relationship that was now predominately asexual. Although the relationship had started out highly charged, within 3 months the frequency of sexual contact had diminished to nothing more than once a year. Frank admitted that he avoided being sexual with Sam in every way—even sleeping in different bedrooms, using the excuse that Sam snored. Frank said his most prominent concern was his fear of losing Sam due to lack of sexual contact.

At Frank's third appointment, when I went to greet him in the waiting room, he rejected my courteous gesture to have him precede me into my office; he had me walk in front of him. I could see that he was growing anxious, as evidenced by his fidgeting in his chair and voicing concerns about my motives as a therapist. He was suspicious that I was finding him attractive and might fantasize about him later. He was careful to sit with his legs crossed and said he thought that I was trying to stare at his crotch. He also admitted that he wanted to walk behind me to avoid the possibility that I was looking at his buttocks.

Frank thought he must have been sexually abused as a boy. He had no memories of anything remotely close to that, but he believed he must have repressed it because of his "unusual sexual ways."

Over the next year, Frank filled me in on his sexual history—which was painstakingly difficult for him. He would start talking about his sexual interests at the beginning of each session but then stop himself, saying he was nauseated at the thought of telling me his deepest, darkest fantasies. But he knew he had to tell *someone*. During some sessions, he would leave to vomit in the bathroom and return only to change the subject.

From the moment he had discovered masturbation, Frank recognized that his sexual fantasies were of other boys his age. He was "mortified" by this and tried hard to think about girls, but to no avail. He stopped masturbating and vowed to wait until he could "condition" himself toward the opposite sex. He told me he was disgusted by both his sexual impulses and his own body. He masturbated often, but hated it after he finished, particularly if he ejaculated on himself. He would shower immediately afterward, feeling intense shame because of his fantasizing about men.

In his twenties, Frank dated women, two in particular, and felt no shame about his sexual experiences with them. However, sex with them was not erotic. Deep inside, he knew that he was performing a chore to "keep them satisfied." If men entered his mind while he was having sex with these women, he would have to stop immediately as he would lose his erection. In its place, he felt intense shame.

Frank told me that after turning 30, he acted on his gay impulses with a male hustler. He could not enjoy the experience, though he stayed erect the whole time. He did not ejaculate while the hustler was present but after the man left. For years afterward, Frank became intensely aroused recalling this sexual encounter, which he'd been unable to enjoy in the moment.

Over the next year of our work together, Frank disclosed more. He told me that while driving to visit his parents in another state, he would insert objects in his anus and experience pleasure from this. He would delight in the fact that the other drivers he passed didn't know what he was doing. He would masturbate to the gay porn he brought with him at rest areas, hoping someone would see him. If they did, however, he would leave immediately—and would shred and discard the porn upon arriving at his parents' house.

When Frank was growing up, his father was an alcoholic who was verbally aggressive toward Frank's mother and often beat her. His mother passively acquiesced to her husband and allowed him to control the house with very strict rules and expectations. He would terrorize and threaten the children with verbal threats. He was physically abusive to Frank a handful of times but never to his sister. One time his father called him a sissy for not fighting back when a bully repeatedly kicked him in front of their house as his friends watched, humiliating him.

Frank: Clinical Interpretation and Treatment

In Frank's case, both his father and society had taught him to be negative about his sexuality, that homosexuality was wrong. He never stood a chance to express his sexuality in any positive way. He was clearly conditioned to be sexually averse to anything of a homosexual nature. For the sexual anorexic, *any* sexual feelings are immediately suspect. Sexual anorexics accuse those who accept their sexuality as "out of control" and "immoral," and Frank accused the gay male community of being both. This made it hard for Frank to trust me, as I am gay and very visible within the community.

Frank entered our work with immediate negative sexual transference toward me.

His worries that I would be sexualizing him as he walked in front of me were rich with his projections of what he was—or might want to do toward me. I interpreted the negative transference in two ways: (1) that he had sexual feelings toward me that he could not tolerate so he projected them onto me; and (2) he may have unconsciously *wanted* me to feel sexual toward him to validate his belief that gay men are nothing but sexual beings.

I educated Frank about negative transference, as I do with all my clients. When I told him I thought he was projecting, he began to cry and told me he wanted help and believed I was the therapist who could help him because I'd helped many of his friends. I explored with him what it might mean if he felt sexual feelings toward me during our work together. He told me he *would* disclose any sexual feelings toward me if this occurred and that he trusted me, based on my reputation in helping his friends. I suggested that if negative transference did surface in the future, it would be therapeutically helpful, and I left it at that.

It would be easy for a therapist to label Frank's behavior as internalized homophobia. I would agree that it's an expression of that, but underneath this symptom, Frank was suffering from sexual anorexia's core beliefs and thoughts.

Also, as Carnes's research demonstrates, many sexual anorexics come from rigid homes where judgmental parents condemn sex in highly negative terms. This was true in Frank's case. In many cases like Frank's, one parent is punitive with their children about sexual issues, but both are authoritative, closed to new ideas, and demonstrate little affection. Children must measure up to their expectations, never being able to negotiate the rules. They're forced to withdraw inside themselves to find affection on their own. For gays and lesbians, *society* is the rigid and judgmental parent. Dr. Carnes's work explains why those of a gay orientation go to such lengths to fight their natural sexual urges.

I placed Frank in a gay men's therapy group, hoping it would reduce his transference toward me and offer him a greater sense of safety. In such a group, he would be able to confide in other men if he felt anything unsafe arising in his therapy with me. Also I wanted him to achieve a sense of belonging and have someplace where he could work on his sexual shame and internalized homophobia.

As Frank grew comfortable working with the group, I encouraged him to talk about the sexual acts he engaged in while driving. I thought this would remove the secrecy and thereby alleviate the shame that was motivating the acting-out behavior. Because other group members had disclosed various sexual acting-out behaviors, I knew this was a safe group for him. It took him a long time to open up, as he worried that all the gay men in the room would sexualize his story. He was still trying to control the sexual impulses of others in addition to his own.

Eventually he did share the secret, and all went well. Frank's next step was to bring in a sample of the pictures of men he felt attracted to. This was my attempt to not only bring out his sexual feelings, but also allow him to receive validation from other gay men—the way straight boys usually do when they begin sharing straight porn as adolescents. This took time too, but eventually Frank agreed.

Overall, Frank improved, allowing himself to feel desire again. Eventually he was able to make more sexual advances toward Sam—and tolerate Sam's sexual advances toward him—which made their relationship closer.

Covert Cultural Sexual Abuse: The Perfect Crime

Covert cultural sexual abuse is the perfect crime because the perpetrator offends, the victim forgets, and the offender gets away scot-free. By the time gay children become adults, they may repress the abuse, deny that it ever happened, and blame themselves for whatever they do recall. Being warned that homosexuality is evil, they grow up thinking that the evil lies within them. Then, blaming themselves, they believe they deserve to be treated poorly. Out of envy, they may even identify with their homophobic oppressors. Your job as a therapist is to help these people realize, after they come out, that their problem lies mainly in what's been *done* to them and is not a result of *who* they are.

Many of my clients insist that some long-ago incident of sexual abuse made them gay or lesbian—even if they have no memory of such an event and have no evidence that it could have happened. Some of this is because of the myth that sexual abuse causes a homosexual orientation, which is completely false. But it also may be due to the fact that these clients harbor unconscious feelings about the effects of covert cultural sexual abuse on them—without knowing what to call it—which they sometimes misidentify as covert sexual abuse.

Those who *were* sexually abused believe that that's precisely why they're now gay. They buy into the old assumption that sexual abuse turns a bewildered child away from his inborn heterosexuality and "makes" him gay. As discussed earlier, sexual abuse may lead to sexual acting-out behaviors, but there is no evidence that it can shape one's sexual orientation, much less create it. The only thing it does do is cloud and confuse people about what their sexual orientation truly is. Again, sexual abuse can influence *behavior*, not basic orientation. And covert cultural sexual abuse can create a barrier to achieving any sense of belonging with other gays and lesbians.

Brian McNaught (1997) put what I call covert cultural sexual abuse into perspective in terms of what happens to a young gay or lesbian child's development:

. . . most gay people have been enormously, if not consciously, traumatized by the social pressure they felt to identify and behave as a heterosexual, even though such pressure is not classified as sexual abuse by experts in the field.

Imagine how today's society would respond if heterosexual thirteen to nineteen year olds were forced to date someone of the same sex. What would the reaction be if they were expected to hold the hand of, slow dance with, hug, kiss and say "I love you" to someone to whom they were not and could not be sexually attracted?

The public would be outraged! Adult supervisors would be sent to prison. Youthful "perpetrators" would be expelled from school. Years of therapy would be prescribed for the innocent victims of such abuse. Volumes would be written about the long-term effect of such abhorrent socialization (as today we lament the ill-conceived efforts to turn left-handed people into right-handed ones).

Yet, that's part of the everyday life of gay teenagers. And there's no comparable public concern, much less outcry, about the traumatizing effects on their sexuality. (p. 48)

McNaught's perspective offers excellent insight into the sexual trauma gays and lesbians experience growing up. By putting heterosexual children and teenagers under the same circumstances that gay and lesbian children suffer, the covert cultural sexual abuse is highlighted and obvious.

Children can be vulnerable to sexual abuse, whether covert or overt—especially in homes where there is physical and emotional abuse and neglect. Children who do not have a sense of belonging or identity and who have troubled relationships with their parents are especially vulnerable to sexual abuse. Lesbian and gay children, even those who come from the best of families, can suffer the effects of covert cultural sexual abuse, internally knowing they don't belong and that their identity is something that could be met with contempt and rejection.

Lacking emotional and intellectual maturity, children automatically trust their caretakers and authority figures and incorporate their beliefs. Gay and lesbian children, then, are particularly vulnerable to covert cultural sexual abuse because they automatically trust their "perpetrators"—caretakers, doctors, teachers, coaches—none of whom necessarily mean any harm, but who are simply expressing the "wisdom" they have learned about homosexuality.

Comparing Covert Cultural Sexual Abuse to Sexual Abuse

If you view lesbian and gay clients as the victims of a cultural rape that unfolded over the course of years, you may well find you can adapt many of the standard techniques used to counsel sexual abuse survivors with surprising effectiveness. In my experience, gays and lesbians who experience the shame of covert cultural sexual abuse as they grow up tend to exhibit PTSD symptoms similar to those who survived sexual abuse, as is illustrated in Table 4.2.

Table 4.2

PTSD Symptoms of Sexual Abuse and Covert Cultural Sexual Abuse

Sexual Abuse Survivor	Covert Cultural Sexual Abuse Survivor
Sexual secret about abuse	Sexual secret about homosexuality
Pretend nothing is wrong and abuse is not happening	Pretend nothing is wrong and pretend not to be lesbian/gay by role playing heterosexuality
Self-perception is hopelessly flawed	Self-perception as gay/lesbian is that you are hopelessly flawed
Confusion about your sexual orientation	Confusion about whether you are gay or straight
Self-hate and blame for what is done to you	Self-hate and blame for being gay or lesbian, resulting in internalized homophobia
Believing you are to blame for the abuse	Believing you are to blame for not being able to suppress same-sex desires
Belief that people who care for you may kill you, abandon you, or be harmed themselves	Belief that people who care for you may abandon you, shame you, or harm themselves upon learning about your homosexuality
Isolation from others out of fear and distrust of intimacy	Isolation from others (especially gays and lesbians) out of fear of betrayal and distrust of intimacy
Deadening of all feelings to avoid sexual arousal	Deadening of all feelings to avoid same-sex arousal (staying closeted)

Sexual Abuse Survivor	Covert Cultural Sexual Abuse Survivor
Self-abuse/injury through drugs/alcohol	Self-abuse through drugs/alcohol and unsafe sex
Suicidal thoughts, gestures, and attempts	Suicidal thoughts, gestures, and attempts
Fear and avoidance of sexual arousal	Fear and avoidance of same-sex arousal
Displays of affection are inappropriately sexualized	Displays of affection are inappropriately sexualized (more so for gay men)
Becoming master of pretense and living out of integrity	Becoming master of pretense and living out of integrity, role playing heterosexuality
Settling for too little	Settling for too little and not expecting much as gay or lesbian
Short-lived and volatile relationships	Short-lived and volatile relationships before fully coming out of the closet

The Legacy of Covert Cultural Sexual Abuse

The trauma of growing up lesbian or gay imprints four core beliefs, which I've adapted from Patrick Carnes's four core beliefs for sexual addicts (Carnes, 2001):

- As a gay male or lesbian, I am basically a bad and unworthy person.
- If people knew I was gay, no one would love me.
- If I have to depend on others, my needs are never going to get met.
- This world is dangerous to me as a gay male or lesbian.

These core beliefs wreak havoc in lesbian and gay people's lives, often well into their adult years. They can lead to depression, substance abuse, and even suicide. They set the stage for personality disorders and make it difficult for people to maintain healthy relationships, romantic or platonic. They erode the very thing that makes us human—our personal identity. In the next chapter I show how the effects of this sexual abuse trauma model manifest for gays and lesbians and how you can best help them.

CHAPTER 5

Post-Traumatic Stress Disorder
From Growing Up Lesbian or Gay

It is not difference which immobilizes us, but silence.
—Audre Lorde, writer, poet, and activist

As a clinician, you know that the effects of trauma surface at different times—sometimes not for years. For gays and lesbians, PTSD symptoms reveal themselves most dramatically when clients are repressing their homosexuality or attempting to come out. The more they push themselves or are pressured toward staying in or coming out, the more they'll have to struggle with PTSD symptoms. Staying in the closet is prolonged trauma. The coming out process reactivates all the trauma that was suppressed—which is one of the things that makes coming out so difficult. Once an individual comes out and is fully self-actuated as a lesbian or gay person, the symptoms of PTSD abate.

Judith Lewis Herman (1992) eloquently described the effects of chronic trauma:

> . . . the features of post-traumatic stress disorder that become most exaggerated in chronically traumatized people are avoidance or constriction. When the victim has been reduced to a goal of simple survival, psychological constriction becomes an essential form of adaptation. This narrowing applies to every aspect of life—to relationships, activities, thoughts, memories, emotions, and even sensations. And while this constriction is adaptive in captivity, it also leads to a kind of atrophy in the psychological capacities that have been suppressed and to the over-development of a solitary inner life. (p. 87)

This explanation of PTSD applies to the experience of growing up gay and lesbian better than any other I've read. It points to why so many gays and lesbians struggle with problems in their inner lives and interpersonal lives.

According to the *DSM-IV*, post-traumatic stress disorder results from exposure to an overwhelmingly stressful event or series of events. The *DSM-IV* talks about how the stressor can be a threat or perceived threat to one's physical integrity. It also addresses the victim's response to the event, involving intense fear, helplessness, or horror. PTSD prompts symptoms of hypervigilance, hyperarousal, and the perception of threat to one's emotional and physical self.

The Case of Patricia

Jane, a therapist I was supervising, was working with Patricia, a 37-year-old hair stylist. Patricia had begun the coming out process and was grieving over the years she'd lost having not come out earlier. Jane did a thorough history on Patricia, learning that she felt she came from a functional family where she was loved and cared for by both her parents but particularly by her father. There was not any alcohol or drug abuse. Jane began helping Patricia through the coming out process, which progressed slowly. Patricia would frequently get angry and upset about not coming out earlier. She knew her family would take the news of her being a lesbian well. She recalled that her father enjoyed playing ball with her and came to all of her soccer games and coached. He often told her she was the "son he never had." She couldn't understand why she didn't feel comfortable, when she discovered she was lesbian at the age of 20, telling them about her homosexuality.

Jane became impatient with Patricia's reticence about coming out, and the more she pushed her, the more Patricia's anxiety symptoms surfaced. This only further agitated Jane, which stimulated countertransference, prompting her to see me for some supervision.

Jane told me that Patricia's father was a police officer whom Patricia described as conscientious, rule-oriented, and full of integrity. Her paternal grandfather had been a police officer as well.

I coached Jane to ask Patricia about her mother's—and particularly her father's—values and beliefs about homosexuality. Sure enough, Patricia had plenty to say that she hadn't said before. Although she maintained that her father was loving and accepting, she also said that her dad was an "Archie Bunker type"—that is, he did not have nice things to say about anyone who wasn't Caucasian, Catholic, and middle to upper class. He frequently made fun of Arabic men, calling them "towel heads," and was very verbal about his negative feelings toward homosexuality, using words like "faggot" and "sissy queer" toward gay males. Although these verbal assaults were never directed at her or at lesbians, Patricia recalled them vividly.

Both her father and grandfather were involved in raiding rest areas where gay men would sexually cruise and hook up. Patricia watched the contempt and disgust both her father and grandfather had toward those "homos." Early in life, Patricia learned that her family's loving and unconditionally accepting attitudes didn't extend to gays. Recalling this was Patricia's "aha" moment. To come out entailed telling her homophobic father that she was one of those "queers" her father always talked about.

At age 37, when Patricia realized it was time for her to tell her father, she started exhibiting what she called OCD symptoms: She didn't sleep, became irritable, and found herself anxiously locking and relocking her house and car as she did when she was a child. Jane had agreed that it was OCD as well.

But this wasn't a case of OCD. These were PTSD symptoms. Understanding this, Jane began addressing Patricia's internalized homophobia, which came from growing up in a homophobic house and society that supports negative feelings toward homosexuality. She was also able to help her with her PTSD symptoms. Without this understanding, Jane would have treated Patricia's supposed OCD, wasting time on an ineffective treatment for a misdiagnosis.

Ultimately Patricia did tell her father, who accepted her instantly, as did her entire family, including her grandfather. They cried together upon learning how hurtful they were to Patricia as a young lesbian girl and apologized for their lack of care around that issue. But now Patricia was left with unresolved feelings of anger and sadness that as a young girl and young woman she did not allow herself the opportunity to come out and actuate her inner identity. She was able to let Jane help her be angry toward her father for the homophobic slurs and at the same time understand she was loved and cared for in every other way. I also coached Jane to help Patricia look at her mother and grandmother's role—they never said anything to her father about his homophobic and ethnic slurs. Their silence, and the implied acceptance of these slurs, contributed to Patricia's trauma.

As you can see it is crucial for the therapist to identify and understand the trauma of growing up gay. There are many clients who will come to you describing terribly dysfunctional childhoods with parents who were addicted, sexually promiscuous, or abusive. It's easy for clinicians to focus on these issues and ignore the trauma of growing up gay. But it's vital to consider trauma with every lesbian or gay client you see. Of course, not *all* gays and lesbians suffer PTSD. It depends on the client's temperament, how severe the abuse was, and how rigid and strict his or her upbringing was.

Silence Is Not Golden

Many parents—even therapists—will argue that children grew up without hearing any homophobic comments directed at them. Usually, they are correct. Direct insults do not always contribute to covert cultural sexual abuse as much as hearing and witnessing negative statements and acts directed toward other gays and lesbians as a group or individually. Another silent assault is perpetrated by the absence of lesbian and gay role models and discussions about homosexuality. Invisibility communicates the message that you don't exist, you don't belong, and that if you do express yourself, you will be alone.

It's difficult to understand the scope and nature of the trauma gays and lesbians experience growing up. To help, I use the following guided imagery exercise, which I've adapted from one written by Brian McNaught (1993). (The exercise here is written for use with a man; if you are using it with a woman, simply change the genders of the characters.)

GUIDED IMAGERY

Think back in your own life to when you were 13 years old. For the sake of this exercise, pretend that regardless of your sexual orientation, you have always been attracted to the opposite sex. Now pretend that when you were a baby, you were adopted by a gay male or lesbian couple. Without trying to figure it out, just go with your feelings of what it would feel like to be raised by either two men or two women who love you very much, are proud of you, and want you to be happy.

In this fantasy family you have an openly gay 17-year-old brother or sister who brings home a boyfriend or girlfriend who is always welcome at the dinner table. Your parents wait up when they come home from dances to find out what a great time they had, and you notice that they are expecting that of you, too. You realize that if you want to be cherished in this family you, too, need to bring home someone of the same gender to make them proud.

At 14 years old, you are on your way to your first day of high school. The bus driver has a song on the radio and everyone on the bus, including the bus driver (and you), is singing along and what you are singing is "I'm gay, I'm gay, I'm gay." What would that feel like? What would it feel like if every billboard you passed featured two people of the same gender? If every comic book hero were gay? If every television program and movie featured only gay people?

What would it feel like if your homeroom teacher were gay? And the librarian? And the principal? And the guidance counselor? What would it feel like if everyone in school thought you were gay, too?

But not *everybody* in this fantasy is gay. There are people sexually attracted to and interested in people of the opposite gender—they're called "heterosexuals." Most people—mean people particularly—call them "breeders," and you've seen bumper stickers that read *Kill a breeder for Christ* and *Make love, not breeder babies*. A boy in your seventh-grade class was hit in the head with a dodge ball because the other students thought he was a breeder. You sometimes read newspaper articles about and see on television small groups of heterosexuals trying to get legislation passed so that they won't lose their housing or employment for being heterosexual. People preach that these people want "special rights" for what they do in the bedroom. In your religious institution you hear that heterosexuality is an abomination and that those who act on it are sinners. You see yourself as a sinner because you know you are a breeder.

A couple of months after you begin high school, you are invited by someone of the same gender to your first dance. Slow dance after slow dance, you are in the arms of a person of the same gender, who keeps nuzzling your neck and whispering in your ear, "Are you having fun?" At the end of the evening, you two walk to your front door and give your first goodnight kiss. You walk inside your house and your gay family says to you, "Honey, you look so cute! Tell us all about it . . . did you have fun?"

So you get a boyfriend if you are a boy and a girlfriend if you are a girl, and you go to gay movies together and hold hands and learn how to French kiss and bring them home to meet your family and you say to them, "I love you."

When you go to college you hope things will be different, but everyone there is dating people of the same gender, too—except a small group of heterosexual students who gather at the student union periodically. Every time they put up a notice of meetings someone rips it down or writes BREEDER across it. No one wants these heterosexual students in their dorm rooms or their social groups, and no one will sit next to them in class.

As a junior you finally have your first heterosexual sexual experience. In a newspaper called the *Heterosexual Community News*, you see an advertisement for a bar frequented by people attracted to the opposite gender, and you want to go because you think you might make a new friend who understands you there. At the bar, an attractive person of the opposite gender smiles at you, introduces themselves, and asks you to dance. The next day, your gay friends comment on what a good mood you're in and ask where you went the night before. What do you tell them?

After dating this person for a long time you decide to live together. But you want to be able to have your gay family and gay friends over, so you get a two-bedroom apartment and put your belongings in one bedroom and theirs in the other. You always pull the shades at night, you get two telephones, you don't let anyone at work call you on the wrong line, and you never pick up their telephone. You don't put their picture on your desk at work and you don't call them from the office because someone might overhear you. You even bring a gay date to office functions.

One evening you arrive home late from work to find that your partner isn't there. Worried, you begin calling police stations and hospitals. After several hours of frantic calls, you discover they were taken to the hospital eight hours earlier. No one called you because there was no ID or indication to contact you in case of emergency—you were afraid that if your wallet was stolen you would be found out. When you arrive at the hospital, you stand behind the plate glass window looking at them fighting for their life all by themselves, and you must decide whether to tell the gay doctors and gay nurses that this person is your significant other—the person you love most in the whole world. You also have to decide whether to tell your coworkers who you really are and why you won't be coming to work for the rest of the week.

This exercise helps people understand what it would be like to grow up straight in a homocentric world. Once the concept of trauma is understood, people are often able to accept and understand gays and lesbians more effectively.

The trauma of growing up gay or lesbian can be acute, but for the most part it is chronic and insidious. These children grow into teenagers and young adults feeling devalued; they have low self-esteem, high levels of anxiety, and are hypervigilant. The result is post-traumatic stress disorder symptoms like those Patricia suffered. PTSD complicates and compromises almost all areas of the lives of lesbians and gays, including the coming out process, relationships, sexual expression, and mental health, along with addictions.

Bessel van der Kolk, a leading authority on the neurophysiology of trauma, wrote that " . . . the younger the age at which the trauma occurred, and the longer its duration, the more likely people were to have long-term problems with regulation of anger, anxiety and sexual impulses" (1996, p. 187). Most overt as well as covert molestation occurs within the context of pseudo-cooperation, manipulation, and coercion rather than overt force. That agreement is part of the problem. The internalization of this trauma can manifest in symptoms such as impairment of basic trust, negative effects on identity, negative impact on play and relationships with others, and excessive interpersonal sensitivity (van der Kolk, 1996).

How Trauma Manifests in Sexual Secret-Keeping

To restore gays and lesbians to intact functioning requires that clinicians learn to discern how the trauma is acted out, as it can be very subtle. In fact, clients themselves may not even know about it. Referring to Table 4.2 in the previous chapter, I will outline how to look for each of the ways the trauma manifests through PTSD.

A look at the existing literature (Maltz, Lew, Gartner) shows that those who have been sexually abused develop in ways that parallel the development of gay male and lesbian adults in terms of their thoughts and behaviors: Both carry the effects of the trauma into adulthood. The most profound trauma similarity between gays and lesbians and sexual abuse survivors is sexual secret-keeping. Like sexual abuse survivors, gays and lesbians are taught that their sexuality is their fault and that if they tell someone about it, they will be harmed in some way, whether psychologically, physically, verbally, or emotionally. Silence is rewarded by the dominant mainstream culture and hiding becomes a way of life. Keeping these sexual secrets can also lead to withholding sexual information from others. Gay and lesbian individuals may find, like sexual abuse survivors, that they are keeping sexual secrets even from themselves. This explains why so many gays and lesbians do not know they are gay before they come out. They are in complete denial.

Like with survivors of sexual trauma, the feelings of fear, shame, and secrecy that lesbians and gays experience lead to loneliness and isolation, helplessness and hopelessness. The intense fear of being "outed" is similar to the fear of others' learning that you were sexually abused. Survivors think there must be something wrong with them; that it's somehow *their* fault for causing the abuse in the first place

The Case of Jerry

Jerry, 28, was leading a comfortable life as a stagehand at a local theater. He fit the widely held stereotype of the effeminate gay man who couldn't pass as straight. He felt good about being gay and was out to his friends and family.

During one of his sessions with me, Jerry recounted a terrible story: One evening, when he was 21 and not yet out or comfortable with his homosexuality, he was approached by two men as he was leaving his fitness club. Claiming to be lost and in need of directions, the men lured Jerry into a rusting red van and promptly raped him anally.

While this was going on, Jerry dissociated—as most rape and abuse victims do. As he described it to me, he felt as if he had left his body and drifted out of the van, into a nearby billboard. The two men called him "faggot" and "queer," kicked and punched him, and then threw him out of their van, naked, before flinging out his clothes and gym bag and speeding away.

The next morning, Jerry dutifully went to rehearsal, worried that if he mentioned the incident, the world would discover he was gay. He feared both his family's rejection and being fired for "bringing his problems to work." As many gays do, he internalized the aggression of the men who raped him and blamed himself for the attack. By thinking of the abuse as "justified," a victim unconsciously identifies with his attacker—thus empowering himself.

Jerry acted as if the whole incident never happened—until 2 months later, when he was diagnosed with a deadly form of hepatitis. The doctor asked if he had contracted the disease through sexual contact. Rather than admit he'd been raped by two men, which in Jerry's mind would call attention to the fact that he might be gay, Jerry said nothing.

Most male victims of rape—whether gay or straight—fear that telling will make others question their sexual orientation. Research shows these rape victims worry about being asked questions like, "Why didn't you make him stop?" It's even worse for a closeted gay male who, like Jerry, is invested in keeping his sexuality a secret.

Jerry's health grew worse. Finally the doctor told him he would probably die if he didn't provide accurate information so the doctor could make the appropriate diagnosis and determine the best treatment. But for Jerry, fear of death was secondary to fear of his family's rejection if they discovered he was gay. Ultimately, he did admit that he must have contracted hepatitis from another man, but he didn't disclose having been raped and made the doctor promise not to tell his family.

Over the next few months, as Jerry was treated successfully, he recovered. Some years later, Jerry finally came out to his family, and they didn't reject him.

Although Jerry's story is an extreme example, it illustrates the sexual secrecy that manifests from the trauma and covert cultural sexual abuse that gays and lesbians suffer, as well as the lengths they'll go to—and even die for—to avoid further abuse and rejection.

How Trauma Manifests as Cognitive Distortions

The negative and shaming messages of covert cultural sexual abuse are learned early in life and develop into cognitive distortions similar to those exhibited by sexual abuse survivors. These cognitive distortions are:

- Pretending that nothing is wrong
- A self-perception that they are hopelessly flawed
- Confusion about their sexual orientation
- Self-hate and self-blame for what is done to them
- The belief that people who care for them may abandon them, harm them, or kill themselves

Pretending That Nothing Is Wrong

Early in life, gay and lesbian children learn to cover up anything that suggests in any way that they might be homosexual. This is when gay males and lesbians begin living out of integrity, which then becomes a rewarded way of life. But the longer they live out of integrity with themselves and others, the more it hampers other areas of their lives.

Many gay and lesbian children hope that someone will see through the pretending—that someone will say, "I can see something is wrong; let me help you." But this rarely happens.

Self-Perception as Hopelessly Flawed

In the early stages of coming out, many gay men and lesbians believe that they are hopelessly flawed. Not yet self-accepting or having formed their full identities as gay men and lesbians, they feel like they are faulty. They also feel ashamed—an emotion different from guilt. Feelings of guilt lead to self-messages like: "My *behavior*—what I *did*—is wrong or bad." The self-message of shame is: "My *identity*—who and what I *am*—is inherently wrong."

My clients have told me they will not and cannot come out to certain people in their lives as they do not want to ruin how they are perceived by them—even when coming out would not jeopardize their safety, job security, or housing. They say things like: "It would ruin how they see me" or "Then I will be seen only as the *gay* friend." This type of self-talk and these beliefs inherently suggest that these clients believe something is wrong with them.

As a therapist you can say to your client, "So what if they see you as their gay friend? What does that mean to you?" or "Why don't you want to be seen as their gay friend?" or "Talk to these people and tell them how you feel that your gayness is just a *part* of you and not *all* of who you are." It is important for clients to understand that they cannot manipulate how others will see them. Exploring their underlying feelings about why they do not wish to be seen in this way may reveal their feelings of being flawed.

Feeling flawed extends beyond one's homosexuality. It permeates how lesbians and gays feel overall in terms of gender, self-esteem, personality, and relationships with others.

Confusion About Sexual Orientation

An enduring aspect of sexual abuse, assault, or harassment is the confusion it creates. Sexual abuse leaves victims—gay or straight—dissociated from their true sexual orientation. Covert cultural sexual abuse forces gays and lesbians into a daze and rewards them for playing straight.

One of the dynamics of sexual abuse is that the perpetrator's sexuality overlays that of its victim. In other words, during and after the abuse, the victim's needs are secondary, if involved at all. For lesbians and gays, the perpetration of heterosexism leaves them wondering whether they truly have heterosexual feelings and desires or if those heterosexual desires are a result of imprinting from the dominant culture.

Because gay males and lesbians typically surrender their innate sexuality to heterosexual standards—heterosexism being the "perpetrator"—it's no wonder that, like sexual abuse survivors, they often remain confused about their orientation once homosexual or homoerotic thoughts and feelings begin to surface. Only when they finally get the courage to rebel and reclaim their own identity does their confusion and indecision dissipate.

By the time such clients arrive in your office, they've become adept at dissociating in ways that are profound and chronic, reflexive and automatic—even about matters that aren't sexual at all.

The Case of Eric

Thirty-year-old Eric was a medical student studying to be an ophthalmologist. He admitted that most of his life was spent "in his head" and said he was more cognitive than emotive in nature. He was about to graduate and wanted to move into the next part of his life, but he was confused about whether he was gay, straight, or bisexual.

This dilemma had prompted him to seek therapy 2 years earlier. Eric was cautious about being in therapy with me. To assure himself that I would not "force him to be gay," he continued to see the straight therapist he'd been seeing weekly for the past 2 years. The other therapist believed that he was more bisexual and could go either way. Eric was looking for someone more pro-gay to help him.

Eric had been in several relationships with women, and he said he had felt romance and love with these past girlfriends. But he was not attracted to women sexually, and he often took erectile dysfunction medications. With men it was different—he was sexually attracted to them instantly, but he never felt an emotional attraction. In fact, as soon as something turned emotional he would become uninterested, which made him think his homoerotic feelings were not about identity and only about sex. Eric had never been among gay men other than those he met online or at bathhouses. His lack of homosocialization was perhaps the problem—he couldn't discover a sense of belonging as a gay man.

Eric: Clinical Interpretation and Treatment

Eric took my suggestions and began attending gay community functions—he went to bars and community, political, and sporting events—but he felt that he didn't fit in at all. He spent 3 years seeing me and his other therapist, which I interpreted as a metaphor for not committing to an identity for himself. He agreed with my interpretation and thought about dating women and committing to that side of himself. I told him that if he did so he needed to tell them that he had homoerotic feelings and interests. He did not wish to do this.

Eric said he could not imagine life with another man in terms of living together and waking up each morning facing each other. He worried what the neighbors would think and how it would affect his professional life as a physician. He was stuck in an ego-dystonic place about how he wanted to live his life, which arose from his being heteroemotional and homosexual. Eric had internalized the condemnation and hostility toward homosexuality from the homophobic culture.

My work with Eric was to help him explore his inner world of emotions, feelings, and values, as well as his core identity, which was very difficult for him. Ultimately he met a man online whom he felt romantically attracted to. As I discuss in Chapter 7 on coming out, many gay men do not connect to their homosexual orientation until they fall in romantic love with another man, which is exactly what happened with Eric. He never did find an outlet within the gay community where he felt comfortable, but over time he created a relationship with this new love, came out of the closet, accepted his gayness, and made a life with his partner and friends outside the gay community.

Self-Hate and Self-Blame

Gays and lesbians internalize the hate we see and read about in the media and watch others inflict against other gays and lesbians. Those who cannot pass as straight receive it directly. This self-hate is learned at an early age. I believe it contributes to self-destructive acting-out behaviors like drug and alcohol abuse, unsafe sex practices, sexual anorexia, and sexual addiction.

Not only do gays and lesbians feel responsible for the homophobia coming their way, but they also find people who will fulfill this belief, as the following case illustrates.

The Case of Arif

Arif, a 30-year-old Chaldean single male who self-identified as a gay man, came to me for therapy after a year with a therapist he felt shamed him for letting down his family by being an out gay man. Arif's family blamed him for not being loyal to their culture, which strongly advocated marrying and having children to carry on the family name. Arif's therapist sided with his mother and father, stating she could empathize with how hard it would be to have a child go against the cultural grain. Additionally, Arif wore his hair long and had mannerisms that were traditionally feminine, which his therapist interpreted as being an "in your face" expression of his gayness and invited abuse and ridicule from others.

Within the Chaldean culture homosexuality is completely unacceptable—particularly for males. Arif's therapist was also Chaldean, and Arif hoped she would understand his plight. To his dismay, he received from her the same judgments he experienced with his family. He felt his therapist, along with his family, must be correct and that he was doing something wrong by being out and open as a gay man and inviting negativity.

Arif filled me in on his history. He initially told his family he was gay during college, at the age of 21. His family threatened to cut him off financially if he "chose that lifestyle," so Arif stopped talking about it. After graduation he took a job out of state to avoid having to deal with his family's negativity and to make a life for himself that supported his gayness. During his time away he enjoyed living a normative gay identity with gay and lesbian friends.

Several years after his move, Arif was let go from his job. Unable to find a new job and no longer able to support himself, Arif decided to move back home to Detroit. His parents told him he had a rent-free place at their home—and promised to pay for his therapy—as long as he did not talk about being gay and considered changing. He agreed to this but knew in his heart that change was not possible.

Arif's therapist explained to him that his homosexual interests might be a rebellion against his family, as he had a strained relationship with his father, whom Arif felt never liked him much as a child. She interpreted his need to be out to his family as an act of aggression and hostility. "It is okay that you are homosexual, but you don't need to act on it and you don't need to make it part of their lives as well," his therapist told him. "Your parents are older, religious, and set in their ways. Why do you seem to need to do this? They are letting you live with them rent-free until you get back on your feet. They are paying your bills and your therapy. What more do you want from them?"

At first Arif took his therapist's words to heart, wondering if he was asking too much of his parents, who were already doing more for him than most parents would. "I've already made them suffer enough," he told himself. "I'm ruining everyone else's life as well as my own."

Then Arif met some other Chaldean men at a local bar and discovered that most of them were living underground lives, marrying the women their parents wanted them to marry, having children, and having sex on the side with other men. Arif did not want to live this way. He decided that he was with the wrong therapist, terminated with her, and started therapy with me.

Arif: Clinical Interpretation and Treatment

When Arif entered therapy with me, it did not take me long to assess how depressed he was and how damaged he felt about being gay due to his family and his past therapist. I helped him see that his family, his culture, and his former therapist were blaming him for his homosexuality and for wanting to overtly be his authentic self and live in integrity. I commended him for his attempts.

The arguments his therapist and family made sounded logical to Arif since he believed that his gayness was simply a behavior. I said to Arif, "But what about talking about where and with whom you went out with at night? What about wanting to talk about dates you go on or give them an idea of the places you frequent in case something were to happen to them or to you and they needed to get in touch with you?"

Living a life of a lie might work for his family but would it work for Arif?

I validated the therapist's well-intended attempts to help Arif in a tough culture where patriarchy and masculinity are revered and homosexuality is seen as being less of a man—and even a cause for being put to death in some Middle Eastern cultures. At best she was trying to protect both Arif and his family and cause the least amount of distress for both. However, to me she was requiring change of Arif rather than of his family, which was where the issue truly lay. This was feeding into Arif's already existing low self-esteem and feelings of self-blame about causing his parents hardship.

I told Arif that he was not committing a crime in trying to be close to his family and be his authentic self with them. I helped him remove the blame from himself and explained that what he wanted in terms of being out and open was nothing different than anyone else wanting to be and feel "known" to those they love. He knew this to be true. Living out of state helped him meet other men and women living as out gays and lesbians and he knew that was how he wanted to live.

Arif's therapy centered on his low self-esteem and his depression. He was trying to suppress how negative he felt about himself for being gay. I commended him for knowing somewhere within his psyche that something was wrong and for seeking out a gay affirmative therapist because of it. I urged him to go to gay and lesbian support group meetings and deal with his internalized homophobia, which both the former therapist and his parents, along with his antigay culture, were able to tap into.

Arif's physical mannerisms made his family uncomfortable but were part of who *he* was. His prior therapist believed they were contrived and had Arif believing this as well. I encouraged Arif to write a letter to the therapist expressing his disappointment in the work they did together and explaining that it further worsened his depression and self-esteem. Arif did this and felt empowered by doing so even though the therapist never responded.

Eventually Arif found a job in Detroit and was able to move out of his parents' house. He continued working to encourage his family to accept him. This was no small task and certainly success was not guaranteed, but it did improve Arif's self-esteem and he no longer felt that being a gay man was something to feel badly about or that he was doing something wrong that needed blame or punishment.

Belief That People Who Care for Them May Abandon Them, Harm Them, or Kill Themselves

Children who are sexually abused—especially by caregivers—learn that to get their need for love and nurturing met they have to comply with the ongoing abuse or risk being abandoned and rejected. Their physical and emotional survival needs are linked to complying with the perpetrator. It is common for the abuser to abandon the abused child once the victim outgrows his or her desirability to the offender.

Parallel to this is that gays and lesbians often fear being abandoned and harmed. They also worry that loved ones may harm themselves upon learning the news of their homosexuality. "Trauma at any age, but particularly trauma that is inflicted by caregivers, generally has a profound effect on the capacity to trust" (van der Kolk,

1996, p. 196). Given that lesbians and gays have been born into "enemy camp" where families may hold negative beliefs about homosexuality, it makes sense that they worry they will be harmed or abandoned. They do not trust that their families will love them enough to work things out and accept and understand who they really are.

Also like the sexual abuse survivor who worries about the well-being of others in the family if they tell about the abuse, lesbians and gays worry about the well-being of their family members as well. You will hear things like, "I cannot tell them—it will kill them" or "It will give them a heart attack. They are already not well, so why put this type of stress onto them?" Here we clearly see the cognitive distortions. No one dies from bad news. I often joke with my clients that I have never heard of a death certificate that reads, "Died from knowledge of homosexuality of a loved one." This helps them see the cognitive distortion more clearly.

It is important here that you check out whether this is a cognitive distortion or whether it is true. Sometimes gays and lesbians *are* abandoned by their families, friends, and colleagues if and when they come out. They are no longer of use to them in that their families' dreams for them have been shattered. Friends may not want to associate with someone who is gay or lesbian. On top of that, they may lose their jobs or housing. It is still legal to be fired or kicked out of one's rental property just for being gay everywhere in the United States.

However, the fact is that this happens only rarely. Moreover, the threat of such losses is used to keep gays and lesbians silenced and closeted. Your work as a clinician is to help the client review which people they wish to tell and what the possible outcomes will be. Issues to examine around this cognition are those of trust, power, and safety. Once they go through some conflict—even major conflict—and negotiate it success-fully, they will be empowered to do it again and remove this cognitive distortion.

Cognitive and Behavioral Symptoms of PTSD

The psychological aftermath of sexual abuse in adulthood again parallels that of covert cultural sexual abuse in that both lead to a similar set of dysfunctional behav-ioral symptomology, with results that include:

- Inappropriately sexualized affection
- Preoccupation with sex
- Deadening of all feelings to avoid sexual arousal
- Isolation from others

- Short-lived relationships
- Settling for very little
- Self-abuse, self-injury, and suicide

Inappropriately Sexualized Affection

Men—gay and straight—sexualize touch more than women. There are many reasons for this. In large part, adults stop hugging and touching boys around age 8—much younger than they do for girls. Males turn to sex for the touch that used to symbolize validation and support. Our culture permits women to touch men, children, and each other with affection, caressing one another's hair and clothes and even holding hands, without anyone thinking it's odd or inappropriate.

Many gay men use sex to fill a void in their lives and to feel wanted; they then confuse this for love. Sex offers instant pleasure and pseudo-intimacy. It is easy for gay men to get caught in frequent sexual hookups because they are looking for connection through the lens of sex. This often leaves their relational intimacy shallow and superficial—but shallow intimacy is better than the total loneliness and isolation that follow in the wake of covert cultural sexual abuse.

The sexualized touch also helps remind gay men they *do* exist—countering the invisibility they experienced growing up. Sex is a way to remind themselves that they're still "there," without having to exert much emotional or mental work.

All of this leaves gay men vulnerable to developing sexual addiction and other sexual-related disorders, which I discuss in Chapter 9.

Preoccupation With Sex

Like sexual abuse survivors, gay men often have sexual difficulties that include promiscuity or trying to meet nonsexual needs through sex. Gay men tend to be more preoccupied with sex than lesbians. Growing up, males receive less affection through touch and emotion, particularly from other males, and gay men learn to exist and tolerate affection with other men through sex. Sex is often their initiation into gay manhood, which makes them vulnerable to sexual addiction (Kort, 2002).

Through the lens of covert cultural sexual abuse, a gay child is like a sexual abuse survivor: In response to his vandalized sexual development, he develops hypersexuality. That's often because when adults recognize that a child is gay, they project adult sexuality onto him before he's developmentally ready to be assigned that adult sexual role.

In Chapter 9, I describe how this manifests among gay men and can become sexual addiction and compulsivity.

Deadening of All Feelings to Avoid Sexual Arousal

Both gay men and lesbians may respond to covert cultural sexual abuse by deadening all sexual feelings. This is different from people who simply have low desire. People who have low desire are not usually *avoiding* sex. If they do avoid sex, it's because they cannot stimulate their desire. Closeted lesbians and gays, on the other hand, try to *repress* their desire and are rewarded for doing so. They learn to have an underlying obsessive hatred and fear of sex, which they avoid by squelching their libido.

Isolation From Others

Like the sexual abuse survivor who feels alone, gay and lesbian children also feel alone. The secrecy and invisibility inherent in growing up gay isolate lesbians and gays from one another. Because of the silence around gay and lesbian children, they do not see each other and are not mirrored in a way that affirms their existence.

Gay and lesbian children do not experience a sense of belonging. In recent years, some schools have created groups called "Gay-Straight Alliance," which bring gay and straight students together as allies and give gays and lesbians a sense of belonging. However, most schools do not offer this and even in those that do, it takes a brave young soul to attend.

This is why it is essential that therapists provide homosocial resources to their gay and lesbian clients and, when possible, place them in gay and lesbian group therapy. Many gay community centers offer social groups that counter isolation.

It makes sense that to ease their pangs of isolation, many gay men and lesbians use alcohol or drugs. To achieve an illusion of belonging, they may hang out at bars, clubs, and circuit parties, or console themselves with porn and gay chat rooms.

Short-Lived Relationships

As noted earlier, it is a myth that gay and lesbian relationships are inherently short-lived and bound to fail. However, the effects of covert cultural sexual abuse often profoundly affect gays' and lesbians' ability to attach to their partners. Like sexual abuse survivors, gay males and lesbians tend to enter into short-lived relationships because their love map and capacity for intimacy have been vandalized—overlaid with someone else's sexual agenda. Heterosexism demands that lesbians and gays role play heterosexuality. If your ability to deeply attach in healthy ways has been negatively affected, how can a relationship move to real love and endure? This is explored further in Chapter 10.

Settling for Very Little

Covert cultural sexual abuse sends the message that gays and lesbians—especially those who choose to be out and open—don't deserve much happiness in life. It follows that people treated as basically worthless will, sooner or later, give up and begin compromising. They may stop attempting relationships completely, or enter into relationships with partners who treat them as unworthy inferiors—whose verbal, psychological abuse only validates their lack of self-esteem.

Self-Abuse, Self-Injury, and Suicide

The rate of adolescent suicide in gay and lesbian teens is 30% (Massachusetts Youth Risk Behavior Survey Results, 1999). Many say the number is inflated; some say it's higher. But I believe this is a fair number when you consider those who attempt suicide and fortunately don't succeed. Also, that number probably includes straight teens who, because of homophobia, might worry they might be gay. Prepubescent boys often experiment sexually with one another, but that curiosity does not make them gay.

Victims of sexual abuse often cut themselves at some point. This behavior is an attempt to bring their inner pain to the surface. I believe that gay male barebacking (unprotected anal sex) and risking HIV exposure are analogous to "cutting" behavior.

"Bug-chasers" intentionally try to contract HIV so they can empathize with others who are "poz" and achieve a sense of belonging. Some gay men purposely infect other men with HIV without their victims' knowledge. The rage inherent in this violent act derives from the self-hate they experience, which in my opinion stems from covert cultural sexual abuse.

The Case of Art

A 24-year-old man named Art came to me after engaging in dangerous sexual acts in an attempt to become infected with HIV. He told me he had been having unprotected anal sex with guys at circuit parties, baths, and public restrooms. Earlier he had contracted Hepatitis B, had it treated, and ignored the potential risk of receiving it again. He'd also contracted genital herpes and gonorrhea.

Art told me that he was intentionally continuing to have unsafe sex with others. "I don't care anymore. If I get the virus, there's nothing more I can lose."

"I know I will catch HIV at some point," Art said. "At least then, I won't have the anxiety of worrying about getting it." He added, "I was not out in the 1970s when sex for gay men was free and easy. I'm not going to deaden my pleasure with latex."

Art was depressed about being rejected by his parents, who said they could not tolerate having a gay son. They cut him off financially, which caused him to drop out of college and live on his own. He tried to contact them but they would hang up. His siblings also wanted nothing to do with him. He was finding himself hating himself and his life more and more.

Art told me that he knew he was gay from an early age. He dressed in girls' clothes and enjoyed playing house and school with the girls in his neighborhood and his sisters. He was teased, humiliated, and bullied by other boys his age. His father told him he was a sissy and his mother tried to get him to play with males and bought him male-oriented toys. Throughout his childhood, Art believed that he was bad, wrong, and that he'd let his parents down.

Art explained that he felt that if he got AIDS, his parents would see how much he was suffering. He believed it would make him less depressed. When I asked him why he thought this, he replied that it would help him cope with the assaults he received from his family and others who teased him in childhood for being a girly boy. "If I got AIDS it would say to the world exactly what I have felt all my life—that I am depressed and I am dying inside and nothing can stop it."

He went on to tell me, "AIDS would be perfect for me. It would give me an identity. It would concretize my pain so that others can understand how much I suffer. It is a virus that can infect my body and destroy me just the way the abuse has destroyed me on the inside. Finally everyone will understand what happened to me."

Art: Clinical Interpretation and Treatment

I've listened to other men involved in these risky sexual behaviors, and I often view them as victims of self-abuse. It's like the survivor of childhood abuse asking (if not consciously), "See how damaged I am? You don't believe me? I'll show you," and revealing his scars for all to see.

I see these men as no different than the sexual abuse survivors who cut themselves. They are trying to destroy the inner feelings of pain from the abuse and from the truth—the truth being that *they* are not the ones who are damaged; those who have *done* the abuse are. They are willing to protect their perpetrators to the end even if it means death.

Through engaging in high-risk behaviors, Art was reenacting his original trauma of being bullied, teased, and humiliated. "More commonly, traumatized people find themselves reenacting some aspect of the trauma scene in disguised form, without realizing what they are doing" (Herman, 1992, p. 40). The therapeutic task was to help Art see he was victimized as a child and connect to that. His anger needed to be directed toward those who harmed him, not toward himself. He learned shame at a very young age, and now as an adult it was time to put the shame back where it belonged—onto the others who placed it on him. The shame was what was *done* to him—not him.

Dysfunctional Coping Mechanisms

PTSD symptoms are often kept at bay by gays and lesbians in four general ways—by displacement, repression, overcompensation, and dissociation—all of which are attempts to shield oneself from the trauma.

Displacement

One syndrome I often see in clients—and even suffered from myself—is displacement. The client diverts or channels his innate impulses into some other fixation that's more acceptable, easier to "explain away." Think of the football fanatic who releases his aggression vicariously on the gridiron, or the abused child who buries his head in books.

As a child, I had effeminate mannerisms and played only with girls. I was very much the gay little boy, and everyone knew it—even me. My peers bullied me, spat at me, and beat me for being gay. Even some teachers laughed at me. Then, in middle school, I became obsessed with a 1970s singing trio, Tony Orlando and Dawn, who served as objects of displacement for my homosexuality.

I discovered that other kids would tease me for liking this singing group—which made me want to like them even more. I became obsessed with them and bought every TO&D iron-on decal I could find. My peers—even some teachers—made fun of my wearing a different one to school every day. But I wore them proudly. I didn't like being made fun of but pushed it more and more, not really understanding why. Now, years later, I see that at the tender age of 11, my obsession allowed my peers to ridicule my star-worship rather than harass me for being gay. It feels vastly more comfortable to be mocked for what one *likes* than for what one *is*.

Repression

Some who experience PTSD avoid and block the feelings of emotional arousal they would have if they let the information about the trauma in. For example, if a woman is sexually abused, she might become asexual to avoid having to reexperience the trauma. The same phenomenon occurs with survivors of covert cultural sexual abuse, as the case of Diane illustrates.

The Case of Diane

Diane was a 33-year-old woman recovering from addiction to alcohol. She had tried sobriety on several occasions and was unsuccessful. She was referred to me for having "possible" repressed sexual feelings. The chemical dependency therapist who had been working with her thought Diane might be lesbian based on her mannerisms and the way she wore her hair and clothes. I made a note of the therapist's remarks but didn't make any assumptions about Diane—I appreciate input from other therapists but never accept their conclusions before talking to the client myself.

As Diane became sober, she began to wonder if she might be "homosexual." She had been instructed not to talk about this during her drug and alcohol treatment, and Diane obeyed. Now, however, she found herself interested in women and entertaining homosexual fantasies while masturbating, albeit infrequently.

Diane had a stereotypically masculine presence: She was tall, spoke aggressively, played sports, dressed in pants and T-shirts, and kept her emotions bottled up. As a child she had been drawn to sports and male-oriented toys. She knew she was different, but did everything she could to not let it show, pretending to be interested in girlish things.

Like many gay children, her self-awareness and eventual coming out were delayed by a religious upbringing. Her Lutheran family was rigid in terms of rules and gender roles. Determined to please them, Diane became rule-oriented and believed—as they taught her—that the Church's teachings were law. She also complied with her self-absorbed and narcissistic mother who demanded obedience. Some of Diane's siblings rebelled, but not Diane, who badly wanted her mother's love and acceptance.

Diane enjoyed the company of other women and felt different around them, but she told herself that her feelings were nothing more than a desire for friendship. She did not have inkling that she was lesbian until she became sober.

Diane married at 24 and lived heterosexually for years—as many gay clients do. She told me that she never felt connected to her husband or her friends. She never enjoyed intercourse but engaged in it to please her husband. Obedient to heterosexist norms, she subordinated herself to his wishes as she'd done in her family, particularly with her mother.

Though her husband was kind to her, it was clear she responded to him by avoiding her own needs and always deferring to him. The only time Diane had a sense of herself was when she played sports. Then, she'd allow herself to become aroused emotionally and her passion could surface. Through sports, Diane met a few lesbians and thought she might be a lesbian, too. However, this was not an option for her as she was married; she could not allow herself to go against her church and her family.

Diane: Clinical Interpretation and Treatment

Given Diane's symptoms of repressed sexual feelings, I felt it was important to ask about any childhood sexual abuse. Her inability to connect to others and dissociation from her sexuality fit the pattern. But nothing in her history indicated any sexual abuse, either covert or overt—so I ruled that out.

Next we explored Diane's possible repressed lesbianism. Growing up, she was not aware of any sexual feelings toward anyone, male or female. Diane prided herself on living out her childhood mission of being a good little Lutheran girl. This supported her avoidant, dissociated stance and kept her from exploring her inner self. She and her husband eventually divorced, but neither bothered to examine why the marriage failed. Once we identified Diane's codependency, she began to identify her needs and make it a priority to act on them first.

During therapy, she realized that she had suppressed and avoided her own needs to the point of not knowing who she really was. It was time to stop being passive: Diane now knew that if she did not deal with her avoidance issues, she would lose her identity all over again. Diane was a lesbian and began the coming out process.

As Diane began questioning the religious tenets of her church and examining her relationships with her family and former husband, she became more aware of her individual identity. She became increasingly comfortable with her feelings of attraction toward women and eventually allowed herself to act on those feelings.

Overcompensation

People overcompensate by becoming the best little boy or girl in the world and excelling in everything—academics, sports, household responsibilities, and so on. Often these individuals act out of shame; they feel defective and flawed.

In some cases, gay male children become hypermasculine and overly focus on male-oriented behaviors and sports. They may even become promiscuous with girls to reinforce that they are heterosexual. Lesbians may become hyperfeminine in ways that do not match their inner sense of femininity but show the external world they identify with mainstream feminine women.

The Case of Philippe

Philippe, a 40-year-old executive, came to therapy because he could no longer keep up with the pace of his life. Heterosexually married with three children, Philippe was struggling to maintain his "perfect" appearance.

In middle school, he recalled, he could never wholly relax, except when resting in his bedroom. Hiding an increasingly significant part of his identity—that he was gay—took so much mental and emotional energy that Philippe became secretly ashamed of himself. He applied much of the homophobic talk he overheard to himself.

As a teenager, Philippe overcompensated by developing a false persona to pass as straight. He pleased his parents by becoming overresponsible and excelling at school and sports, all to avoid being disparaged as the flawed man he felt he was. Philippe realized that if he received good grades and did exactly what his parents, teachers, and other authority figures wanted—even anticipating their needs before they asked him to do something—he would be rewarded and praised. He felt that if they really knew his thoughts, feelings, and desires, he would be rejected.

As an adult Philippe became a workaholic, but his workload was beginning to overwhelm him. He presented as emotionally shut down; he intellectualized his inner and outer worlds. He was suffering from depression over his anxiety that he was not performing well enough as a husband, father, or employee.

Philippe: Clinical Interpretation and Treatment

Philippe was working hard cover up what he felt was damaged and corrupt—his homosexual self. Winning awards for employee of the year, father of the year, and best husband in the neighborhood is all fine and good but it will not erase the feeling of being damaged goods. Philippe was working overtime and I helped him see that he was no longer going to be able to maintain a perfect exterior without damaging himself physically and certainly psychologically.

Philippe went on antidepressants and gradually began slowing down his work performance. He attended a gay/bisexual married men's group in the area and spoke about his shame and guilt for being a gay man in a heterosexual marriage with children. He was able to see that he was pushed into making decisions that were not in his best interest or others' best interest because he wanted to please and be accepted by others. This trumped everything in his inner world.

Dissociation

Trauma specialists speak of the integral aspect of dissociation when trauma is happening—and long after it has occurred. Basically, an individual isolates the memory of the painful event and stores it in another compartment of the mind, along with any associated strong feelings and emotions. We know that children who are abused at home dissociate to get through each day and be functional at school, sports, religious institutions, and anywhere they need to perform. The dissociative split allows the rest of the personality to achieve and thrive as if nothing has happened. Dissociation can help suppress anxiety-provoking knowledge about the self and make life more manageable. As trauma survivors begin the process of reintegration, those repressed memories can leak out and interfere with everyday functioning. The individual is left disconnected not just from himself, but also from others.

The way gay and lesbian children dissociate is by going into a heterosexual trance. The literally grow up believing that they are heterosexual and deny homosexual feelings and impulses by renaming them or giving them different meanings.

The Case of Rhonna

Rhonna, 35, came to see me after frustration with her past therapist, whom she felt was imposing negative judgments and not allowing Rhonna the freedom to decide for herself whether or not she was lesbian. Rhonna was having difficulty identifying for herself whether or not she was, in fact, lesbian; she had recently fallen in love with a woman and developed sexual feelings for the first time.

Prior to meeting this woman, Rhonna had been with and was attracted to only men. Her sexual experiences with them were less than satisfactory and she blamed them each time for not satisfying her enough. She was currently living with a fiancé of 3 years and was not sexually satisfied, again holding him accountable for meeting only his needs sexually and not hers.

When Rhonna enrolled in a graduate-level class at a local university, she immediately found herself drawn to a female teaching assistant, Gayle, who was around her age. Week after week she would look forward to the class, not for the content but to be around Gayle. She began to recognize that she more than simply liked Gayle; she had sexual and romantic feelings toward her.

Rhonna met with Gayle after class to get "extra help" on her homework, though Rhonna had other intentions. She felt compelled to move toward Gayle and see if Gayle felt the same way. Rhonna had never acted this way before.

After the class ended the two women became friends. Eventually Gayle came out to Rhonna as a lesbian and Rhonna found herself hoping something could happen between them. "I had never felt that way before—ever!" she told me. "Not even with my fiancé."

Over the next year Rhonna and Gayle decided to take a vacation as best friends. Before going, Rhonna told Gayle about her feelings, and during the vacation their friendship turned romantic and sexual. Upon returning from the trip, Rhonna felt tremendous guilt and shame, and she entered therapy. She told the therapist that she did not self-identify as lesbian at all. She also did not see herself as a woman who would have ever cheated on her fiancé. Yet she was engaging in lesbian sex and romance—and was cheating.

Rhonna's previous therapist asked if Rhonna ever had any inkling before that she might be lesbian. She asked about her history, which was stereotypically female and gender-conforming in an ego-syntonic way. Rhonna had dated boys during adolescence and fallen in love and gotten her heart broken by several men before becoming engaged to the man she called "the love of her life." She was not attracted to other women; even now, the only woman she had sexual feelings toward was Gayle.

Rhonna did have a history of being sexually abused by a best friend's brother at the age of 14. One night she awakened to find him kissing her breasts, with his finger in her vagina. She froze and pretended to be asleep, not knowing what the boy would do. She lay there until he breathed heavy and she felt warm fluid hit her face. Startled, she jerked back, scaring him out of the room. Thinking he had urinated on her, she wiped it off and never told a soul.

Rhonna's therapist was convinced that because she had no history of typical lesbian-type behaviors—like being a tomboy or feeling attracted to other girls—that Rhonna was not lesbian. The therapist told Rhonna that she was acting out her sexual abuse and once the abuse work was resolved she would no longer desire to be with Gayle. The therapist also told her to stop her relationship with Gayle as it was cheating on her fiancé.

Over the next year Rhonna couldn't stop seeing Gayle, even though she knew she was going against therapeutic recommendations. The therapist continued to condemn the behavior and helped her to work through the trauma of having been raped by her best friend's brother. Rhonna went back and forth wondering about her identity. Was she straight and in love with a woman or was she a lesbian engaged to a man? She didn't know.

Rhonna: Clinical Interpretation and Treatment

Rhonna was completely dissociated from her sexuality identity. She adapted and adopted heterosexuality as a means of survival. The therapist, in my opinion, made a poor judgment connecting her lesbianism to her sexual abuse. The fact that Rhonna did not have an inkling about her sexual identity is the norm for those growing up gay and lesbian—particularly for women, as I discuss in Chapter 7. Connecting the abuse to her homosexual behaviors was something to consider but not to make as a final decision. It is the client who should have the final say on his or her sexual orientation—not the therapist.

The sexual abuse Rhonna experienced only served to confuse her; it wasn't an acting-out behavior. What the therapist should have done is help Rhonna work through her sexual abuse issues while simultaneously helping her with her identity crisis. Rhonna also needed to decide what to do in terms of her fiancé and living out of integrity. This was a major concern for her as she did not want to want to lose him or hurt him.

It is understandable how, from a developmental perspective, this shame and trauma causes a natural splitting. Lesbians and gays hide anything that might expose them. Many will tell you in therapy that they changed their speech, their walk, the way they dressed and moved their hands, and their interests. To avoid being discovered, they bury a frozen inner self—a splitting that causes problems with identity and relationships.

Because of this splitting, many of your clients will appear characterological—that is, they will present with borderline or narcissistic personality disorders. Your job is to understand if the client's problem is characterological or a result of the splitting.

To help one client of mine connect with himself and stop the dissociation that contributed to his self-abuse, I had him write a letter to his perpetrator, who infected him with HIV.

The Case of Terry

Terry was hiring male escorts and paying for sex when he traveled for his job, which he did on a regular basis. He no longer felt any sense of belonging within the gay community. As a clean-cut man in his twenties, he had exercised religiously, shaped his full head of hair in the style other gay men wore, wore the right clothes, and went to all the right clubs. He was constantly sought after by other gay men—and even some straight ones. But as he entered his later thirties and forties, his job grew busier, and he no longer worked out like he used to. He gained a good 40 pounds, lost most of his hair, sported a goatee to make up for it—and no longer attracted men as he once did.

Throughout most of his adult life, Terry had attended circuit parties. Now, most of his friends were dead of AIDS or other health problems stemming from wear on their bodies, or were addicted to party drugs to the point where the only way he could socialize with them was to use as well. Otherwise, they had nothing in common. Terry had never learned to create much of an identity beyond the superficial one that he adopted at these parties.

No longer feeling attractive, Terry didn't feel entitled to claim a space in the gay community. So he began paying hustlers for sex. As he told me, this was easier than risking rejection and criticism in the gay bars or online. He was a bottom, and found that paying a rent boy circumvented the relational and social work of cruising.

Terry ensured that the rent boys wore condoms, and for the most part they were affirming and kind, behaving nicely toward him. But after they left, he felt lonely and depressed. He grew increasingly uncomfortable with this solution and recognized that he might even have a sexual addiction.

Then, one night, Terry was receiving anal sex from an escort and felt him pull out his erection. When the man reinserted, Terry experienced a different sensation, but he never suspected that the man had removed his condom, as they had talked beforehand about the importance of safe sex. He realized what had happened when he felt the dampness running down his thighs. He was frozen in shock. Neither of them said a word as the escort put his clothes back on and left.

Terry: Clinical Interpretation and Treatment

For therapeutic reasons, I asked Terry to write the rent boy an anger letter, even though he couldn't mail it because he couldn't find the man's address. The point was to help Terry understand that he was acting out from covert cultural sexual abuse, access his anger instead of his depression, and get beyond the distorted belief that he somehow "deserved it."

I wanted him to read the letter aloud, but he asked me to read it instead. He said he did not want to weep and wanted to distance himself from his feelings because this was so hard for him. So I read it aloud. I'm reprinting it here with Terry's permission.

> You won't remember me. We had a brief encounter in my hotel room last year. Our meeting was probably nothing out of the ordinary for you—you must have many such encounters in your line of work. But it changed my life.

You infected me with HIV, and I have to believe you meant to. Our encounter had been safe right up to the point when you deliberately removed our protection. After 6 weeks, I had the symptoms of acute HIV infection and was diagnosed as positive.

Since then, I've been holding myself to blame: I was a consenting partner, aware of the risks with someone I'd met on the Internet, and had taken such risks for some time. Maybe my luck was bound to run out.

On reflection, though, that's too easy. The fact is, on my other encounters, the play was always safe. So why did you remove our protection? Was it just recklessness on your part, a wish to play dangerously? I think you knew you were positive and had every intention of passing on the virus. But either way, what you did was wrong, and had the same consequences I now have to live with.

I can't change what happened, but believe me, I agonize over how it did. For a brief physical pleasure that would otherwise be soon forgotten, I must suffer the memory of how easily and cheaply you cut my life expectancy. For the time I have left (hopefully years, not months) I will suffer a reduced quality of life to protect my health. I may never find a life partner. Perhaps worst of all, what will this do to my family and friends?

Were these thoughts going through your head when you went out of your way to infect me? Did someone pass the virus to you in a similar way? And therefore, drive you to seek revenge on others? I can only imagine this is the retribution you sought.

How easy it must be to become a victim, blaming everyone but yourself and making a career (literally) out of passing on the infection. But you have to stop. You have to get the anger out of you and stop the chain of suffering. I am trying to find room in my heart for forgiveness, trying hard to control my anger and act responsibly towards others and not become a risk to them in the way you were to me.

I guess I'll never know your reasons or what became of you. It's ironic that you won't remember me, and I will never be able to forget you.

CHAPTER 6

Developmental Insults

> If you can't get rid of the skeleton in your closet,
> you'd best teach it to dance.
> —George Bernard Shaw

Sometimes your lesbian or gay clients will remain stuck—unable to move forward in their personal lives and relationships—even after you have implemented all of your knowledge about growing up gay (in terms of the trauma, covert cultural sexual abuse, and PTSD), have made a correct diagnosis, and have assessed them perfectly in terms of the *DSM-IV.* I have found that in these cases, the issue they are struggling with is not about being gay at all but rather relates to a developmental insult and wound that is blocking them.

These developmental wounds often appear to be related to the clients' gayness, but in truth the issue has little or nothing to do with the clients' orientation. The clients' gayness may be what is forcing the developmental wound out, however. In other words, the block in their life around being gay is a symptom and not the problem. Additionally, developmental insults sometimes leave clients with apparent disorders of character and personality. Other times, a client may seem mood disturbed. But neither may actually be the case.

I highly recommend Jean M. Baker's book *How Homophobia Hurts Children.* This book offers an excellent overview on lesbian and gay identity development. Gay and lesbian children go through the same stages of development as heterosexual children, but their sexual orientations present unique hurdles centering around their perceptions of being different from both their peers and their parents (Baker, 2002).

In this chapter I discuss some of the most common developmental injuries I've seen in my office with adult gays and lesbians, and I talk about how they might manifest in your office. I have found that Erik Erikson's developmental stages of attachment, exploration, identity, competence, concern, intimacy, and responsibility can be used as a framework to help your clients get unstuck.

For example, being stuck in the identity-confusion stage of coming out may reflect a developmental error in the client's childhood identity formation (see Chapter 7 for a detailed description of the stages of coming out). Being stuck in the identity-tolerance stage of coming out may reflect a developmental injury during the childhood exploration stage. As you identify these developmental insults and help clients heal from them, you will find that the therapy begins moving forward again.

Attachment

Attachment style and the ability to bond with another are determined early on in childhood (Ainsworth, Blehar, Waters, & Wall, 1978; Bartholomew & Horowitz, 1991; Siegel, 1999). Humans are all born wired for attachment to our caregivers. Three developmental processes are created that are then associated with a child's development of emotional competence, a sense of well-being, and skills for successful relationship development. These processes include the need to be physically close to a primary attachment figure; when upset having an emotionally secure, stable attachment figure to turn to for soothing; and after repeated experiences with the attachment figure, an internalization of the relationship as secure so that the child can hold it in mind for a sense of comfort when physically distant from the caregiver (Solomon & Siegel, 2003).

The effectiveness of how a child goes out into the world is based on how he learned to attach and build a secure base with his caretakers. This "template" becomes the basis for all future close relationships throughout childhood, adolescence, and adult life (Bowlby, 1988).

According to psychological attachment theory, mothers need to be available to their babies at least 60% of the time, to touch them and attend to them in loving ways. Their children then grow up into healthy adults who can attach to others. Otherwise, problems occur, creating unhealthy attachment disorders—vandalized forms of the ability to bond to others through love and friendship. In its most severe form, the sufferer cannot form attachments and becomes isolated and a loner. Knowing this is crucial to understanding what may be disrupting your client's attachment to friends, partners, and even you as the therapist.

Attachment and Internalized Homophobia

It would make sense that if an individual forms an insecure attachment in his first year of life, he might have later problems with coming out. Internalized homophobia has also been found to be related to one's attachment style. Mohr and Fassinger (1998) indicated that attachment insecurity increases fear associated with the tasks of identity development, thereby compromising exploration that may be critical in developing a positive gay identity. Participants in their studies who had insecure attachment styles, especially the avoidant type, were more likely than others to fear judgment based on their orientation, less likely to disclose their sexual orientation to work colleagues and heterosexual friends, less likely to identify with or interact with others in the gay community, and more likely to report high internalized antigay values.

Clients demonstrating developmental blocks around attachment issues may have come out to themselves but have great trouble trusting you as their therapist. They may not share their feelings with you for a long period of time, much as they want to. In other cases, these clients may ultimately come to trust you but not trust anyone else, regardless of your efforts to reassure them that it's safe. They may seem paranoid—which is not surprising given that growing up gay requires a high level of paranoia.

The Case of David

David was a 28-year-old gay male who came out in college to himself but not to his family or any of his friends—all of whom were straight. He also never established a social life with other gay men or lesbians. He entered therapy with a straight clinician, Rachel, over depression, which he attributed to feeling lonely and isolated.

Over the first few months David's depression improved as he met with Rachel on a weekly basis. Eventually Rachel started to talk with him about why he was not out to his parents or his straight friends.

"They would never understand and I have such good relationships—I don't want to jeopardize them. Besides, they don't need to know what I do in bed," David responded. He denied any problems growing up. He believed he had normal, hardworking parents. He was the oldest of three with two younger sisters. He denied any abuse or neglect and felt if there were any problems it was when he was a teenager and he used marijuana. "My parents caught me and we fought a lot about it but I eventually stopped and we stopped fighting too."

Rachel began working on David's internalized homophobia and fear of rejection and abandonment, teaching him these concepts in terms of gay affirmative therapy.

It all made sense to David and yet he was resistant to doing anything about it. He would agree with Rachel and come back the following week without having made any progress in the coming out process. After 2 years in therapy David was in the same place socially as he had been when he entered therapy.

Rachel sought me out for supervision and I encouraged her to address David's lack of follow-through more directly, challenging his assertion that he wanted to end his isolation. If he really wanted to become less isolated, why didn't his behavior indicate this? I was sure she would invite negative transference from him, and sure enough she did. I believed that within the negative transference would lie other issues that he was not able to consciously speak about.

In her next session with David, Rachel commented on how he agreed with her in every session, developed plans about going into the gay community at his own pace, and then inevitably failed to follow through on these plans. David offered some polite responses, but Rachel stayed with her gentle confrontation of him. Finally, David accused her of having an agenda for him. "I am not going to be a flag-carrying gay guy. I don't need to come out to anyone—I just need to meet some gay friends," he told Rachel. This only reinforced Rachel's concept that GAT was what David needed in terms of addressing his internalized homophobia and coming out issues.

In the next supervision with me, I told Rachel I thought differently. I had seen clients like David before and felt that his resistance to making behavioral change was taking too long given that he had been out to himself since college. I coached Rachel to stay with the negative transference and challenge his lack of behavioral change in a supportive but stern manner.

In the next session Rachel did just this and David started to get angry. "So are you going to fire me as a client if I don't do what you ask?"

"Why would you ask me that?" Rachel replied.

"Because you seem invested making me more out than I want to be, and you are rushing me and being critical," he told her.

Rachel knew this was not the case and explored this with David.

"I'm not used to someone being on me so much like this. You haven't been this way before. I know you mean well but get off my back!" David shouted. Then he started to cry. "I'm sorry. I didn't mean that. Please don't let me go as a client. I will try harder!"

Here was the material that needed to be addressed. Something was lurking that Rachel could not see before. She sat with David and asked him what it was like when his parents pushed him in directions that were in his best interest. And the rest of the story came out.

"They didn't really push me in any direction. They traveled a lot. My father's work demanded a lot of travel so we were with a nanny most of the time," he reported.

"But why did your mother go with him so often?" Rachel asked.

"She liked to travel," David said.

"So they did not track you much or very well? Is that fair to say?" Rachel asked.

"They did the best they could," David replied.

"But David, they needed to be around more to encourage you and nudge you to be everything you could be. Children need a parent tracking them closely, looking over their shoulder making sure they are on the right path. Your parent's didn't do a good enough job in that. So when I try to be the good parent to you in coaching you toward the very things you asked me to, it makes sense that you try to push me away or think I will push you away. That must have been your defense as a child."

David agreed and this became his working space in therapy. The issue was less about being gay and more about having an insecure attachment issue from having been left so often by his parents.

Exploration

It takes inordinate courage for lesbians and gays to explore the gay community. Even going to a social gathering looms as a huge challenge. If this persistent difficulty keeps clients from exploring avenues for socialization and establishing a peer group, explore what their caretakers were like and what the rules and norms while they were growing up were. Did their parents foster exploration and a well-rounded curiosity? Did they give them a sense of confidence that they could explore their own world and be okay? Or did they instill rigidity, warnings, doubts, and caution?

In this second developmental stage, a child needs to learn how he differs and is separate from others. It is also a time for developing an innate curiosity about the world. If this exploration is thwarted or made threatening, the child may grow up to have difficulty separating from the family and developing a healthy curiosity about his own culture.

If this stage of development goes well for gay and lesbian children, the coming out process will be easier for them as adults. But if it doesn't, their sexual exploring and coming out may be fraught with much more turbulence and angst.

For example, a client may be reluctant to explore the gay community. You may have great ideas and suggestions about going to local gay community centers or different groups, but the client simply won't go. He may have trouble meeting others and adjusting to going from a straight lifestyle to a gay one, and he may blame the gay community for this. In fact, however, the issue is more about his vandalized exploration stage than about the community.

One needs a healthy sense of being able to explore the world, particularly a new culture like that of the lesbian and gay community, which is not visible and very foreign to most people. Finding it and navigating through it can be scary. Clinicians need to be familiar with how to guide clients toward the best types of groups and organizations.

It is extremely important for the straight clinician to constantly push gay and lesbian clients out into gay and lesbian social groups. Allowing their reactivity around this to surface will help you know what direction to head in terms of their therapeutic work.

Obtaining a good history is essential here. Questions to ask when clients seem stuck in this stage include: "What messages did you get as a child about being away from your parents?" and "Were your parents overprotective?"

Identity

To avoid pathologizing gays and lesbians for the ways in which they create their adult identities, you need to be aware of what's normalized within their communities. For example, in one of my gay-affirmative trainings, a straight woman said she was bothered by the way gay dating personal ads spell out what men want sexually in terms of body types, top or bottom practices, and even fantasies. It made sense that a heterosexual woman might be offended by a man's personal ad leading off with what he enjoyed and wanted sexually, as that's not culturally acceptable in the straight world. But I explained to her that it was normative among gay men to do that. In general, a gay man creates his identity through his body and his sexual practices. Understanding why this is so from a developmental point of view is crucial.

The longer clients remain closeted and suppress their core identity, the more likely they are to display behaviors that mimic psychiatric disorders, actually create full-blown psychiatric disorders, or mask genuine disorders through acting-out. This is addressed further in Chapter 12.

Often you can identify what stage of psychological development lesbian and gay clients are struggling through based on their progress in coming out. Failure to develop a positive lesbian and gay identity in childhood is perhaps one of the biggest deficits that gays and lesbians can suffer. By this I don't mean sexual identification, but rather the normative identity development that all children and teenagers should successfully undergo. For gay and lesbian children, their inner core becomes forbidden, their true identity walled off.

To develop a secure sense of self, children create their identities through playing with toys, usually between the ages of 3 and 4 years old (according to Erikson's model), and later through playing with others in school and on the playground. But, as I mentioned earlier, many gay and lesbian children have their toys of preference taken away from them and are shunned on the playground. Suffering this kind of developmental insult can produce later problems in identity formation. It can manifest by way of cognitive distortions in terms of clients believing something is inherently wrong with them.

Every child should have a sense of belonging. But from childhood on up, gays and lesbians have been taught—if only by subtle slights—that their essential identity is disappointing, inferior, and something to be despised.

A new time of identity formation occurs in adolescence (Erikson, 1997)—but not for the gay or lesbian teenager. For them, this second stage of identity formation occurs in adulthood, though more and more teenagers today are coming out earlier.

Gay and lesbian identities are very different from one another. That said, certain commonalities do exist.

Gay Men

A common stereotype of the gay man is the slim, effeminate, soft-spoken individual. But many gay men take the opposite tack, striving to achieve a type of hypermasculinity. Here you will see the developmental wound in full bloom. These men have overidentified with the macho, patriarchal, bully-type male in terms of their overly muscular physical builds and their cognitive beliefs on what it is to be a man.

Gay men are punished from childhood for their natural desire to be softer and gentler and have romantic feelings for another male. The resulting developmental wound is to be out of integrity with one's self in terms of masculinity.

After years of being called "pansies," "sissies," and "mother-dominated mama's boys," and after years of being referred to as "more like women," "underdeveloped in their masculinity," "less than a man," "weak," "innately vulnerable," and "cowardly," it is no wonder that some gay men go to such extremes to project a masculine identity. Unfortunately, however, avoiding such slights by becoming hypermasculine constitutes a trauma in and of itself.

Straight-Acting Guise

"Circuit boys" are gay men, usually age 21 to 50, who attend circuit parties across the world. These events cram together shirtless gay men who dance to loud, rhythmic music and often do drugs and have sex right on the dance floor. These parties have different themes and usually run all night into the late morning and even afternoon. It's a bit like a gay boy sleepover that was missed out on during childhood.

The typical circuit boy is muscular, sometimes overdeveloped. He may abuse steroids. Some psychologists refer to this hypermasculine look as *muscle dysmorphia*: The man doesn't see himself as being as muscular as he "should be," even though he's developed far beyond buff. In these men's eyes, the more masculine-looking they are, the better; it is an unconscious attempt to cover any femininity.

To achieve a sense belonging, these men want to be "a man among men," which they failed to be while growing up. When I am around circuit boys, I often feel surrounded by the very bullies and homophobes who ridiculed and humiliated me when I was younger. I have to remind myself that these are my gay brothers, and that they only *look* like those other, patriarchal men.

Like sex parties and sex clubs, circuit parties offer many gay men a niche, a place where they can finally fit in—which makes them so compelling to so many. Observed from the outside, circuit boys seem to exude freedom, connectedness, and authenticity. But circuit parties are fueled with drugs, alcohol, and barebacking. Many circuit boys fly from city to city to attend the parties, worshiping the DJs and enjoying pseudo-intimacy with one another. To achieve a sense of belonging, these gay men risk STDs and HIV infection, overdosing on drugs or alcohol, and recklessly wasting time and money on the next party they can find. They often spend all of their free time on superficial people they describe as their "close friends" even though they see them only a few times a year and only at these parties. They miss out on real relationships, careers, family—and, inevitably, on life.

When the party is over, men in their forties and fifties will come to see you, regretting having expended so much on something that gave so little in return. I see this as a direct result of covert cultural sexual abuse.

Misogyny

Another way to identify a developmental insult at the identity stage is to track the language of woman-hating by gay men. Aversion to women does not create orientation, though it can contribute to anger toward women and anything feminine. Some gay men do hate woman and are misogynists. Others appear to be antifemale but instead are showing their identity wound by shaking off anything female within them to reaffirm their own masculinity.

A gay comedian once quipped, "I like my women like I like my coffee. I don't like coffee." His audience laughed uncomfortably. Some women in the audience booed him. Did he mean he just wasn't interested in women sexually or romantically, or that he hated them?

Femininity is not generally acceptable among gay men. Countless times I have heard gay men say of their more effeminate counterparts, "If I wanted a woman, I would be straight" in a negative and hostile way. Many gay men accept and tolerate drag and feminine talk and behaviors among friends in the culture but declare this taboo in relationships. Just read the many personal ads seeking "straight acting" guys, or "masculine, no fems."

Some gay men refer to each other as *she* or *her* or *Mary*. Although this can be said in jest—a way of "owning" femininity through humor—there are times I think it goes too far and becomes a way to channel hostility, sexism, and misogyny. It is a manifestation of an identity developmental wound that should be explored in therapy.

Questions to ask your gay male clients are:

- How were you treated by your parents in terms of masculinity?
- What were the gender roles and stereotypes in your family?
- What happened when you did or did not conform?
- How were you treated by your peers for the type of male you were?
- What was your relationship with your mother like?
- How did your father feel toward women?
- Where did you get the strongest messages about what it meant to be female and an atypical male?

Lesbians

Much of lesbian identity is tied to relationships and to politics. Having been suppressed by patriarchy, sexism, and heterosexism, lesbians take a different route when coming to terms with their identity.

The Lesbian Anti-Ideal

By trying to look as masculine as possible, gay men try to become like the straight men who demeaned them as teenagers and excluded them from the male fraternity and spurned their advances. But lesbians do the opposite. Many lesbians pass through a stage—perhaps during the coming out process—during which they stop shaving their legs and underarms and forgo makeup, dying their hair, and wearing nail polish. This is done in an effort to distance themselves from the patriarchal sexist norms that so many straight women must endure. After coming out, lesbians often cut their hair short, wear more comfortable shoes, and adopt a less traditionally feminine appearance to counteract the myth of acceptable beauty and what it means to be a woman (Krakauer & Rose, 2002). This defiant phase can settle into a way of life in which a lesbian decides that wearing as much makeup as she used to and dying her hair isn't what she wants or needs for herself as she develops her identity. This is necessarily not due to a developmental wound, rather, it can be a way of developing a healthy identity.

Lesbians also use their "physical appearance to be recognized by and to recognize similar others" (Rothblum, 1994). In other words, adopting such an appearance allows lesbians to identify one another and become distinct from women in the dominant culture. Appearance norms are one way to establish a group identity.

Among lesbians, identity issues relating to physical appearance are different than those of gay men and have changed over time. As Barron (1998) stated, being a lesbian "is a body issue":

> Becoming lesbian is partly about reclaiming the neutral from being defined as masculine. For instance, hairy armpits are not masculine; they are human and as sensual as a woman's bush. Shoes that allow one to walk naturally are not masculine; they are human. (p. 9)

Barron goes onto say that her lesbian identity is about caring less about male approval or disapproval. This concept of the damage male patriarchy has done to women comes out in the competence stage as well.

Politics

For lesbians, how they identify themselves takes on far greater meaning than for gay men. For many of them, being referred to as "lesbian" rather than "gay" is extremely meaningful. I used to advertise my workshops for lesbian and gay male couples with a flyer that read, "Gay and Lesbian Couples Workshop." When I spoke to other therapists and lesbians, they told me that many lesbians would not come because the flyer did not read, "*Lesbian and Gay* Workshop." In fact, lesbian couples regularly tell me that if I don't have female assistants—preferably lesbians   that they will not attend.

I must admit that at first I thought it was ridiculously nit-picky for anyone to use wording and gender as reasons for not attending a workshop. But I've come to understand that behind this apparent pettiness is profound logic. To date, the best overview of some reasons behind this issue is in Adrienne Rich's article "Compulsory Heterosexuality and Lesbian Existence" (Rich, 1980). This still-popular, commonly referenced article describes how patriarchy and sexism—characteristics of male power over women—render lesbians invisible, forcing them to face an additional level of trauma. In other words, what might be misconstrued as lesbians' anger over slights and preconceptions is really about *existence*. In fact, Rich uses terms such as *lesbian existence* and *lesbian continuum* instead of *lesbianism*, a word she feels is limiting in terms of what it means to be a lesbian.

Clinicians can understand lesbian clients more fully—as I have managed to do in my workshops—by thinking along these lines rather than assessing them wrongly as hostile feminists. Validating their anger, mirroring their experience without judgment, and holding a safe space for them to talk about these issues are what they need.

The Relational Identities of "Butch" and "Femme"

This concept—or dichotomy—was more prevalent in the 1950s, when one female partner often dressed in a more "feminine" manner and the other was more masculine. This allowed lesbians to identify one another as well as express themselves as separate from the dominant culture (Myers, Taub, Morris, & Rothblum, 1998).

Some lesbian couples still do role play, with the "butch" engaging in "packing," or wearing a dildo to represent the "male" role in their relationship. She is stereotypically more masculine in dress and behavior, sporting short hair and men's clothing, whereas the "femme" pays attention to her makeup and dress. Many therapists think that a butch lesbian is trying to be a "man," but this is not the case. The butch is usually trying to take on the character traits of being empowered and in control. Again, therapists must recognize whatever homophobia and prejudices this may evoke in them.

Adopting butch and femme roles is not necessarily an indication of a developmental injury. However, in some cases it may be. For example, some lesbians assume a hyper-butch persona, acting as if nothing can bother them and projecting an attitude of not caring about a thing. They are often confrontational—with straight people, men, and other lesbians alike—and come off as having a chip on their shoulder. Underneath, however, these women are extremely sensitive and care deeply about being accepted. This may be the lesbian version of the circuit party/boy sleepover: the adoption of the masculine identity they were never allowed to have as children, now manifested as hypermasculinity. You can see how both of these personas ultimately cause further abandonment and emotional pain for these gay men and lesbians.

Misandry

Rosanne Barr has a standard joke in her stand-up comedy act where she says, "I don't know why people think lesbians hate men. They don't have to have sex with them!" Everyone laughs because they know the stereotype of lesbians hating men and they know how some straight women despise men for not meeting their sexual needs.

In fact, some lesbians do hate men and build their identities around anything that is not male. They might decide to spell women "womyn" and distance themselves from anything that has to do with men at all. As clinicians you have to assess whether this is healthy or unhealthy: Is it a case of true male-hating or simply an attempt to honor their identity as separate from the patriarchal model?

A *misandrist* is the respectable feminist equivalent for the misogynist, according to the *Oxford English Dictionary*. Even in *Webster's*, little to nothing can be found on misandry, the hatred of men! *Misogyny* was a known word in Latin and Greek and according to the *Oxford English Dictionary* was first used in English in 1656. *Misandry* was first used in 1946, three hundred years later. Some books—*Misogyny, Misandry, and Misanthropy*, for one—use the word in their titles, as do some articles. But little is out there to explain the concept fully.

Both misogyny and misandry are gender-neutral: Misogynists and misandrists can be either men or women. In general, however, usually women hate men and men hate women. Perhaps because of the horrors of sexism, our culture had to go very far in one direction and only look at what men have done to women. Some accuse feminist activists of being misandrists, and some are—but most aren't.

The developmental wound here for lesbians is that of having to be hyperfeminine and behave and dress in ways that were not in line with how they saw themselves as the types of females they knew they were.

Clinicians catching this language and mindset in their lesbian clients can ask them how they have been treated by males—especially by their fathers and older brothers. You can ask your lesbian clients:

- What was your response to how your father wanted you to be?
- What were you rewarded for and punished for in terms of the type of female you were?
- What were your family of origin rules about gender—overt and covert?
- What kind of a woman was your mother in relationship to men?

- How were you taught to be female?
- Did your mother go along with what the traditional female should be like or did she give you some leeway to be the kind of girl she were?

Betrayal Bonds

Our understanding of the manifestations of these identity problems comes from the concept of "trauma bonds." A *trauma bond* is a dysfunctional attachment to an abusive and neglectful person and situation that occurs in the presence of danger, shame, and exploitation. The core of it is abandonment. For lesbian and gay children, their cores and identities are neglected, which causes deep shame.

Patrick Carnes (1997) called them *betrayal bonds*—a term I like better as well. He called them this "because in most circumstances a fundamental betrayal took place" (p. 32).

When an intense, traumatic experience or betrayal of trust takes place, an equally intense relationship and bond with the perpetrator may form. As van der Kolk wrote: "Still others recreate the trauma by identifying with the aggressor, and perpetuating the same acts on others that were once exercised upon them . . . ."(1988, p. 286). Similarly, gays and lesbians may exhibit dysfunctional attachment by overidentifying with the patriarchal male model. This is an attempt to keep themselves safe and defended against further pain, but in fact it just causes them further pain. The circuit boy is running, doing drugs, and lacking relationships with others and himself. The hyper-butch lesbian loses out on relationships as well, as she does not allow herself to be the vulnerable and sensitive person she truly is inside. Both have internalized the very thing that caused them pain to begin with.

Trauma bonds can occur to all children, straight or gay, who are victims of abandonment, neglect, and trauma. For gays and lesbians, covert cultural sexual abuse is at the crux of the trauma bond. It is about being loyal to adults and caretakers who consciously or unconsciously enforced compulsory heterosexism and gender conformism.

Treatment

Clinicians need to teach their clients about betrayal bonds and explore the ways they may have been betrayed in terms of gender formation growing up. It helps to explore how their internalization of the perpetrators' characteristics might have manifested. These clients often feel unique and enjoy the "special" way they are in terms of how they live, dress, and keep their patriarchal stance. Clinicians need to help disrupt their beliefs around their uniqueness and the meaning they have attached to them by teaching them they may be continuing the same bad behavior that they were victimized by in childhood. In other words, show them that what they are doing is perpetrating the original abuse by doing to themselves what was done to them.

Competence

In the fourth stage, the child develops a sense of personal power and a drive to achieve. If negatively influenced, he may feel incompetent now and later in life, or overly competitive with others. Many gay boys who aren't athletic and don't do well at sports are made to feel incompetent and belittled by coaches who deride them for not being a "team player." Gay athletes feel that by "passing"—by fitting the patriarchal ideal of what it is to be male—they're essentially phonies and that if others knew the truth, they'd be devalued and outcast.

Gay men and lesbians are highly competitive with each other as a result of wounds in this stage, which disrupt their ability to form cohesive groups. Their extensive past wounding leaves them feeling incompetent. Every child needs to feel that what he does and thinks about is competent. If he doesn't get this from caretakers or authority figures, he'll grow up to feel incompetent, competitive, or both. We are taught that how we think, act, and feel is wrong. How can we support and empower each other if we can't do it for ourselves?

Clinicians should look for overachieving traits in gay and lesbian clients. It is common for gay and lesbian teenagers to adopt this strategy to hide their homosexuality. Their adaptive thought and behavior is: "If I overachieve, people will like me and not see me as the damaged goods I am."

As an openly gay therapist writing books, doing trainings, and giving public lectures and workshops, I have had my share of negative transference from lesbians and gays. I've also noticed differences in how I am treated by lesbians and how I am treated by gay men.

At almost every public lecture I do, I am confronted by either a lesbian or gay man who, although well-intentioned, wants to add his or her expertise and story about being gay or lesbian. Usually it starts as a question that even they believe they have. However, as soon as they start their question it turns into a presentation and suddenly I have a co-presenter. Rarely if ever have I had a heterosexual individual do this at my presentations.

At first I was taken aback by this and did not know what to do. I would politely find an opportunity to ask them to sit down and wait for the question-and-answer part of the presentation, but this only served to make them angry and give me a negative evaluation.

Later I discovered that what was happening related to the fact that as a group we have been silenced and held incompetent. In standing up in front of a group of people and sharing my expertise, I am breaking all the rules. Unconsciously, participants are feeling permission to do the same. However, it is inappropriate for them to interrupt my presentation, and it would be inappropriate for me to interpret their interruption. Usually what they have to say is solid and good—it's just bad timing.

I have actually had lesbian and gay men tell me after a talk that they could do a better job. One woman actually had me removed from a speaking engagement and used herself as the replacement. Others have told me what I need to include to be better at what I do.

Now I begin my talks by saying, "There will be one or more of you in the audience who will experience a reaction to what I am saying either positively or negatively, and you are going to want to add to my presentation. You will think you are raising your hand to ask me a question, but once you start talking you will find yourself becoming my co-presenter, and I will be in a position of having to interrupt you and ask you to sit back down and wait. To avoid that, please know I provide time at the end of my presentation for you to add anything you wish, as I learn from you, too. Until then, please keep any questions you have to simply clarification of my thoughts and not adding any of your own opinions yet."

By saying this I am letting them know that they will have a voice, that their opinion counts, and that they are competent. I never say that my opening remarks are directed at gays and lesbians because that would be offensive to them, but the truth is that it is usually a gay man or lesbian who wants to contribute. I also do want to hear what they say, as it might help me say it better or differently next time, and I may even learn something I did not know.

As a straight clinician, you must be prepared for this kind of negative transference as well. Remember that it is coming from the pain of being silenced and rejected, and that what the client needs is your validation and willingness to listen. You will represent all the straight people in their lives that invalidated them and deemed them incompetent. This is different than what I represent to them as a gay male therapist.

Concern

Most children develop healthy empathy for others—as long as those others are heterosexual. In fact, children are strongly encouraged *not* to feel concern or show positive regard for gays and lesbians, including their peers. Males, in particular, are rewarded for showing contempt and disgust for anything or anyone that seems gay. Gay and lesbian children, too, are encouraged to empathize with heterosexuals only and to "edit" their own identity development by developing a distorted self to present to the world.

Any adolescent's peer group becomes a vitally important influence. As adolescents develop a stronger sense of self, they separate from—if not actively rebel against—their parents' values. But in most schools, gay peer groups do not exist. Passing as straight bypasses the normative process of developing one's true identity.

The degree of psychological damage depends on how the adolescent adapts. With their sense of belonging critically impaired, they may withdraw and isolate themselves. Not until the coming out process begins can their identity development take place, as they find their niche in the gay or lesbian community.

During this stage, which Erikson termed the "identity crisis," teens refine their authentic self. To figure out who they really are, they hang out with like-minded peers who offer a sense of belonging. They try to choose a coherent self-image from many different templates: jock, leather-jacketed rebel, SAT scholar, computer geek, "most popular" or "most likely to succeed," or just an all-around good sport. Socially isolated teenagers are often believed to be gay—even if they aren't—and because everyone wants to avoid them, they remain isolated.

Later, as a delayed step in achieving a sense of belonging, gay men will desire to start a diet or increase a workout regimen—hoping to become the very types that other gays find attractive. Their sense of identity is often created by achieving perfect gym bodies: sculpted chests, buns of steel, and well-defined biceps. Gays and lesbians may also work to ease the negative impact through sex, overachievement, and politics—and by joining a subgroup with extremely (often obsessively) narrow interests. All of this is an attempt to go against the grain of the way they were influenced at an early age—or as psychologists say, imprinted.

To build a sense of one's own worth, one needs a feeling of belonging. This is the essential starting point from which one can add, remove, and modify where one came from originally and where one is headed—emotionally, mentally, and psychologically. In psychosocial development, this is a crucial stage for every child to complete successfully. The foundation of a sense of belonging begins with the family you're born into and continues with your socialization in school, on the playground, and in your house of worship. It is in these places that you learn relational skills and how to get along with others.

Often developmental wounds occurring in the concern stage will manifest in clients talking about someone different within the gay community in a negative way. They will talk disparagingly and contemptuously about certain people. You might mistakenly identify it as internalized homophobia, as it will look similar. But you will notice that the client lacks concern not only for other lesbians and gays but also toward others who are different. The way they present it will seem at times juvenile.

For example, I had a 24-year-old lesbian client who was primarily a loner but wanted to be in a relationship and have other lesbian friends. She described herself as a "gothic" type woman, wearing dark makeup and dyed jet-black hair over one eye. She said that people needed to love her the way she was and if they didn't, they could "kiss her behind."

I placed her in a singles relationship group mixed with straight, lesbian, and gay individuals. It was a 6-week group and I learned a lot about her during those weeks. She was judgmental of the conservative lesbians coming from work in their business clothes, the gay men wearing their "typical" muscle shirts, and the "totally predictable" straight individuals. Her concern for others was almost completely absent, yet she desperately wanted it for herself.

Even in the "goth" community she felt isolated and was judgmental about the members who attended the bars and goth functions. I gently confronted her on her extremely judgmental attitudes and beliefs and we talked about how she worried that others would treat her the same. She had always felt different growing up and was an outcast. Even at home her parents questioned why she chose the "goth" lifestyle and criticized her.

Her wound was not about being lesbian as much as it was about her sense of belonging and not feeling as though she fit in. As a result she developed a judgmental attitude toward others to keep them at bay. Once she realized this, her work in therapy became about being more empathic and accepting of others. It was shocking to her to learn this about herself because she had always seen herself as open and nonjudgmental.

Intimacy and Sexuality

For gays and lesbians, perhaps the biggest developmental hurdle is not being able to experiment, sexually and romantically, with their own gender and being forced to role play at heterosexuality.

According to Erikson, adolescence, between ages 12 and 18, is the most crucial stage, when all the earlier stages of growth become integrated. Do young people display a strong sense of independence, a sense of basic trust, and strong feelings of confident competence? Do they feel in control of their lives? If individuals can manage this stage successfully, they will be ready to head out into the world in a healthy way, ready to plan for their future. But if not, the teens will feel frustrated and incompetent, have difficulty making decisions, and remain confused about their sexual orientation, future career, and general role in life.

Gay and lesbian adolescents face even more challenges than the common ones Erikson talks about. They feel confused about their sexual identity largely because they're not allowed to explore it in a positive, instructive way.

At this stage of development, love relationships become central. Erikson believed that no matter how professionally successful one may become, he's not *developmentally* complete without intimacy. If all goes well, the young adult will bond with others and enjoy a secure sense of identity. If not, he'll avoid commitment and feel unable to depend on anyone. Many gay men find themselves isolated in just this way, because homophobia and heterosexism have kept them from developing intimacy.

Falling in love places anyone—gay or straight—in an endorphine-altered state. For gays and lesbians still in the earlier stages of coming out, developing crushes can accelerate the process (Coleman, 1981). Romantic love supercharges the desire of wanting to tell the world that "gay is good" and to tell others that now they have a partner. Achieving the traditional, cultural promise of a committed, loving relationship offers gays and lesbians "proof" that those who told them that same-sex relationships can't succeed were wrong.

Sexual Abuse

During childhood, overt sexual abuse can vandalize healthy development. As I noted earlier, there is no evidence that sexual abuse can shape, much less create, anyone's sexual orientation—it can only confuse young people about what their orientation really is and what actually happened to them.

Sexual abuse can tarnish anyone's ability to love and have healthy sexual boundaries. Sometimes clinicians overlook sexual abuse when their clients come in with intimacy and sexual problems simply because they don't want to be politically incorrect by assuming that because they are lesbian or gay, they have been sexually abused. However, it is okay to ask. With good therapy and healing, abuse victims can come to know their true sexual and romantic orientation—be it gay or straight.

The Case of Darren

Darren, 42, came to me regarding problems in his relationship with Spencer, his partner of 5 years. The two had moved in together just 3 months before, and Darren no longer knew if he wanted to stay with Spencer. Darren enjoyed the sexual openness that the two had shared before moving in together. He had promised that once they moved in together, they would be monogamous—but now he was having second thoughts. He wanted to be monogamous, but he also felt compelled to play around.

"Most gay male couples do this," Darren told me, "and I want to be able to be one of them. I always thought I wanted monogamy, but now that I'm living with someone, I can see I don't."

Darren had wanted a relationship for some time. He had come out at the late age of 30, dated many different men, and had short-term relationships with some of them, but he never found anyone he felt secure and in love with—until he met Spencer. Darren explained that Spencer was right for him in almost every way. He was a successful landscaper with a flourishing business, and he was very masculine. Though he enjoyed men, he wanted children. Darren couldn't believe he was willing to sacrifice this relationship, for which he had waited for so long, just to be nonmonogamous.

I obtained Darren's history. He said that as an only child, he was left alone most of the time while his mother worked. His first sexual experience was at age 13 with a 35-year-old man named Hans. Hans had taken a special interest in Darren and took him out for ice cream, to the movies, and to sporting events. Darren slept over at Hans's house when his mother worked late.

As Darren told me this, I asked, "So you were sexually abused?"

This made Darren irate; he insisted it was *not* sexual abuse. He explained to me how his mother had worked two jobs after his father's death, and she'd become friends with Hans from work. When Darren was 13, Hans introduced him to oral sex by fellating him. By then, Darren knew he was gay and wondered how Hans could tell. "He must have known I was gay, or he would not have given me my first sexual experience," Darren told me.

Over time, Hans "taught" Darren how to fellate him in return, how to masturbate, and eventually about anal sex—with Darren being the receiver.

When Hans took a job in another state, Darren's mother paid for Darren to spend weekends and a couple of weeks in the summer with him. They spent their time together doing things that Darren enjoyed, including being sexual. "Hans was the father I never had," Darren told me. "Hans was my first love."

Darren: Clinical Interpretation and Treatment

In my mind, there was no doubt that what Darren experienced with Hans was sexual abuse. In working with him, I took many opportunities to point this out, explaining that a 13-year-old is not developmentally ready to handle adult sexuality, especially not with a 35-year-old. But Hans's abuse had felt like love to Darren, and he wasn't going to let me or anyone else get in the way of what he believed.

Spencer had also told Darren that Hans was a perpetrator, but Darren got angry with him, too, and soon Spencer stopped talking about it.

I explained to Darren that there had to be some reason why he felt compelled to sabotage the relationship of his dreams by acting out sexually. He agreed that something was driving him, but denied that it had anything to do with Hans.

Darren was willing, however, to hear my thoughts on sexual abuse, despite refusing to connect them to Hans. He was also willing to consider that covert cultural sexual abuse was contributing to his urge to be promiscuous. He was willing to read the book *Victims No Longer*, which I hoped would help him realize that Hans's behavior was abuse, but it didn't. The more I pushed him to understand what Hans had done, the more he rebelled and started skipping appointments.

I decided the only way to help Darren understand what he had suffered was to put him in group therapy with other gay men—to reduce the negative transference he was placing onto me. In other words, he was projecting his problem onto me, taking the accountability off Hans. My simply identifying it as abuse caused Darren (albeit unconsciously) to blame me for calling the problem for what it was.

Darren agreed to enter group therapy. Over the course of 6 months, he began to accept that what Hans did was actually a "form" of sexual abuse and was interfering with his desire to remain monogamous.

However, Darren made it very clear to me and the group that even though he saw that what Hans did was a *form* of sexual abuse, he still believed that Hans had loved him and that if not for Hans, he would have had no love growing up. Darren said he would not let the group or me take that away from him.

In my years of practice, I have met many gay men like Darren—gay men who were sexually abused by a much older male. But because it was done in an affectionate way, they viewed it as "their first sexual experience" and not abuse.

This is akin to the straight male whose first sexual experience is with a much older woman. The difference is that it's been easier for me to help straight men understand what happened to them than to help gay men see the abuse for what it was. The difference, I believe, lies in the isolation, loneliness, and feeling of being disenfranchised that gay children grow up with. When a perpetrator approaches them in a friendly way, they perceive it as love and not abuse because covert cultural sexual abuse has made them feel so unlovable.

It is important to explore the developmental insults that might be related to clients' lesbianism and gayness but not be the main source of it. Darren is a great example of this: His sexual abuse affected his homosexuality, but his homosexuality was not the real issue.

Responsibility

When treating overly responsible, "workaholic" gay and lesbian clients, it is appropriate to consider that they are responding to covert cultural sexual abuse by trying to be "the best employee/partner/family member possible." However, it is also crucial that you tease out any possible developmental wounds related to the client's family dynamics to assess whether this overachieving behavior stems from growing up gay or from something else.

The Case of Joey

Joey was a 32-year-old gay male who lived with his mother and father. His two sisters, both much older (ages 42 and 45), were married and living out of the house with children. Joey had been out since he was 16 and felt that he needed to stay home and care for his elderly parents (ages 80 and 81). He believed in family and giving back what he felt he received—a good childhood.

Joey came to therapy due to feeling depressed, which he thought might be about not having long-term relationships. He had one that lasted a little over a year, but when it came time to talking about moving in, Joey refused to move out of his parents' home. His boyfriend, however, did not want to live with Joey's parents. Unable to come to a compromise, they broke up. "If I cannot get a guy who understands my situation, then they are not for me," Joey told me.

"Understand what situation, Joey?" I asked him to explain.

"I had understanding parents who did not give me a hard time about being gay when I told them at age 16. I was bullied and harassed and they were there for me. In turn, I did everything I could for them. My sisters were useless and would not drive them to their doctor's appointments or come by to see if there was something they needed. They started their own lives and families and never looked back," he said angrily.

In fact, this was not the case, as I learned when I asked further about the situation. The sisters came around and called quite often, but Joey would intercede and do what his parents needed, telling his sisters not to bother. Joey did not rebel during his adolescence as his two sisters did. "They gave my parents hell and I vowed never to do that," he said.

"Why?" I asked. "That is the job description of an adolescent—to develop an identity through a bit of rebellion."

Joey then told me that his father and mother always saw him as the good child. They told him they never had to worry about him and he always did the right thing.

Joey was a "surprise" to his family, as he was unplanned. He knew this growing up and made the decision to be there for his parents as much as he felt they were there for him. His parents never encouraged Joey to stop what he was doing, to get an adult life, or to move out. When I explored this with Joey, I received a verbal shower of anger and rage. He believed I was trying to fault his parents when I was only trying to understand why they were not encouraging him to move on.

Joey: Clinical Interpretation and Treatment

Perhaps if Joey were not gay, the same dynamics would have held for him in terms of his overresponsibility for his parents. However, it seemed to me that the issue related both to his being gay and to developmental issues. His parents' unconditional acceptance of his gayness made him feel obligated to them, and the fact that he was a "surprise" who arrived late in their lives perhaps made him feel like he owed them something extra to make up for their inconvenience.

I explored this gently and paced myself slowly, bringing these things up and tying them back each time to his lack of adult relationships and friendships. I told him that as long as he was preoccupied with taking care of his parents and not asking his sisters to share the responsibilities, he would remain alone and isolated. I worried aloud with him that after they passed away he would be alone. I also suggested that his focus on his parents was preventing him from offering his caretaking "expertise" in other situations that would benefit from it. This motivated him to divert some of his caretaking away from his parents and toward others in the gay community. He got involved in some grassroots gay organizations and eventually began forming relationships with people in the gay community.

Lesbians and gays often become overly responsible as children to cover their inherent feelings of being damaged. Family members often support and reward this behavior without helping them see that they don't have to be as overresponsible as they are. When this is the case, it is important to look at how the family dynamics are being played out.

It is important as a clinician to look under ever rock and rule in or rule out every possible cause of a client's problems. Developmental wounds play a part in all of our client's lives. No parent can successfully get a child through each developmental phase without some wounding occurring, whether severe or light. Examining this with your clients can help them understand where they might be stuck and how to move forward.

CHAPTER 7

Coming Out

We do not choose to be gay . . . we are chosen.
—Suzanne Westenhoefer, lesbian comic

Most clinicians don't realize that the coming out process has predictable, observable stages. Once you become familiar with the stages, you can help clients know which one they are in—and what they can anticipate.

The stages do not necessarily occur in order. Clients may jump back and forth, skip one or two, or linger in some as well. Along the way, those going through the coming out stages struggle with internalized and outward homophobia. Some linger at one stage longer than others. It may be years before they move on.

As the therapist, you have to walk a fine line. It's essential to proceed at your clients' pace, not yours. Rushing them can prompt them to regress in stages or stay stuck in the one they are in. However, not coaxing them along and failing to advise them on when and how to move to the next stage can stall their process.

Keeping the covert cultural sexual abuse trauma model in mind is crucial when working with clients in the coming out process. Remember that coming out demands that clients relive the trauma that put them into the closet to begin with, which can result in PTSD symptoms (as discussed in Chapter 5). This is often not understood by clinicians, who may treat the process as a "coming out" issue and nothing more. Within the closet are more issues, such as family dysfunction issues, bullying, and gender shaming, to name a few. Reexperiencing these traumas of suppressing one's homosexuality can lead to many problems, which clinicians need to anticipate.

The Case of Maggie

Maggie, 28, had recognized her lesbian feelings for many years. She knew that to live an authentic and affirmative life, she would have to act on these feelings and no longer hide and suppress them. To discuss this, Maggie chose a straight therapist, Barb, who was gay friendly and gay affirmative. She encouraged Maggie to approach gay and lesbian settings where she could build solid relationships with others like herself.

Barb, unaware of what was available, referred Maggie to a lesbian bar that she had heard of from her other lesbian clients. The following week, Maggie returned to therapy and reported being—in her words—"turned off" and "disgusted" by the women she'd met, who behaved in a "masculine manner." She was also appalled at being approached by several straight men wanting to "score" with a lesbian twosome. Barb aligned with Maggie's experience by saying, "I don't know why so many lesbians are masculine." Inadvertently, she also echoed Maggie's annoyance at straight men trying to pick up lesbians.

Next, she referred Maggie to a local gay and lesbian community center, where Maggie also saw masculine lesbians, some of whom came on to her—even those already in relationships. Maggie commented that lesbians must be unable to commit and that they all seemed like they wanted to be men. "If I wanted a man I would not be coming out!" she said.

Disappointed in the lesbian community, Maggie was now disinterested in investigating any further. She was angry with Barb for not better preparing her for what she would expect to find at the lesbian clubs, accusing Barb of being unaware and incompetent. Maggie even threatened to find a gay or lesbian therapist who would be better able to help her. Although Barb supplied her with names of some lesbian therapists in the area, Maggie never followed through and stayed in therapy with Barb. Barb sought supervision and became informed on resources that she passed on to Maggie, but Maggie remained angry with her during treatment.

Maggie: Clinical Interpretation and Treatment

Here, problems arose because the therapist didn't know how to navigate a gay/lesbian socialization process for someone just coming out of the closet. Barb assumed that a lesbian bar could serve as Maggie's first introduction to the "lesbian scene"; however, she should have cautioned Maggie that some straight men and swinging couples tend to frequent these bars—even though the management tries to keep that to a minimum.

Next, Barb should have addressed Maggie's internalized homophobia about masculine lesbians, which was manifested in Maggie's being "disgusted" by them. By validating Maggie's sense of disgust (by saying she did not know why they acted like that either), Barb fueled Maggie's internalized homophobia and increased her reluctance to attempt more homosocialization. Barb needed to tell Maggie that her reaction to seeing masculine women was her own internalized homophobia, that it was normal to feel this way in the early stages of coming out, and that it would diminish over time as she became more comfortable with her own lesbianism.

Maggie also needed to be aware that she could enter the lesbian community through many different doors. To help ease Maggie's transition—particularly at this early stage of coming out—it was Barb's job to know about the alternatives, and to treat Maggie's internalized homophobia, not inflame it.

Finally, Barb needed to address Maggie's unconscious negative transference toward her for not preparing her for what to expect in the lesbian community. The real source of Maggie's anger was probably related to her parents and society, who let her down and did not prepare her for a lesbian identity. Unlike heterosexual children, lesbians and gays do not receive a roadmap on how to socialize and date.

When Barb sought me out for supervision, I asked her to address Maggie's negative transference toward her about Barb's being heterosexual. I knew this had to exist, as Maggie kept belittling her skills and threatening to see a lesbian therapist. It seemed as though Maggie needed to deem Barb incompetent and keep her that way to stay closeted and not move forward in her coming out process.

Barb asked Maggie whom she thought Barb was standing in for given that Maggie had so many negative feelings toward Barb for not helping her more. At first Maggie was defensive but she then began to cry as she got in touch with her feelings of being left on her own without help from her family and friends. She badly wanted to talk to them about her feelings. She had even told her sister she thought she was lesbian and asked her if she would go with her to the bars but her sister declined. Her mother was insensitive to her struggle of coming out, saying, "Well, this is what you wanted, so this is what you get."

With this breakthrough, Maggie was able to get in touch with the lonely feelings she'd grown up with and denied all of her life. Now, as Barb addressed the covert cultural sexual abuse Maggie had been subjected to, Maggie recognized how abandoned and rejected she had felt all of her life. She began feeling more positive toward Barb and the therapy began to help her continue in the coming out process. Maggie started attending lesbian functions once again and worked on her internalized homophobia, finding lesbians with whom she felt she could relate.

If Barb had seen Maggie's crisis only as a coming out issue and interpreted Maggie's unhappiness with the therapy as a sign that Maggie was unhappy with Barb's sexual orientation, she would have missed the hidden issue of covert cultural sexual abuse. Negative transference is always an important therapy tool that can be used to uncover hidden information—but only if clients are willing to stay and work through it, and if therapists can tolerate their clients' being angry with them for a while. Fortunately, Maggie and Barb were able to use the negative transference to help Maggie.

The Six Stages of Coming Out

Various theorists have developed and defined the stages of coming out and discussed how clinicians can use them as a framework and tool for clients. By discerning which stage a client is going through, you can best prepare him or her for the next one.

Vivienne C. Cass's Homosexuality Identity Formation model (Cass, 1979) best reflects the stages I've observed in my clients. According to her, the stages of identity formation are:

Stage 1: Identity Confusion
Stage 2: Identity Comparison
Stage 3: Identity Tolerance
Stage 4: Identity Acceptance
Stage 5: Identity Pride
Stage 6: Identity Synthesis

These stages are not necessarily linear or consecutive. Many individuals go from stage 1 to 3 and back to 1, depending on many factors, such as their personality and the circumstances in their lives.

During the first three stages, clients are most at risk for stopping the coming out process and regressing back into the closet. These are the most vulnerable stages in that clients' emotions are raw and their sensitivity to judgments of others is high. Safety, both emotional and physical, is crucial during these early stages. The work during these stages is often internal in that clients are mentally and emotionally deciding within themselves what their identity is, comparing themselves to others, and deciding whether or not they can tolerate it. Your job as a clinician is to help them remember the reasons why they wanted to come out to begin with. It is also important to allow them to start and stop at their own pace. Just as with other trauma survivors, the goal is to let *them* feel in charge of their own psychological material.

The final three stages are more affirmative, as clients become increasingly certain that they are on the right track and can accept and claim their authentic gay identities. The work is more outwardly focused; clients venture out into the gay and lesbian world and begin learning relational and socialization skills that help them become more social and intimate with other gays and lesbians. Therapists need to assess what is creating any difficulties or snags for their clients during this time and watch for any developmental injuries such as issues pertaining to a dysfunctional family of origin or repressed memories of abuse. Depression and anxiety may also surface and interfere with the coming out process.

Stage 1. Identity Confusion

Those who begin to acknowledge their attraction to other members of the same sex may not see themselves as even remotely gay. This isn't pretending; they still honestly identify themselves as heterosexual. At this stage, their homosexual feelings are completely unacceptable to them. They are looking for anyone who might tell them they are not gay.

Men may have sex with other men but define it as something other than gay or bisexual behavior. Terms like "on the down low" and "kinky" can help a man stay closeted to himself. Women might be sexual with other women and consider it merely experimental, or they may think of having sex with another woman as something for their male partner and his desires—not theirs. For many people, that may be true. For others it is the beginning of a natural gay or lesbian identity surfacing.

Once individuals recognize that a homosexual nature does exist within them, they often become very sensitive, highly anxious, and self-conscious. This is the beginning of reexperiencing their PTSD symptoms. Pushing them too far in this stage can cause too much psychological discomfort and potentially keep them from moving on to the next stage.

Many clients at this stage do not use the word *gay* or *lesbian*, as it would reflect affirmation and positivity. If anything, they'll usually self-identify as "homosexual" or "heterosexual with homosexual fantasies." Therapists need to stick with their clients' terminology to avoid rushing them or blocking them from continuing with their process, again keeping in mind the covert cultural sexual abuse and PTSD.

At this stage, clients are ready to seek information, often by logging onto the Internet to explore various websites about homosexuality. They are also vulnerable to getting married heterosexually, genuinely hoping for the best. Your job here is to support clients in being honest and open with their potential opposite-gender mates about their homosexual urges, thoughts, or feelings so that their potential partners can have informed consent.

When clients enter your office in this stage of coming out it is an opportunity to intervene and help them identify and understand the true nature of their sexuality.

The Case of Drake

Drake, a 24-year-old college student, came to me after completing a recovery program for alcohol addiction. He told me he thought he "might be homosexual" and hoped that his sobriety would make his homosexual feelings go away—but they only grew stronger.

Drake filled me in on a history of what he called "being a little kinky." He told me that he'd experienced homosexual urges since he was 12, when he started masturbating, but thought they would go away. He was not, he believed, innately gay. When he told his chemical dependency counselors about his homosexual feelings, they told him it was related to his distant relationship with his father and brothers. Drake was the only nonathletic child of four boys and his father took a strong interest in them and not in Drake. They promised him that once he became sober, worked on his "father hunger," and found a girlfriend, his homosexual urges would disappear.

However, Drake was not hopeful about this. The vast majority of his masturbatory fantasies were about males, and when he viewed heterosexual pornography, he focused primarily on the male bodies and on what the males were doing to the females.

He told me he could not imagine a gay life. He always dreamed of having a "normal" life with a wife and children. Being gay was not an option for him. He had a high level of social anxiety and knew that if he lived a life as a homosexual, he would not be able to tolerate the negative judgments.

Drake: Clinical Interpretation and Treatment

Many therapists explain homosexual feelings as stemming from anything other than an innate homosexual orientation. The belief is that clients will eventually recover their innate heterosexuality through work on whatever "caused" the homosexual feelings. This does tremendous psychic damage to those who are truly gay and lesbian. It discounts the possibility that the client is beginning a process of self-recognition of being gay or lesbian and is in the identity-confusion stage.

My work with Drake was to help him decide this for *himself*. I educated him about the many possibilities that exist when people have homosexual feelings and interests: There are heterosexual men who have homosexual feelings, fantasies, and behaviors but are not gay or bisexual. Their sexual tendencies with men are a result of early childhood sexual abuse, father hunger, sexual addiction, availability, and opportunity, just to name a few. I used the word *homosexual* when working with him, as this was the word that he used. When I slipped and use the word *gay*, he would cringe and worry that I thought he actually *was* gay. What I thought mattered greatly to him. I explored this as negative transference (as he knew I was gay) and asked if he thought I had an agenda to make him gay. (As a straight clinician you may ask your clients if they think you have an agenda to make them straight.) He replied that he did think that. I reassured him that this was not the case and we explored the weight he gave to me about determining his sexuality. I told him it was normal for him to feel this way and that my only agenda was to help him resolve any shame around his identity and coach him to look within for the answers.

We started the work about Drake's distant relationship with his father, as this was in the forefront of his concerns. He talked about it in detail, and during the course of the work he told his father about his grief and anger over their strained relationship. He had always wanted his father to mentor him and support him in becoming a man but his father worked long hours and seemed disinterested in him. Over the first year in therapy he became closer with his father and he did not act on his homosexual feelings other than to masturbate while looking at porn. He tried to prevent any homoerotic thoughts and fantasies but always found himself "relapsing," as he called it.

In the second year of his therapy, Drake admitted that his homosexual feelings persisted and in fact were stronger. This is common to all people in this stage of coming out if they are truly gay or lesbian—their innate homosexuality surfaces. He could admit now that he was "homosexual" but would not use the word *gay*.

I told him that if he wanted to know if his homosexuality was more than just about sex, he needed to homosocialize. I warned him that doing this, however, could make his homosexual identity stronger, and that if he did not want this to happen, he needed to consider that. Again I was helping him make his own, conscious decisions by openly stating the consequences of them. I gave him a list of local gay 12-step groups for his alcoholism and a calendar of community gay events. This made him very nervous but he believed that he needed to follow through and took the literature.

After this session, Drake missed his next scheduled weekly appointment with me. Usually this means a client is acting out his resistance or transference, so I called him to ask why he missed. He denied that it had to do with our discussion of his socializing among gays and said he forgot—even though he'd had the same weekly appointment for the last year.

I realized that he might have felt pushed toward the next step too fast. Even though he had told me he wanted to be pushed, his behavior said otherwise. I pointed out this discrepancy to him and he agreed that the idea of going into the gay community was too scary for him; however, he knew he needed to do it. He asked me to coach him more and lean on him to go. I interpreted this as his father transference directed toward me and translated the word *coach* to *father*, as his father did not mentor him into becoming the man he wanted to be. I told him that this positive transference of the good father directed at me was a good sign, as it was an opportunity to work through in a reparative way his negative issues with his father. I told him that I could be the "good father" therapeutically for him and we talked about it. I did as he asked and we agreed if it was too fast for him he would speak up about it, which at times he did.

I also kept in mind that Drake's socializing with gays and lesbians would potentially activate his PTSD symptoms from the covert cultural sexual abuse, which were kept at bay by being closeted. I talked with him about this, explaining what covert cultural sexual abuse was, and told him that he might experience PTSD feelings and that they were normal given his history and the stress he displayed regarding coming out.

Ruling Out MSM and WSW

Men who have sex with men (MSM) and women who have sex with women (WSW) are not necessarily gay or bisexual. When they show up for therapy, a therapist may, in an effort to avoid being homophobic, immediately label them homosexual and place them in stage 1 of the coming out process. But this may not be true. Behavior is not always attached to one's sexual or romantic identity. There is a difference between sexual orientation, behavior, and fantasy. A client's fantasy or behavior might be a manifestation of childhood sexual abuse or an escalation of sexual addiction, where "taboo" behavior adds a thrill. Some bisexual or biattractional tendencies have nothing to do with a person's core sexual identity. Furthermore, sexuality is not a dichotomy of gay versus straight but rather exists on a continuum, including everything in between.

One's sexual *preference* takes into account the desired sexual actions and fantasies with a partner, whereas sexual *orientation* encompasses a sexual *identity* with all the thoughts, feelings, fantasies, and emotions that cause us to become sexually excited. Thus, there is a distinct difference between a gay man and a "male who seeks sex with another male." A gay man's sexual orientation is characterized by lasting aesthetic attraction to, romantic love of, and sexual attraction to exclusively others of the same gender. A gay man's sexual thoughts, fantasies, and behavior are aligned. It is an identity based on affectional, emotional, spiritual, psychological, and sexual feelings exclusively or mostly toward men. Although some gay men can enjoy women as part of their sexual fantasies and behaviors (for instance, being sexual with a woman while with another man and his wife), the gay man is mostly if not totally attracted to men and left cold by the woman if a man is not involved. I often explain it to my clients this way: If a gay man were walking on the beach, he would be sexually drawn only to men; he wouldn't notice women in such a way.

MSMs, on the other hand, might fantasize about men, but on the beach, they're staring at women. They sexually and romantically desire women, not men. These are heterosexual men who engage in sexual behavior with other men for a number of reasons. They are *not* gay, nor are they bisexual. Their same-gender sex acts are about physical release and sexual behaviors, not about attraction to or desire for another man. MSMs are turned off and left cold by naked images of men. Instead, they are sexually aroused by and attracted to women. These men typically want to bond with and need affection from other men. Their behavior may also reflect a desire to experiment, or an expression of problems and conflicts with their sexual feelings and desires—which have nothing to do with being gay. More often than not, these are the men whom I counsel or whose wives come to me in such frantic states.

Clients who are not MSMs or WSWs and are in stage 1 of the coming out process often will be in an ego-dystonic state, which means their diagnosis is usually "sexual disorder not otherwise specified" in the *DSM-IV*. Informing clients about the stages of coming out will help them understand that their ego-dystonic state is likely to be short-lived. However, if this stage persists beyond 2 years, it is likely that the issues involved are not about homosexuality but rather about a developmental insult that occurred in the childhood identity-formation stage. You may need to delve into issues such as how the client's identity development was handled during childhood.

Stage 2. Identity Comparison

During this stage, clients begin to accept the possibility that they *might* be homosexual. They still typically don't describe themselves as "gay," because they associate the word with a particular way of life. The word *homosexual* lets them start exploring from a "safe" distance.

Some clients may accept their *behavior* as gay or bisexual while still rejecting homosexuality as their core identity. Or they might accept a homosexual identity but, paradoxically, inhibit their gay behavior by, for example, deciding to heterosexually marry and have anonymous "no strings" sexual hookups. Of course, this kind of compartmentalization—a fracturing of behavior and identity—leads to problems later on.

Some lesbian and gay clients may attempt to embrace a heterosexual identity out of internalized shame and guilt. These clients are particularly vulnerable to the promises of reparative therapy. Because of their self-hate and hope for a "cure," they are eager to be rid of these unwelcome thoughts and feelings.

Other clients, after exploring and experimenting, may decide to pursue a heterosexual life but do so *not* out of shame or guilt—they simply don't connect to a gay identity. Just like adults raised in one organized religion who decide to convert to another, they're entitled to choose the identity that fits them best. They don't change orientations; they change how they live out their identity. In other words, they are still inherently gay or lesbian, but they self-identify as heterosexual and decide to live this way.

When treating clients in this stage, it is important that psychotherapists (particularly gay and lesbian therapists) not force the issue of whether their client is gay, straight, or bisexual, as doing so can cause damage. Again, I cannot stress enough that it must be the *client* who leads the way during these early stages, with you helping in the background.

The Case of Rita

Rita, a 30-year-old Catholic woman, had known since childhood that she was homosexual. In recent months, she had made efforts to come out as a lesbian: She bought books on lesbianism and surfed the Internet for information on lesbian life, and she was attending a lesbian social group at her local gay community center. However, she was having no success in accepting and embracing her lesbian longings. The problem was the strong conviction of her religion. Rita simply could not reconcile her Catholicism and homosexuality.

Rita had read about Dignity, a supportive Catholic organization for gays and lesbians, but she decided not to look into it after she discovered that it was not sanctioned by the Catholic Church. After many months of struggling over the decision of whether or not to come out as a lesbian, Rita decided to live a heterosexual life. This prompted her to see Jan, a Christian psychotherapist, who in turn asked me to supervise the case.

Jan was struggling with how to approach Rita: Should she encourage her client to attend a Dignity service, or should she support Rita's decision to seek out groups that help people who are gay or lesbian to live heterosexually? The problem with these groups is that they don't see *any* homosexuality as positive.

Rita: Clinical Interpretation and Treatment

I supported Jan's telling Rita that any decision should come from within herself and not be based on internalized shame and homophobia, which—as Rita needed to understand—can only block the process of either coming out or deciding to live a heterosexual lifestyle. I advised Jan to help Rita understand that for most individuals who have a homosexual orientation, coming out as lesbian is the appropriate and best option. But for others, it's not—especially if the client is struggling with other issues such as religious beliefs. I informed Jan about the inherent sexism, homophobia, and heterosexism of reparative therapy, and had her address this with Rita to assess for herself how much of her desire to distance herself from homosexuality was about self-hate. These factors should not influence a person's decision to not to define as gay.

Rita ultimately chose to keep her homosexuality at a distance and left therapy. She recognized that reparative therapy was not effective for her and instead chose to attend a Catholic group that supported chastity for homosexuals.

Jan felt that she failed this client. She believed that successful therapy for Rita would have entailed helping her to come out as a lesbian. I, however, disagree. Although coming out is the best answer for most lesbian and gay clients, it was not for Rita. She made an informed decision to not self-identify or live as a lesbian, and Jan needed to accept this decision. Jan had succeeded in providing a space for Rita to decide for herself how she wanted to self-identify, which is all we can ask for as therapists with any client.

I have helped many clients reduce or eliminate the shame they felt about their homosexuality, but then supported them in living heterosexually because that is what *they* wanted. I am aware of the fact that living a closeted life often leads to depression—something no therapist would want to foster in a client—but ultimately my main goal is to help clients live how *they* want to live, not how I personally think they *should* live. Although this is politically taboo in the homophobic climate in which we live, clients have a right to make their own decisions about how they wish to live their lives. Some simply cannot adjust to a homosexual identity or lifestyle.

I don't, however, condone remaining in the closet. I support these clients to be out and open in terms of their homosexual feelings. I encourage them to be up front and honest with a partner when they enter in a relationship with the opposite sex so their partners have informed consent. Nor do I try to fool these clients into thinking they can change their orientation. They do *not* change their sexual and romantic orientation. Instead, they create a heterosexual life for themselves.

Gay and lesbian clients who decide to live a heterosexual life need to be warned of the possible depression this can create, and I refer my clients to studies that show this. I also warn them that their defenses against homosexuality may eventually wane, explaining that this can cause problems for both them and their loved ones if they are married and have children. But again, the clients are the ones who have the responsibility of deciding for themselves how they want to live their life.

That said, letting the client make *too* many decisions may not always be wise, and you should recognize when it is best to coax or coach a client struggling with how to self-identify. Giving clients too much room to explore *not* being gay might result in their staying closeted and aligning with what they think you (and others) want for them. Avoiding this can be tricky; you need to have a solid working relationship with your client. Generally the best approach is to avoid framing the issue as an either/or, coming-out/not-coming-out decision. Instead, explore what will work best for the client now and in the long term.

During this stage of the coming out process, clients who are on their way to a healthy lesbian and gay identity begin to feel positive about being *different*. They like that there is something inside them that is waiting to come out and be expressed, and they feel special inside themselves. The shame about their sexual secret turns into something ego-syntonic and integrated as part of their sense of self.

Your job as a therapist is to support this shame reduction by helping clients honor their specialness and uniqueness. Clients may worry that you, as a straight therapist, will not understand their feelings of being special—or they might not tell you about them at all for fear that you will think they are strange.

You can predict for your clients that during this stage a feeling of specialness and uniqueness arises and that is normal and healthy in the coming out process and part of moving to the next stage.

Stage 3. Identity Tolerance

At this stage, individuals accept the likelihood that they're homosexual in a positive way and begin to move toward describing themselves as gay or lesbian. This entails "trying on" a homosexual identity to see if it fits. Clients may still hesitate to venture into the gay culture, but they do begin to see a need to end their social isolation and loneliness.

Clients' experiences moving toward homosocialization within the gay and lesbian community have a significant impact on the rest of their coming out process. If the experiences are positive, the individual will continue moving forward in the coming out process and begin an affirmative identity. If they are negative, the individual might stall or revert to stages 1 or 2.

When clients have negative initial homosocialization experiences, it is your job as a therapist to be supportive and validate that they had a negative experience but assure them that this is just one negative of the many positives they will have. Remind them there are positive and negative things they will experience and normalize that attaching to the negatives is their internalized homophobia. For example, one of my former clients—an attractive 57-year-old man—came to a session very upset. He had just begun going to gay bars and said that he felt invisible, as though men were looking right through him. He had never had this experience with women and always found at least one woman—even if unattractive—to talk with. But at the gay bars, he had no luck at all. I explained to him that in the gay male culture, being over 50 is difficult, particularly at gay bars where youth is revered.

He was also upset because he saw men having sex in the bathrooms and back-rooms, and he concluded that the heterosexists and homophobes were correct in thinking that the entire gay community is strictly sexual. I challenged this homopho-bic thinking by saying that if the entire gay community were like this, lesbians would be acting the same way. In my judgment, what he witnessed was a *male* experience and couldn't be generalized to the entire gay population. I also told him that it was unfortunate that he had these experiences, but that they were more about the bars than gay males themselves. This helped the client understand that he simply had to find other venues—and there are many—where he could mingle with men who would want to connect with him on a more meaningful level.

Other clients are afraid to achieve this stage or fear that they'll get stuck in it. "I don't want to become a gay man waving a rainbow flag around," they say. I reassure them that this needn't happen and also explore their potential homophobia. I teach them that they will be able to become the kind of gay or lesbian individual they wish to become and will find or create their own niche.

By the end of this stage, clients have learned that there are both healthy and dys-functional gay people, just as there are healthy and dysfunctional straight people. There are also hundreds of subsets within the gay community. If clients feel over-whelmed, help them explore what niche they might feel most comfortable in. Make sure you inform them that there are many niches to choose from—they just need to search.

Culture Shock

Therapists must also understand the culture shock clients experience when they first step into the gay community and help their clients anticipate this. Like all communities—whether they are religious, ethnic, professional, and so on—the gay community has its own social customs. Clients who have not been exposed to such customs may not know how to interact with or respond to other gays and lesbians.

For example, I remember my first time entering a gay bar. I was 19 years old, alone and frightened. I ordered a drink and stood near some other men who were standing at a wall. Unbeknownst to me, I was at the "meat rack" (a place where men who want to be chosen for quick sexual hookups congregate). I soon noticed a man staring at me intensely. Every time I looked away, he'd always be there when I turned back. I tried walking to another part of the bar, but he still glared at me.

I recall thinking that my mother was right—going alone to gay bars would get me killed, and this was the man who was going to do it. Though I can laugh about it now, at the time I was frightened, self-conscious, and overwhelmed. Fortunately a nice man started talking to me, explaining that guy was "cruising" me (giving a sexual predatory stare to initiate immediate anonymous and casual sexual contact). I was lucky to have been befriended by this man—many first-timers have no idea what is going on.

Another problem occurs when gays and lesbians interpret this culture shock as a sign that they are not gay or lesbian or, even if they are, they are not meant to live their lives as such. This is again where they are vulnerable to going back into the closet and into stage 1. They get scared by looking around and not seeing images that mirror them or images they would like to be. They do not feel psychologically safe; returning to the closet is about returning to safety.

The clinician's job is to help clients stay emotionally safe and assure them that there are plenty of environments where they will see themselves reflected in the way they wish. It is crucial as a clinician that you know of other lesbian and gay groups and activities to talk about and refer them to.

Stage 4. Identity Acceptance: The Beginning of a Gay Adolescence

This is when people move from simple tolerance to accepting themselves as gay. They discover a new sense of identification and belonging in the gay community as a whole. They feel increasing anger at homophobic segments of society, which is healthy for this stage of identity development. All the doubts and self-hatred they once directed inward are now turned outward at more deserving targets.

At this time, individuals begin to process conflict between their own self-perceptions of their homosexuality and those of society. They begin to become more vocal and take small risks. They also may distance themselves from people and situations that would disrupt their new way of thinking. This healthy reaction is very similar to that of adolescents, who have just gone through puberty and start identifying with their burgeoning sexuality. Just as teenagers experience an acute need for privacy in which to forge their new identity—closing their bedroom doors, adopting music and fashions they know their parents won't like, and bonding with peers who recognize their newfound sexual selves—the "newly gay" distance themselves from family and old friends to explore their privacy. Few parents delight in a teenager passing through this stage, but school counselors and therapists know it's nothing to worry about—it's a necessary, appropriate step toward a sense of belonging and a personal identity. Friends of a "newly gay" person may feel the same. Like adolescents accepting their new sexual identity, "newly" gay men and lesbians of any age may choose new friends and hangouts, if only to shield themselves from gay-negative views—theirs or anyone else's.

The Case of Jeff

Crying in his therapist's office, 48-year-old Jeff talked about the years he'd lost by staying in the closet. He'd recently begun meeting many young gay men in their twenties and thirties and imagined what his life would have—could have—been like had he been out and open in his younger years. He did not regret having married; he deeply loved his wife and the son they had together. But he said he also was depressed at having missed out on having a gay youth.

Jeff expressed anger at society for pushing him into a straight life and anger toward his conservative family, whose beliefs he described as "Republican and narrow." His blue-collar father and his stay-at-home mother lived in a working-class neighborhood that he described as "macho guyville."

Jeff had recently begun separating himself from heterosexuals, whom he accused of being antigay, and dropped most of his straight friends. He grew increasingly distrustful of straights, frequently calling them "breeders" who were insensitive to the needs of gays and lesbians.

Jeff's therapist responded to these comments by pleasantly replying, "Not all straight people are like that." He also tried to help Jeff see that he at least had begun coming out before it was too late in life, and that his discomfort was not the fault of straight people but rather of his being raised in an environment of patriarchy and heterosexism. But Jeff did not want to hear this. Because his therapist was straight,

Jeff had even more ammunition for his anger, and he used his therapist as the target of his negative transference at heterosexist straights in general.

I advised the therapist to mirror Jeff's anger rather than challenge his logic. That is, instead of trying to curb Jeff's anger by being reasonable and rational, it was more practical to understand the source of the anger and to locate Jeff's progress in the coming out process.

It was also important to help Jeff through his grief over losing heterosexual privileges, as well as over not being able to explore his gay orientation during his youth. Now that Jeff was identifying with part of a marginalized subculture, he was angry at how unfair this was. The therapist needed to validate Jeff's grief and loss and help him work through his feelings, not argue about them.

Grief and Loss

The case of Jeff illustrates one of the common aspects of stage 4: As clients take more risks, entering gay affirmative establishments where people of all ages are out and open, they typically begin experiencing grief and anger over their "lost" years of living heterosexually.

Using Elizabeth Kübler-Ross's stages of grief in dealing with death and dying (Kübler-Ross, 2003) can help you assist your clients as they go through the sorrow of losing heterosexual privileges:

1. *Denial.* During this stage, clients are in denial about the loss they are going to experience by living as a straight person to now identifying authentically as gay or lesbian. They also deny others they tell the right to have their reaction to their sexual and romantic identity and deny any other reality but their own.
2. *Anger.* The anger begins to grow toward heterosexism's forcing them to play it straight. Heterosexuals become the target of their anger, as if all heterosexuals are heterosexists.
3. *Bargaining.* This happens more in the early stages, where clients try to keep their homosexuality at bay and bargain with their higher power to be good and hope the feelings go away. In this stage they might consider only being out in certain places to ensure everyone else's comfort and forego their own. This bargaining is an attempt to help keep the peace.
4. *Depression.* So many circumstances add to this stage—from coming out later in life to heterosexually marrying to getting infected with HIV. Whatever the depression is focused on, it is real and usually predominately about the loss of heterosexual privileges.
5. *Acceptance.* In this stage, clients fully accept that they are—and want to be—

truly gay or lesbian. This prompts stage 5, in which they force the world to just get used to it!

While waiting for others to adjust to their news, clients must brace themselves for the distancing or loss of friends and family relationships or even their livelihood. These losses may also trigger feelings about other past losses the client may have experienced.

Stage 5. Identity Pride: Gay Adolescence in Full Force

In this stage, gays and lesbians immerse themselves in their subculture. They have much less interaction with heterosexuals and often begin to confront straight people. They do not distinguish between straight people who are heterosexist or homophobic and those who are not. All their previous repression is now explosively directed outward, and they want to come out to the world. They devour gay books, magazines, and weeklies, absorbing all the culture's earmarks and trademarks. Disdain for the straight world surfaces; they tend to think it's "them against us." The person in stage 5 also begins correcting heterosexuals who assume they're straight (Kort, 2003).

This stage energizes the best activists. The combination of anger and pride impels them to become heavily, passionately involved in gay rights organizations and gay pride marches. Those in the forefront of these marches are often predominately those in this stage of coming out.

Stage-5 individuals are teenagers trapped in adult bodies—and minds. Again, like adolescents who do all kinds of things to underscore their "emerging" as individuals—dying their hair, shaving their head, piercing themselves, wearing T-shirts with slogans that discomfort their elders—gays and lesbians assume a similar "in your face" attitude. They delight in shocking behavior that's over the top. They relentlessly tell everyone they're gay. They wear T-shirts that say *I CAN'T EVEN THINK STRAIGHT.* They're rebellious and promiscuous. They French-kiss in public. They love to draw attention to themselves, but their critics—and they themselves—don't realize that this is only a phase of development that they missed at their age-appropriate time. The difference is that their "gay age" doesn't match their chronological age. Whereas such behavior is appropriate for teens, it doesn't seem appropriate for adults.

Therapists who aren't aware of stage-5 behavior may misdiagnose clients as suffering from oppositional disorders, personality disorders, or sexual addictions. These therapists may also unwittingly shame their clients by displaying their own discomfort over their clients' stage-5 behavior.

Homophobes like to condemn lesbians and gays for their "bad" behavior on the grounds that being promiscuous, obnoxiously vocal, and indulging in too much partying and chemical abuse exemplifies what gay life is all about. However, that acting-out behavior is a *stage* of coming out—usually lasting only 2 to 3 years—and has little to nothing to do with gay identity. Typically, clients are *relieved* to learn that they're only going through a stage, as they feel uncomfortable about being compelled to act this way.

The Case of Roger

Recently divorced from a heterosexual marriage, Roger was a 50-year-old executive at one of the Big Three auto companies and a father of two teenage sons. He sought therapy after 2 years of promiscuous behavior. Worrying that gay life was "all about sex," he told his therapist that he'd met many men with whom he'd hoped to share romance but after having sex, both safe and unsafe, they would drop him. He repeatedly promised himself to stop having sex with men, but found himself doing it all over again.

Though he took pride in being authentic, true to himself, and able to act on his being gay, he also felt chagrined at what he saw in the gay male community as well as at his own lack of sexual boundaries. He'd never before exhibited any sexual acting-out or impulse-control problems. He admitted that his behavior was putting him at risk of contracting STDs.

Shamed by his behavior and not feeling understood by his therapist, Roger made an appointment to see me. He told me his past therapist had chastised him for conforming to the promiscuous behavior that the media portrayed as being typical for gay men. Astounded by the therapist's remark, Roger stopped seeing him.

In assessing Roger's behavior for a diagnosis and treatment, I asked questions that explored possible sexual addiction, bipolar disorder, borderline personality disorder (BPD), and reenacting of childhood sexual abuse. The behavior of individuals in stage 5 imitates these syndromes, so it's vital that you make these distinctions in order to plan appropriate treatment. Roger's behavior fit many criteria for these disorders, but it seemed to me that his promiscuity derived from delayed "gay adolescence." I talked with him about stage 5 to help him make sense out of why he was experiencing a loss of control. I explained that it is not uncommon for gay men—particularly heterosexually married men—who have long repressed their needs to become sexually compulsive for a *temporary* period. As discussed earlier, they can act like teenage boys whose hormones suddenly kick in.

During stage 5, reason goes out the window. I suggested that Roger remove the gay pride bumper sticker he'd put on his car because his 16-year-old son drove it, too. It made sense that he wanted to proclaim his identity as any "adolescent" would, but his son might have to explain to his pals what the sticker meant. I reminded Roger that his son was straight, and that he needed to be sensitive to his son's feelings. Roger agreed that he had placed his own "adolescent" needs over his son's genuine ones.

Roger wept while we talked about this. He felt ashamed about the way he had treated his son. He knew better than to act like this, but his anti-establishment feelings were very strong. However, learning that his behavior could be understood as a stage in his coming out process relieved him of the toxic shame he felt and allowed him to do right for his son. Roger removed the bumper sticker.

As Roger's coming out process unfolded, his urgency and compulsive acting out diminished to a normal frequency, as it naturally would for anyone moving toward identity development after a delayed adolescence. He became more in control of his sexual life, and he began to date more and have boyfriends for months at a time.

Many men and women in this stage beat themselves up and experience high levels of shame over long-suppressed behaviors that they now feel compelled to act on. The therapist's job is to help them understand what is happening to them and how best to navigate through it.

Individuals in stage 5 often proclaim that they're gay and proud even if they don't yet fully understand their own behavior and feel a little foolish. You may also detect tremendous grief inside them: They wish they'd made this change years earlier in life. Although their behavior can be mistaken for a midlife crisis, I redefine it for them as a life-awakening opportunity and educate them on the stages of coming out, reassuring them that they're just in the "adolescent" stage of "identity pride"—a necessary step for their eventual self-actualization as gay or lesbian. Upon learning the *name* for their experience, they almost always breathe a sigh of relief.

Stage 5 can last up to 2 to 3 years. It can be painstaking and fraught with emotional turmoil—humiliation, frustration, and heartbreak. People in this stage frequently meet potential flames who swiftly flicker out. (Formerly married clients who come out later in life tend to have forgotten the trial and error involved in dating and naively expect that "love at first sight" will evolve into a long-term relationship.)

Therapists need to remind clients who are experimenting with sexuality and promiscuity of the importance of safe sex. Clients in stage 5 need to monitor their sexual behaviors. They also need to remain alert for signs of dependence and abuse if they're using drugs and alcohol.

If your client remains in this stage longer than 2 to 3 years, it's no longer merely a stage. Using your clinical skills, explore the possibility of a mood or personality disorder (see Chapter 12), sexual addiction, or chemical abuse/dependency. You should also begin exploring if they are stuck in some unresolved trauma or stage of development from childhood (see Chapter 6).

Stage 6. Identity Synthesis

At this stage of integration, the "them and us" concept breaks down. Gays and lesbians begin to understand that not all heterosexuals are homophobes. Like older adolescents, they can now relax their militant stance and reintegrate themselves into society. They understand that there are "good straights" as well as "bad straights," that heterosexism and homophobia needn't dominate their lives, and that they can relate to both gays and straights without any loss of self-confidence.

As I mentioned earlier, these stages do not always occur in the order presented; they are simply meant to be used as a guide for therapists, just as Kubler-Ross's stages of loss are. For instance, although most lesbians and gays do go through stage 5 and have a gay adolescence, some don't. Anticipating it for clients is the best approach, so that if and when they experience some of the symptoms and dynamics particular to the stage, they will know what is happening to them.

Even with the recent increased acceptance of homosexuality, these stages persist. Children and teenagers are still not allowed to explore and know their homosexuality, so a coming out experience will always need to occur for the identity to be integrated.

What *has* changed with time is that lesbians and gays are coming out earlier. They are feeling safer and witnessing a shift in acceptance for the better. An observation I have made and others have concurred with is that many of today's young lesbians and gays, who are coming out more in late adolescence and young adulthood, tend go through the stages faster and sometimes all at the same time, being angry and proud and tentative and outspoken all at once and vacillating rapidly between feeling ashamed and apparently secure. Knowing this as a clinician can help you normalize it for yourself and for your clientele.

Phases of Coming Out

In addition to the previously described stages, there are also *phases* to coming out. The phases are:

- Coming out to one's self
- Coming out to close friends
- Coming out to family

Typically, gays and lesbians come out first to themselves, then to close friends, and finally to family. Your job is to normalize and anticipate each phase so that clients understand what they are going through. A good book to help your clients deal effectively with the coming out stages and phases is Michelangelo Signorelli's (1996) *Outing Yourself: How To Come Out as Lesbian or Gay to Your Family, Friends, and Coworkers.*

Usually years of self-exploration precede coming out to oneself. From a psychological perspective, safety and security are extremely important. Individuals then come out to friends (especially gay and lesbian friends), as they are the next safest. Being rejected by friends is more tolerable than losing relatives. Friends may serve not only as a sounding board but also as a practice ground.

As you guide clients in their coming out process, tell them what has worked for other clients during the same phase. For example, gay males have a better and easier time telling their mothers first and then their fathers, whereas lesbians have it easier when telling their father first and then their mother. Generally the parent of the same gender as the client has a more difficult time be accepting. Also tell clients that it is important to come out to themselves and feel solid first, and then to close friends before their family, as they will probably not receive they support they would like from their family and will need their friends at that time. Also encourage clients to make some new friends—preferably gay and lesbian—so that they have supportive individuals to turn to if they are met with distancing and rejection from their family and straight friends.

Coming out to family—especially parents—is the hardest, bravest thing your clients will ever do. Few gays and lesbians want to hurt their parents, and they know that this information very well might cause hurt and other feelings they're not eager to engender. These issues are discussed in more depth in Chapter 8.

Gender Differences

Lesbians generally come out later than gay men (Hanley-Hackenbruck, 1989). Studies show that males tend to be aware they're gay by age 13, whereas females tend to know by age 19. One reason is that girls can touch, hug, and kiss each other, and even dance together, without raising an eyebrow or being labeled "queer." Women also tend to act on their acknowledgment several years later in life. They tend to realize their orientation in a special same-sex friendship, whereas men tend to seek sexual experiences for their own sake, not necessarily in any long-term relationship context.

Once a man falls in love with another man, he's forced into awareness that his feelings are more than sexual. Men are not supposed to have any feelings at all, let alone romantic feelings toward another man. Men learn they'd better keep their emotions at bay. Thus, when feelings arise toward another male and can no longer be pushed aside, a man must recognize that he might be at least bisexual.

For women, it's just the opposite. It is when she has sexual feelings for another woman that her awareness of being lesbian surfaces. Our society permits women to love each other, use terms of endearment, and even touch each other affectionately. However, having *sexual* feelings toward another woman will prompt the woman to consider her lesbianism.

The Case of Caroline

Caroline was a 36-year-old mother of three children. She was married to her high school sweetheart. Overall she was happy with her husband—it was a safe and secure marriage and she loved him very much. But they'd always had sexual difficulties. He wanted to please her but no matter how he tried, she didn't respond, and she blamed herself. At first, Caroline told herself that she had a low libido. Later, she blamed her husband for wanting sex too often. Over the years, it became more of a chore for her; she dreaded sex and complied only to please him. She did not think this situation was problematic, however, as she talked to other married women who were in similar situations.

Then Caroline met Tina, a 30-year-old lesbian who was involved in one of the sporting events Caroline attended. They became friends and it was obvious that Tina was interested in Caroline. Caroline felt flattered and told Tina she was straight. Tina said she was more interested in straight women than gay women and saw this as challenge. Tina, a masseuse, offered Caroline a free massage, which she accepted.

Tina began giving Caroline, who was naked, an erotic massage. At first, Caroline fought the arousal she began to feel, but ultimately she decided to enjoy it. She realized that she'd felt sexual feelings upon first meeting Tina—sexual feelings that were becoming increasingly difficult to hide. The two began having sexual contact. Caroline felt herself come alive sexually, experiencing feelings she never had with her husband. For the first time in her life, she had no trouble becoming and staying aroused.

The relationship between Caroline and Tina became a yearlong affair during which Caroline realized that the sexual trouble in her marriage was not from her poor libido or her husband's overactive libido. The issue was that she was lesbian. Never in her life had Caroline thought of herself in this way. She'd coached her children's sporting events and was involved in adult women's sports, but she never thought of the women she met as anything more than friends. Now she was angry that she had suppressed her own sexual identity for so many years, depriving herself of enjoying a full sexual experience with another person.

Caroline's therapist, however, did not think Caroline was a lesbian. She told Caroline that women have a more fluid sexuality than men do and that one can fall in love and even have sex with another woman but not be lesbian. The therapist also said that if Caroline were truly a lesbian, she would have had some inkling of this earlier in her life. The therapist was relying on what she'd heard from her gay male clients, who said they recalled always being aware of their sexual orientation.

Because she'd never been attracted to women before, Caroline was relieved to think that she wasn't lesbian; it meant she could return to her happy life with her husband and children. The therapist worked with her to frame the behavior as a phase that would eventually pass. However, Caroline soon found herself sexually attracted to other women in addition to Tina. "I had been repressed my entire life," she said, "not realizing that my true sexual and romantic attraction was to other women." The "phase" was lasting longer than Caroline felt comfortable with.

Caroline: Clinical Interpretation and Treatment

Caroline's therapist was misinformed and uneducated about lesbians; she also didn't realize that women repress their homosexuality differently than men do. The therapist was aligning with Caroline's hope that she was not lesbian by promising her that it was not true given Caroline's past.

The therapist needed to be informed of not only male homosexuality but of lesbianism as well. Although there are lesbians who report they knew something was different about them, it is more common not to know. Women report that they had loving and strong feelings for their girlfriends, teachers, and coaches but never considered it was anything more than a strong relational bond and attachment.

Caroline's therapist, whom I was supervising, admitted to me that she had had a sexual experience with another woman during her twenties and it was nothing more than a sexual expression of their love for one another. It happened a few times and was a passing phase for both of them. I helped the therapist understand that this was not the case for Caroline. As a therapist, she needed to pay attention to the other things Caroline was saying in terms of her attraction to other women and diminishing desire for her husband.

Caroline was coming out, as most women do, with a lack of awareness that she was a lesbian. And Caroline's therapist needed to put her countertransference in check and acknowledge that her client was having her own journey.

Disclosure of One's Gayness or Lesbianism

It would be erroneous for me to claim that all gays and lesbians must be completely out and openly gay in every aspect of their lives—I do not believe that. I have seen, however, that even when clients decide not to come out at work or within their families for legitimate reasons—because they know that they might be fired or lose their housing, for example—they still send negative messages to themselves. That is, they say to themselves, *There's something wrong with me or my relationships that I must keep secret.* This needs to be addressed therapeutically, but often isn't. Clients use the old excuse, "There is nothing I can do about it."

For example, it may be unwise for an employee to come out at work and risk being fired. But she still has to face the emotional and psychological consequences of staying closeted. For example, at office functions, she'll have to edit out any references that might imply that she is lesbian. She won't be able to introduce her partner as anything more than a friend. She'll have to limit the number of times she takes phone calls from her partner.

Although it is true in these types of situations that coming out is not an option, clients need to safeguard against the negative messages they send themselves by being and staying in the situation. As a clinician you can tell your clients that not telling and playing it straight—while important in their specific situation—is not good for their self-esteem. To help them through the process, have them do some written work or self-talk reminding themselves why they are hiding and pretending, and encourage them to do the least amount of lying possible.

At the very least, clients should come out to themselves—which doesn't necessarily have to involve informing anyone else. Many people don't understand the need for gays to come out, saying, "It's nobody's business if I'm straight." But heterosexist society assumes that *everyone* is straight—unless they declare themselves otherwise. Gay men get asked about their wives or girlfriends; lesbians about their boyfriends or husbands. To answer such questions, lesbians and gays must lie, change the subject, or explain exactly why the question doesn't apply. Gays and lesbians often convince straight clinicians that they can't or shouldn't come out when they're actually suffering from conflict avoidance or PTSD from their accumulated shame and concealment. Clinicians need to challenge their denial because visibility increases self-esteem.

Staying closeted results in personality disorders, which I address in subsequent chapters. Staying in an incongruent state, being out of integrity with oneself and others, and living a life of chronic deceit and concealment distorts one's personality.

Coming Out: A Lifelong Process

Coming out is not a discrete event or milestone but rather a lifelong process. Various life situations change over the years, necessitating new instances of coming out (for example, when someone begins a new job or makes a new friend). Changing doctors and telling them one's sexual orientation can be difficult, yet it is necessary so for the best possible treatment. Single clients may not have felt the need to come out to extended family and have told only when asked. However, when partnered they often feel a desire to tell, with pride, that they finally found someone. Whatever the life circumstances are, they change throughout one's life and each situation is unique and calls for another coming out.

Coming Out Is Not a Cure-All

National Coming Out Day, which occurs each year on October 11th, encourages individuals to liberate themselves, promising happiness and increased self-esteem. But this positive message fails to acknowledge that locked within that closet are other issues waiting to come out: family dysfunctions, childhood trauma, grief, and loss, all of which have been hidden along with one's orientation. Your clients may tell you, "Okay, I have come out of the closet, told everyone there is to tell, and I feel worse than I did before!" Typically, they assumed that everything would fall into place once they came out. But as addicts in recovery learn, things don't always get better; sometimes they get worse. There's plenty of baggage in the closet that has to be addressed once the door is opened.

Repressed memories can leak out through the coming out process, for example. I often refer to these issues as "dust bunnies" that need to be addressed along with sexual orientation. Depression can also arise from trying to release a lifetime of repression and erroneous messages and beliefs in a day, a weekend, or even a month of gay pride. As therapists, we need to anticipate these possibilities and treat them as they arise.

Treatment Considerations

As a straight clinician, you may have lesbian and gay clients who display positive and negative transference around coming out issues. Following are some brief guidelines for dealing with this.

- *Watch for clients' desire that you can cure them.* Some clients hope that while they're still in the early stages of coming out, you might have some secret behavior-modification technique to help them revert to being straight.
- *Realize that you are standing in for the good, accepting parent.* Many clients invest a great deal in their therapist's acceptance and approval—which they do not expect to get from their parents.
- *Anticipate that when the client reaches stage 5, you might become the target of heterophobia.* Because this stage is about seeing the world as "the straights against the gays," you as a straight therapist are likely to become the target of your client's negative transference. I recommend informing your clients that this is likely to happen.
- *Educate your clients that a full public declaration about their sexual orientation isn't necessarily the best decision for everybody under all circumstances.* Help them determine the social costs and psychological benefits for their particular situation.
- *Coach clients to be sure they feel comfortable about being gay or lesbian* before *telling others.* They need to resolve their guilt or depression before coming out to family or other straight people. If they don't, others will assume that they're unhappy because being gay is not what they really want.
- *Inform your clients that they may surprise, anger, or upset the people they tell—at first.* Teach them not to react angrily or defensively, and to let others honestly express their initial feelings, even if negative. Initial reactions are seldom long-term or permanent. Any initial distancing usually changes over time—but clients should realize that in some cases, reactions like this can become permanent.
- *Make sure that clients are well enough informed to answer questions with confidence.* Refer them to dependable books and websites they can quote as resources, if need be.
- *Help them never lose sight of their own self-worth even if people reject them.* Remind them that by coming out, they shared an important part of themselves. Ask them if they really desire a relationship with someone who rejects them for coming out. You can ask, "Were they really *your* friends?"
- *Remind clients that coming out is one of the most difficult things they'll ever do.* It won't always go well, nor does it need to—but most of the time, it is a very liberating experience.

Countertransference Considerations

Check your own countertransference by differentiating what *you* want for the client from what the *client* needs and wants. This is true for all your clients, of course, but it is especially imperative when working with gays and lesbians during their coming out process. Taking an overaffirmative stand, trying to be too gay friendly, can ultimately push clients out too fast for *their* comfort.

You also must remember that gays and lesbians can hold homophobic beliefs themselves. It is important not to align with their internalized homophobia as a result of your own unresolved feelings. For example, if you are uncomfortable with blatant vocalizations of gay pride, your countertransference may activate, or even fuel, a client's negative transference about people who attend gay pride events.

Following are a few guidelines about avoiding countertransference.

Remember that the decision to come out is your client's, not yours. Never pressure your client into coming out before he or she feels ready.

Be clear about your own homophobia and heterosexism. Many therapists will be initially supportive and open to their clients' being gay—until the clients start addressing issues such as promiscuity, sex, and "in your face" activism, wanting a premature living-together relationship or gay marriage, and challenging religious teachings (which may include yours).

Get comfortable with your own sexual feelings and impulses. It is not uncommon to have your unresolved feelings about your own unacknowledged and unresolved homosexual impulses and homoerotic feelings get in the way of treating gays and lesbians, particularly if you are working with someone of the same gender.

Remember that clients in stage 5 may become angry with you. As a straight person, you represent heterosexists, so be prepared to deal with their feelings. Tell your clients that anything they have to say about heterosexuals is perfectly fine in your office so they feel safe in examining their grief and anger during this stage. Of course, this is not an invitation for them to abuse you as a therapist, but it is a time to hold a space for their anger and allow them to use you as an antenna for all the heterosexists who have betrayed them. You can teach them to vent appropriately and respectfully. Give them permission to vent with you as a stand-in for all heterosexists.

CHAPTER 8

Helping Families of Lesbians and Gays

We are the only minority born into enemy camp.
—A client to his therapist in Jack Drescher's
Psychoanalytic Therapy and the Gay Man (1998)

When I was 18, I told my family I was gay. My therapist, though helpful in other ways, had led me to believe my gayness was the result of a smothering mother and a distant father. So I dutifully blamed my mother for being overprotective and told my father it was his fault for leaving us to start a new family when I was 3.

I was angry. I wanted them to feel guilty. We all went into family therapy—with a new therapist who also believed that my being gay was the result of their shoddy parenting. "Joe," she asked, "why would you tell your family? And why did you tell them in this way?" What I really needed to hear was how brave and courageous I was for telling.

Finally, at age 21, I found the courage to come out of the closet completely, let my parents off the hook, and become responsible for myself by presenting my gayness in a healthy way. The second time around, my family was more accepting. We probably spent more time healing from what therapy did *to* us than from my coming out.

This chapter is about helping your gay and lesbian clients and their families have an easier time coming out than I did. The first step, for you as a therapist, is educating yourself about the coming out process as it pertains to family of origin issues.

Straight therapists working with gays, lesbians, and their families often apply their knowledge of minority families as a guideline. But that approach is flawed in a number of ways. First, most minority families are a *united* minority. Members learn how to think and behave as they see themselves mirrored in other family members. Most children of minority families are offered a prejudice-free zone at home, and their parents suggest ways of dealing with discrimination outside the home. Gays and lesbians, however, are minorities within their own families. Learning to role play and pretend—even to themselves—that they are like the rest of their heterosexual family contributes to problems for them and their families alike.

Some straight clinicians use the concept of adoption as a template for what it must be like to be gay or lesbian within one's biological family. But that model also falls short, because adoptions imply that the children are coming from outside. Provisions and allowances are made to include those children and integrate them as full-fledged family members. Their differences are respected, especially if they are of a different race or ethnicity.

Another approach sometimes used by clinicians is to borrow from the guidelines for an adult child dating or marrying someone outside of the family's race, religion, or ethnicity. Because the gay adult is now interested in being with members of another minority, that paradigm seems to make sense. This model applies if one views coming out as a sudden change in the family. However, although the family may view their loved one's coming out as a sudden change, it isn't a sudden change for the gay or lesbian family member. In keeping with the gay affirmative belief that homosexuality is innate, it's vitally important to remember that gays and lesbians have been minorities *from the start*—they were born into their minority status.

In your lesbian and gay clients' coming out work, much of their anxiety and depression will focus on their families. In fact, the concept of family is so important to lesbians and gays that they even use it as a code word: Saying "he [or she] is family" is a way of communicating that the person is also gay or lesbian without outing the person in public.

As mentioned earlier, by the time lesbians and gays do tell their family, they've usually come out to themselves and their friends. Because one's family is seen as the highest risk for rejection and abandonment, clients worry about what reactions their disclosure will engender. They see coming out to family as risky, something fraught with fear and danger. For example, over the years, gay and lesbian clients have told me,

> "I cannot tell them—they're already too old. They won't understand."
> "They are very religious; they'll never accept it."
> "I'm their only son [or daughter]. They're counting on me to give them grandkids."
> "If I tell them, it will make them physically ill or even kill them."
> "They will never let me be alone with my nieces and nephews."

Parents have told me such things as:

"I would rather my child be a murderer than a homosexual."
"It's all my fault! What did I do wrong?"
"They can change, but they don't want to."
"Why did he tell us this? Is he trying to hurt us?"

Yet gays and lesbians usually *want* to tell their families to be closer to them. Their very urge to come out demonstrates their commitment to maintaining healthy communication, interactions, and closeness. But once they do, they'll have a whole new set of challenges for you to help them with.

Helping families build bridges across such a turbulent, difficult topic is no easy task. To effectively facilitate this process, you must know clients' family dynamics and issues as well as their own personal judgments and agendas.

Recognizing your own homophobia and heterosexism is essential. Growing up, we were all imprinted with some form of homophobia, and for any therapist to deny that would be itself a form of covert homophobia. It's too easy to get caught in your clients' heterosexist webs and collude with their reasons not to come out to their families.

The Case of Alice, a Psychotherapist

Jennifer, a 30-year-old lesbian, came to Alice for issues around her coming out. Initially uncertain that she really was a lesbian, Jennifer began confirming her identity through her therapy with Alice and had a long coming out process that lasted over 2 years. She developed a group of lesbian friends, began dating, and finally fell in love with another woman.

Now that her orientation was increasingly clear, she wanted to tell her parents that she was a lesbian. But she was concerned about how they would take it. She worried that, at ages 75 and 77, they were too old to be able to handle the information. "What would telling them now do for them or for me?" she asked Alice. "What if it kills them? It feels selfish, because it will do more for me than it will for them. I want them to live out the rest of their years in peace, not grief for having a dyke for a daughter! But I also want them to know who I am."

Alice concurred that Jennifer's hesitance was warranted. She added that bad news probably would not *kill* Jennifer's parents, but that it was something to consider. "What if that did happen?" Alice asked. "And what good would it do for them? Is this for you or for them?" She also explained that Jennifer didn't need to advertise or promote her sexuality: "Most adults don't share their sex lives and behaviors with their parents, so why should you?"

Jennifer agreed with this. But she also felt torn; she was very much in love with the woman she'd begun dating, and she wanted to be able to share this happiness with her parents. Alice, however, cautioned her against it: "You are in romantic love, and should enjoy this honeymoon period. But your parents won't be in the same place, so why do that to them?"

"But they might feel better knowing I have someone," Jennifer replied.

"But what if they don't? Then you've not only made them unhappy, but you may have harmed your relationship as well."

Jennifer accepted Alice's point of view and kept her new relationship a secret from her parents for several months. But as her love with her new girlfriend grew and she felt more assured in her lesbian identity, she spontaneously told her parents, expressing her excitement and hoping they'd be happy for her.

Mortified and angered, her parents at first did not believe her. Jennifer, crying, insisted that she was lesbian and tried to open up a dialogue with them. But they stopped the conversation and asked her to leave their house. Over the next few months, she had very little contact with her parents.

Alice questioned why Jennifer had told her family so impulsively. She thought that together, they had agreed she would remain quiet about it and keep her private life private so "no one would be harmed." Alice then explored Jennifer's "unconscious rage" toward her parents, manifested in what she called "acting out her hostility" by telling her parents so impulsively.

Assessment of Jennifer's Therapy With Alice

Alice was colluding with Jennifer's internalized homophobia, as well as expressing some of her own. What Alice should have done for Jennifer was prepare her: give her the pros and cons of coming out, tell her what she could reasonably expect following her declaration, and inform her about how other declarations typically had unfolded. But Alice lacked the information to help Jennifer effectively navigate her coming out process. In addition, her agreement with Jennifer's concerns about her aging parents' ability to handle the news, and her advice to keep her "private" life private, were symptoms of her own countertransference and homophobia. No therapist would advise heterosexual clients to tell their parents that their new romantic interest was "just a friend."

The harm in not telling was twofold. Jennifer wasn't able to have her relationship respected, and by being evasive, she compromised her own self-respect by being out of integrity with herself as well as her parents.

Jennifer's telling her parents impulsively was not out of unconscious rage toward them. Rather she was in stage 5 of the coming out process—identity pride. Experiencing the rush of exhilaration and excitement that anyone feels when starting a new romance, she wanted to tell the world about her identity and new love. Treating such behavior as "unconscious rage" is not just ineffective—it's actually damaging.

Realizing that her work with Alice was not helping her coming out process, Jennifer terminated therapy. She and her parents experienced a temporary period of distancing—as is usual when families learn that someone they love is gay. But Jennifer's relationship with her parents had been close throughout her life, and after a couple of months, her parents did come around. They did not, however, want to talk about Jennifer's "news" and referred to her girlfriend as "your friend."

At this point, Jennifer needed support to deal with her parents' conditions. She needed to understand that while her parents' discomfort needed to be respected by her, her discomfort needed to be respected by them, too. She shouldn't have to be silenced about who she was. At the same time, the parents didn't have to pretend that they accepted the situation when they did not. Both positions made sense; both deserved validation. She and her parents needed to explore a happy medium. They way through this was dialogue and constant communication with both sides hearing and validating the other's points of view.

For example, would Jennifer's parents be willing to listen to Jennifer's life as a lesbian with some limits, and could Jennifer be okay with that? Could her parents be willing to stretch themselves and hear more than was totally comfortable for them—within limits of respectability, of course? Both Jennifer and her parents would need to stretch for the other in terms of their comfort zone; neither's reactivity should be allowed to trump the other. Both had points of views that needed addressing.

For a while Jennifer's parents would not ask her about her life, and Jennifer came to her sessions angry. I encouraged her to talk to her parents about her life anyway and let them have their reactions—which they did. I supported her in responding that although she could accept they would not ask about her life, she would tell. Even if there was silence on the other end, it was better than her being silent.

After a while her family did ask about her life and her girlfriend. Elated, Jennifer talked about things going on. I encouraged her to tell her parents how good it made her feel to be asked.

However, at the first family gathering since Jennifer began her relationship, her parents said they would rather she not bring her "friend." Jennifer chose not to go and was angry. I coached her to express her feelings in therapy but to honor her parents' request and for them to honor her decision to not go if her girlfriend could be with her. Before the next family gathering, Jennifer's parents did not ask about her girlfriend. Jennifer was determined to just bring her. I talked her out of that and convinced her to tell her parents that she really wanted to attend but only if she could bring her girlfriend. Her parents hesitantly agreed.

All of this took time and back-and-forth and communication. It is your job as a clinician to help your gay and lesbian clients understand their family's perspective, just as the family needs to understand the perspective of the client.

Before Coming Out: Typical Family Patterns

When gays and lesbians do *not* come out of the closet, they follow three typical patterns to avoid their families' rejection or abandonment Brown (1989):

- *Maintaining a rigid emotional—and often geographical—distance from the family.* Gays and lesbians may run away from home for a life on the streets—particularly in their teen years, when boys are young enough to get involved in hustling. They may move to another state or across the country—to gay meccas like Atlanta, New York, or San Francisco—keeping their private life secret from the family and visiting only rarely. They may also call and visit less to avoid being asked questions about their personal lives so that they won't have to lie.
- *Adopting the "I know you know" pattern.* Today, we'd call it "Don't ask, don't tell." According to Brown (1989), "The gay person relates to his family . . . with the unspoken agreement that no one will talk about [his] personal life" (p. 68). Everyone knows that his "friend" is more than that, but no one dares say so.
- *Selective sharing, as in "Don't tell your father."* The gay son or daughter is officially out to one parent or sibling, who responds with support but with a warning not to tell certain family members.

Privacy Versus Secrecy

Obviously, these are unhealthy patterns. You can help your clients be more open with their families by explaining the difference between privacy and secrecy. Clients may tell you things like, "My parents don't tell me about their sexual behaviors, so why should I tell them about mine?" My response is usually that of course some topics, like finances and sexual practices, are nobody's business and should be kept private, but being gay or lesbian isn't one of them. Being gay is not only about sexual preferences but also about whom you love and how you live your life.

Secrets keep people feeling ashamed and inauthentic. To be fully out and confident, a gay man or lesbian should tell his or her parents. The only exception is when the client feels that telling the family will put him or her at risk for physical or mental harm.

Disclosure: Getting Your Client Ready

Most therapists and their gay or lesbian clients struggle with when and how to tell their families. There's really no best time for this type of news. Before gay children can reveal something so deep about themselves, their families must first establish an atmosphere of affection, openness, and safety. Most of the literature advises not telling family members during the holidays or special occasions, as it can create a worse reaction and generate more problems for all concerned.

The most important factor is that clients are fully out to themselves—and to some friends for support, in case the reaction is very negative. They need to feel confident and positive in their homosexuality; parents and relatives should not see them showing any ambivalence or negativity about being gay. This is an important point: Some gay men and lesbians appear ambivalent because they weep, but those tears are often shed over the fear of impending rejection and abandonment, not because of any ambivalence about being gay or lesbian.

Also, gays and lesbians need to understand that their families have a right to their reaction, negative or positive, and need the time and space to experience it. As the gay person comes out, the families immediately go into the closet. The family, in other words, is at stage 1 of their own coming out process of having a gay child, whereas their gay or lesbian offspring might be at stage 5 or 6.

A religious family, for example, might become more devout. If there's alcoholism, the drinking might increase even more. Family relations that were strained before become even more distant—and family members often blame all these changes on their gay son or lesbian daughter, who, even worse, tends to believe the family's dysfunctional reaction is somehow his or her fault.

Helping clients brace for their families' reaction is extremely important. The family's reaction to unexpected news in the past will indicate how they might react to this new development (Ritter & Terndrup, 2002), so you can ask clients how their families have handled previous crises and stressful situations. Understanding that their families' reactions are not really about them can also help your clients not take things personally. Exploring these issues will arm clients with helpful coping strategies that allow their families to go through their own reactions.

After a Child Comes Out: Typical Negative Reactions

Kübler-Ross's stages of grief—denial, bargaining, anger, depression, and finally acceptance (see Chapter 7)—apply not only to the person coming out but also to the family members, who must deal with the sudden realization that many of their hopes and dreams for the gay family member are lost. Following are some of the typical negative reactions family members may have.

- *Seeing it as a "stage" or "phase" that won't last.* Often parents say things like, "So you *think* you might be gay?" or "Don't make too many decisions as this might be a passing phase for you, dear." Parents of gay or lesbian teenagers often ask, "How could she know at such a young age? She hasn't even been with a boy!" Of course, straight teenagers do go through phases when they experiment with others of the same sex; these teens know what they are doing and their peers understand that they are trying the latest fad. Parents, then, of course are hopeful that their child's announcement is just this—a trendy fad. However, usually the gay or lesbian teenager or young adult is clear that "this is not a phase or a stage—it is who I am and always have been." This is hard for parents to believe or understand, which is why they cling to it's being a "stage."
- *Magnifying existing family dysfunction.* If the family is already struggling with a parent who is alcoholic or physically abusive—or if there have been marital problems, affairs, a divorce, or anything other issue that exists within the dysfunctional family—family members may blame their child's homosexuality on that. These dysfunctional family issues become exaggerated and are used as an excuse for the child's sexual orientation. Blaming family dysfunction *is* the dysfunction in and of itself. Rather than deal with they dysfunction, family members look at the symptoms as a way to avoid dealing with the real issues.
- *Refusal to acknowledge a romantic partner's existence.* Families who do not want to acknowledge their child's homosexuality often won't talk about their significant other. They won't ask about him or her, nor will they recognize the person as anything more than a "friend"—if they acknowledge the partner at all.
- *Blaming the partner for "seducing" the child into homosexuality.* This is very common in families who don't believe their child is truly gay or lesbian. They blame

the partner for "turning" their child gay. This stems from the belief that homosexuality can be learned. The family is also unconsciously worried that something they did turned their child gay, so they use the partner as a scapegoat.

- *For ethnic families, seeing the child as being a traitor to their culture and ethnicity.* These families view their child—especially male children—as turning his back on their culture and not reproducing and keeping it within their ethnicity.
- *For religious families, becoming more religious.* I have heard clients tell me that their families were not particularly religious before the child's disclosure but began "quoting the Bible" upon learning about their homosexuality. Some parents start attending church or synagogue regularly.
- *Taking it personally ("How could you do this to me?").* Some parents take a child's disclosure as a direct assault, as if their child is using his or her homosexuality to hurt them and humiliate them.
- *Trying to send the child for reparative therapy.* One of my clients reported that his father regularly put out religious pamphlets and books on organizations that promote "healing homosexuality."
- *Ignoring the issue, sending the inadvertent or deliberate message that "You don't matter."* These families will never bring up anything about their child's gayness, and if the child brings it up, they won't respond. They will ask their child if he "has a girlfriend yet" or if his partner "has found the right girl yet," totally dismissing that their child is gay.

During the time of the "outing," judgments fly, and the result can resemble a Salem witch-hunt in miniature. Though it is usually the parent of the same gender as the child who has the most difficulty accepting the child's homosexuality, other family members may have a hard time as well. Family members struggle to find reasons or excuses for the child's homosexuality, and they look around for someone to blame—often the gay child, but also other family members. To make sense out of something they don't understand, families search through past issues that they have long acknowledged but until now have been unwilling to confront: parental divorce, a distant or workaholic father, a controlling mother, an alcoholic parent, and so on.

Similarly, when the truth is spoken, other uncomfortable and unexamined truths tend to "come out of the closet" as well—making the core issue seem even heavier than it already is. I've had clients talk about how, once they told their families they were gay, other family secrets—such as their parents' sexually open relationship, a family member's chronic mental or physical illness, or a child's being adopted out of the family—came spilling out. These types of family secrets tend to come out because the child's disclosure makes family members feel that they, too, have permission to reveal their secrets. The important point to remember is that although this secret-telling can be painful or shocking, it sets up a safe space for more honesty in the family.

The "Change Back" Syndrome

Family members often try to get the gay or lesbian to return to who they thought he or she was—or who they want the person to be. Family members will do anything to get the person to *change back* so that they don't have to face the truth about the person or about themselves.

From family therapy theory we know the concept of homeostasis, which is that the family—or any organized system, for that matter—tends to resist change and seeks to maintain its customary organization and functioning over time. You can teach your clients and their families about homeostasis and how it is not helpful to the family, as coming out requires the family members to change and adjust to the news. It is helpful to predict with your gay and lesbian clients that they will potentially be seen as the problem and that family members will work hard to "fix" the problem by talking them out of being gay.

You can also ask your clients how their families dealt with change in the past. This will offer some insight into what they might be able to expect.

Magnified Family Dynamics

When a gay son or daughter comes out, most families' existing dynamics become exaggerated. The family is plunged into a temporary crisis and reverts to old, familiar behaviors—dysfunctional or not. Current dysfunctional patterns may also be magnified, which the gay or lesbian family member may be blamed for.

Families that are not very open or have a "don't talk" rule have an especially difficult time dealing with the coming out crisis, as the gay family member is breaking the rules by raising a controversial issue. The same goes for families that are inflexible and rigid and families who have trouble letting their children grow up and differentiate (Laird, 1998).

The Case of Brenda

Brenda, a nurse, had spent most of her life living with her parents, caring for them as they aged. The last of seven children, she remained single while the others moved out, married, and started families.

For a while, Brenda had thought she might be lesbian, but she never acted on it—nor did she believe she ever would. In her thirties, much to her parents' and siblings' delight, she had explored entering a convent. But halfway through, she realized it was not for her and returned home.

When Brenda was 40 her father died, leaving her to live with her mother, who began to lean on her, asking Brenda to accompany her on errands and attend family functions with her by her side. Brenda's mother did not know how to handle finances or manage the house, as her late husband had handled most of these things. Brenda stepped in and helped her mother do this. Her family was accustomed to seeing her as the one who should stay home to care for her mother.

Then, Brenda fell in love with a female doctor, Darcy, who worked at the hospital. Though Brenda still cared for her mother, she spent more and more time at Darcy's house and was home less and less. Her mother complained to her other children, who then started calling Brenda, upset and disappointed that she was not doing her "job."

At first, Brenda felt guilty. But ultimately, with Darcy's help, she realized that her brothers and sisters needed to step in and help their mother too, now that Brenda was creating a life for herself. Her siblings did not see it this way at all and grew angry when it became apparent that Brenda was not going to comply with "the family's" wishes and resume her full-time role as their mother's caretaker. Brenda then told them she was lesbian and had fallen in love. Although she still wished to care for their mother, she no longer wanted to do it alone.

The family—including the mother—accused Brenda of being selfish and looking out only for herself. They also blamed Darcy for "influencing" her to become a lesbian and abandon her place in the family. In an angry, reactive stance, Brenda moved out of her mother's home and in with her new partner, leaving her family to hold gatherings without her.

Brenda: Clinical Interpretation and Treatment

Brenda came into my office, crying that her family had rejected her. She told me that they mailed her pamphlets on how to "heal" her lesbianism. This was very hurtful to her, but being alienated from family gatherings bothered her the most. She was considering leaving Darcy and going back to her mother and her place in the family.

Quickly assessing her family situation, I explained that this had less to do with her being a lesbian and more to do with her relinquishing the role of "good daughter," which she created to hide her lesbianism and be accepted by the family. When I asked what her mother thought of the situation, Brenda said her mother had "blamed" her for moving out and not continuing to care for her. She also refused to consider Brenda's lesbianism as authentic; she felt it was an excuse that Brenda was using to leave her.

I explained to Brenda that her mother had a covert form of narcissism and helped her see that she had carefully groomed Brenda to be her caretaker ever since she was a girl. Brenda told me that her mother hadn't wanted a seventh child and had "accidentally" become pregnant. She even had admitted to Brenda that she tried to abort by subjecting herself to strenuous exercise. It appeared that Brenda's mother decided to single out Brenda and use the girl for her own needs.

Brenda understood that this was probably why it had taken her so long to come out and lead an independent life. Now, her lesbianism was a convenient distraction for her siblings and a reason to be angry at her for forcing them to have to step up and care for their mother.

Knowing your clients' family system is always imperative, but it's particularly so when homosexuality is involved. Homosexuality has many issues attached to it, including religion, sex, and politics to name a few. Some questions you might ask your clients about their families to get a sense of how they might react to their being gay are:

- Does your family talk about sex? If they do, is it too much, inappropriate, or within normal limits in your judgment? If they don't, what happens when the subject of sex comes up?
- How religious—if at all—is your family?
- How does your family deal with change? Tell me about the three most recent changes in your family and how the family members dealt with them.
- What are your family's politics? Have you seen this affect your family and if so, how?
- How does your family deal with differences among other family members? Are they open-minded and accepting or closed and rejecting?

The Case of Alan

Alan, age 25, was an only child. He came from a Baptist Christian home where he felt judged and learned that homosexuality would send him to hell. Throughout his childhood, he kept most of his inner world a secret, but after leaving home for college, he came out to himself and his friends at school. He also met and fell in love with a man, with whom he was now in a committed relationship. Now, as he prepared to return home to look for employment after finishing an out-of-state master's program, Alan realized that he wanted to tell his parents who he really was and face their judgment in an effort to be closer to them.

Armed with literature and support-group handouts, Alan was prepared for any reaction they might have. To his surprise, when he revealed the news, his parents said they had always known. Martha, his mother, said she'd found some gay pornography in his bedroom, and Cliff said he "just had a hunch."

Although Cliff and Martha embraced Alan and told him they still loved him, they were not accepting of his being gay and told him they would pray for him to change. Martha voiced her worry that he would go to hell. Cliff was more critical, saying to Alan, "Well this is *your* choice!" This comment led to an argument, in the middle of which Cliff turned and walked away—as he always had done in Alan's life. Alan expected his mother, who had always been accepting and supportive, to ask more questions and follow up with the information that he had given them, but in the days and weeks that followed, neither she nor Cliff asked him anything about being gay. It bothered Alan, and the longer they "ignored" the issue, the more he felt rejected and isolated.

When Alan explained his feelings to me, I told him what I tell all of my clients: "You have to be the one to keep the dialogue going." It would be great if his parents asked follow-up questions and even planned to go to PFLAG (Parents, Friends & Family of Lesbians and Gays), but most family members don't know what to do—or what to say or ask. To play it safe, they adopt a "don't talk about it" rule. I told Alan that his job was to create a dialogue and insert new topics on being gay into conversations.

Hearing this, Alan became angry. He felt it wasn't fair that he was expected to do all the work in coming out to his family. This brought up his memories of being emotionally neglected while growing up. If he did not talk to his parents about his schooling and grades, they would never ask. He even had to rely on school counselors and friends when considering college, as his parents didn't encourage his attending or even ask about it.

Alan: Clinical Interpretation and Treatment

Alan had two issues to resolve. One was the typical way many families deal with learning their child is gay—which is to be silent and distant. The other was that he wasn't comfortable with the way his family normally operated, which left him angry about his childhood. His work in therapy was dealing with his feelings about being neglected as a little boy.

I coached Alan to talk to his parents about his socialization while coming out, urged him to mention what types of organizations he had discovered (including PFLAG), and even suggested that he give them a copy of the local gay newspaper. I referred him to several articles and the books *What the Bible Really Says about Homosexuality* (Helminiak, 2000) and *Prayers for Bobby* (Aarons, 1996; about a mother who prayed for her son to change and ended up contributing to his suicide). Alan followed my advice, but he often found things left, untouched, where he'd put them, and if he did bring up the subject, his parents would not ask him to elaborate. So I encouraged him to talk to them about their lack of follow-up questions. He worried that doing this would cause even more problems, as they were already upset each time he brought up his being gay. I told him that although it upset his family to talk about it, it upset him *not* to talk about it—and that the three of them should address this together.

Alan did go to his parents about this, and they all wept together. His parents said they didn't know what to say or do and were trying to avoid hurting him with possibly ignorant and hurtful questions. Through her tears, Martha said she worried about his catching HIV and asked if he was being careful. For the most part, Alan's father was silent but tearful and attentive to the conversation—even though he looked away.

I asked Alan to have his parents come in for some family therapy sessions and they did. It was apparent that Martha was in the initial stages of grief over the loss of having a heterosexual son. Both the parents were cycling back and forth between denial, bargaining, and depression. They were not angry, however.

Over our next three sessions, I told Alan's parents that their son was clear about his being gay and wasn't going to change. I explained to them that when the gay or lesbian family member comes out, the family often has a hard time with it—initially. Gently, I told them that now *they* needed to do some work on accepting their gay son—that problem was theirs.

To this, Martha reacted angrily: "Are you telling me it's our fault that he's gay?" She then stated that she thought she must have caused Alan's gayness by being too overbearing and smothering as a mother. I normalized her reaction and educated them by saying that parents cannot cause a child's gayness, although it's typical for them to think they did. I told them the issue was not about Alan's gayness as much as it was about their acceptance.

Cliff commented that he still had trouble with Alan's homosexuality and said he would never accept it. "I don't think he has been with enough women to know," he remarked. "Maybe he's had bad experiences with them. With women, it wasn't easy for me at first either. I did everything to make this boy straight by putting him in

Cub Scouts, sports, and even leaving my copies of *Playboy* around for him to see. But nothing worked!"

I asked Cliff about his own childhood relationship with his father. It came out that as a boy, he'd been sexually abused by a priest and neighbor boy, and for a while had felt confused about his sexual orientation. Nothing had ever been done about the abuse, nor had he told anyone until now.

Martha and Alan were in tears. For Cliff, this was the real issue: The news of Alan's being gay had brought out his own unresolved material. As mentioned earlier, this is very common dynamic: When a gay or lesbian comes out, other family issues surface as well. And usually family members blame (or in Alan's case, ignore) the gay child rather than examining what is causing their distress.

Several weeks after this session, Alan gave the following letter to his parents.

Dear Mom & Dad,

I wasn't doing a very good job of educating you guys, because even with all of the reading I have done I wasn't totally prepared for talking with you. The bottom line is that I am who I am, and this is who I have always been. And I don't care what anyone says, this is not a choice. I was born this way and I finally get to be who I am and I can honestly say that I am the happiest I have ever been in my entire life, finally!

I don't ever want to hear "you can go back" or "it is a choice." I believe that God/Jesus/whomever made me this way and he wouldn't make something that he thought was evil or bad. True, people can turn into evil or bad, but I was not born that way because I am gay. And by the way, the Bible also says that God will be the one to judge us, not our parents or our siblings or our friends or anyone else, so I would also appreciate you saving the judgment for him to pass.

I know it may sound as if I don't care if you guys accept me or not, which is not the case, but I had to go into this whole process being true to myself and being proud to be who I am. And I can tell you with 100% certainty that I am. I hope that we can continue to have the same or a better relationship now that I am honest with myself and everyone around me, but if that is not possible, I totally understand. That is not to say that I am expecting you to come around today, tomorrow, next month, or even in a year or two. Take as much time as you need. I do understand that this comes as a shock and it takes time to adjust no matter how you end up dealing with or accepting it.

Please know that I love you both and I am the same person I was yesterday, and for my entire life for that matter. I am just much happier than I have ever been and I am actually very proud of myself for finally being able to be true to myself.

When you are ready (and again, I will wait for you to tell me), I would like to talk about how my significant other or whatever you would like to call him fits into this picture. I know that may not be easy but accepting me will also include accepting him as the wonderful human being that he is.

Talk to you guys soon.
Alan

Alan waited a good year before his father came around. He talked with his mother regularly and though she cried each time he brought up his sexuality and his relationship with his partner, she listened. Ultimately his father's way of making peace was to say that it would be God's judgment in the end and should not be his. Although Alan was not 100% pleased with his father's "tolerance," I helped him see this was the best his father could do given his religious beliefs.

What Parents and Families Need to Know

As therapist, you need to know how to help the parents in addition to the lesbian and gay client—even if the parents never come in. Family therapy sessions are particularly helpful, but you can also help your clients educate their families on their own. Parents receive little to no support from others for having a gay or lesbian child. In terms of comfort and empathy, they actually would receive more support if the child had died.

Parents need to know that their child's orientation is not their fault in any way. They need to be reassured that they did nothing to cause it, shape it, or develop it. The more you can help them understand they are not to blame or the cause, the more they will be able to accept their child's homosexuality.

Next, it is helpful to talk to parents about the closet they are in now that their child has come out. They now have to deal with telling or not telling their friends and family that their child is gay. Prepare them for what they might feel when they hear homophobic slurs—mad, sad, afraid, ashamed—and what, if anything, they intend to do about it.

Discourage parents from telling their child not to tell certain family members.

Remind them that it is their issue, not their child's. If they need some time before their gay child tells, that is fair, but making blanket statements like, "I don't ever want you to tell so-and-so" is not fair to their child. Help parents see their own issues that arise around why they would not want certain people to know.

Also it is important to teach parents and families that their reactions are their own. They have less to do with their child's homosexuality and more to do with how they react to news that is upsetting. Help them understand what about their child's disclosure bothers them the most.

The following questions are helpful when working with parents:

- Do you feel it is your fault and if so, why?
- What is the general way you deal with sexual issues?
- How were sexual issues addressed in your family growing up?
- How were differences viewed among family members' personalities and interests in your childhood growing up?
- Is this affecting your marriage? If so, how?
- What concerns do you have about your child being out in the world as a gay man or lesbian?
- Does this conflict with your religious beliefs and if so, how?

For further support you can refer parents to PFLAG (Parents, Friends and Family of Lesbians and Gays). There are chapters all around the country. You can also refer them to the Internet (www.pflag.org), which lists information about local chapters. It is especially helpful to have some hardcopy pamphlets and brochures for them to read. Educate them on the benefits of going to a support group of people who have experienced what they are experiencing and can share stories that may help them.

The Case of Mary

Mary, a 42-year-old mother, told me her 20-year-old son, Jacob, had just told her that he was gay—and she was sure this wasn't so. Her husband, Howard, who was Jacob's stepfather, wasn't interested in attending therapy, so she came to the appointment with only Jacob. (Jacob's father died when he was 3, and Howard functioned as Jacob's principle father figure.)

Mary began the session by stating that Jacob "didn't know what he was" and that she wanted to provide some help. Apparently, Jacob had come out to her only 2 months before. Mary was devastated, claiming that Jacob, her youngest, was closer to her than her other two children. She even stated that she felt closer to Jacob than to her own husband!

Jacob assured her that nothing had changed, that he loved just her as much as before. He said that he was *not* in fact struggling with his sexual identity, and knew that he was gay—for sure. Mary took this as an affront. "Why are you trying to hurt me like this?" she implored.

Over several more sessions, it became clear that Mary's relationship with Howard had been weak for years. She had given very little to the marriage and received little in return. Able to ignore her marriage, she had put all of her energy into her daughter and two sons.

Jacobs's brother and sister had moved to other parts of the country, which she took as personal rejections. "I never believed I couldn't see my kids every day." The children kept in constant contact with her and visited with her four times a year, but that was not enough for her, she reported. She still felt alone and abandoned. Now, Jacob had told her he was gay, and he was spending less and less time with her.

I assured Mary that the fact that her son and daughter felt comfortable living elsewhere—and stayed in regular touch—was a sign of her good parenting. Her children felt secure, able to make their own lives for themselves. But Mary insisted that this was *not* a positive sign. I also praised her for having raised a gay son who was willing to share his authentic self with her, but this didn't calm her either. So we moved on to the real, underlying issue, which was her distant relationship with Howard.

I asked that Howard come to our next appointment, which he did—tentatively. Immediately upon entering the therapy room, Howard stated that he was there only "to support his wife," and he refused to participate in our conversations. I honored that, giving him credit for being there at all.

During the session, I explained to the parents that Jacob was on his way to a healthy gay identity, if not already there. The issue was really about them coming to terms with having a gay son—and a marriage based on parallel lives, with not much overlap as a couple or as parents. Howard worked many long hours and was an avid fisherman. Mary had repeatedly asked him to spend more time with her, but Howard had rebuffed her. I recommended that if therapy continued, it should be marital therapy for Howard and Mary, without Jacob—which sent a message to the whole family.

Howard wasn't pleased with this suggestion, as he felt his marriage was fine and had no interest in working on it. But after Jacob stopped joining his parents for therapy, the three of us spent a number of sessions on Howard's ambivalence about marital therapy with his wife. Ultimately, he agreed to try it, and they created a stronger, tighter marriage.

Becoming more confident about herself and her husband, Mary was no longer so emotionally needy with her children. Their interactions were more appropriate. She also developed healthier relationships with her friends and relatives. She and Howard were able to resolve other issues in their marriage—all thanks to Jacob's integrity and courage.

It can be hard for parents to deal with the behaviors typical of a gay or lesbian child or teenager coming out of the closet. They worry their child will be bullied, humiliated, harmed, and endangered either physically or emotionally. It is normal for parents to have these concerns. As a therapist, normalizing their child's behaviors (without condoning the dangerous ones) is important.

Following is an email I received from a concerned parent. It is typical of what many parents struggle with as their child goes through the coming out process.

Dear Joe,

I hope you don't mind that I am sending you this email, but I am kind of desperate. My son is 20 (just finished his sophomore year in college) and told us a couple of months ago he is gay. My husband and I are coming to terms with this—we really are. We love Jordon and would do anything for him and we only want the best for him.

The problem is this: I think he is way too sexually active and sometimes practices unsafe sex. He seems to spend hours and hours on various gay male websites talking to guys. Then he goes out and hooks up with them (I think). While he was at college, we were obviously not there so we don't really know, but for the week that he has been home he has done this twice. I don't have a problem with him meeting gay guys and hopefully someday developing a deep relationship but I feel like he is kind of whoring around right now and I am torn apart inside. I'm not sure he tells us the complete truth about what he does—not that we want details. We did find out that he had tried drugs with these men he had met and we came down on him pretty hard about that. He swears he will never do it again and that he only did it a couple of times. Can we trust him? I'm not sure.

We really need help with this because it does not seem "normal" to me that he spends so much time talking on the Internet with guys. He is basically a nice kid, just with such low self-esteem that I am scared to death for him. Please let me know what you think—I know it's hard to say anything without meeting a person but WE ARE DESPERATE!

Thank you,
Ashley

My response to them was as follows:

Dear Ashley,

Although I cannot speak specifically for your son because I don't know him, I can tell you that what he's going through is normal. He sounds like he is in stage 5 of the coming out process, which is like adolescence, only delayed. Most straight teens do what he is doing in middle and high school, and straight teens don't have to go online because they can date openly and have the resources and openness to do it.

Your son is probably more like age 15 in the romance/sexuality department. It is VERY scary to hear he is having unsafe sex and experimenting with drugs. On the other hand, he is no different than any teen having unprotected sex and experimenting with drugs. I am just trying to give you a normative concept so you can see what he is doing is normal—just different in terms of his age and how he meets guys. The number one way gay men hook up is online. Honestly it is better than the bars, where he could fall in with the wrong peer group who do drugs on a regular basis.

This is a stage he is going through and it could last 2 to 3 years, like with any adolescent. After people get this stage out of their system, they settle down with Mr. Right or Ms. Right, just as your son will probably do.

It sounds like you and your husband have done all you can do. I would recommend keeping the conversations open and honest as they sound like they have been. Also, have you heard of PFLAG (Parents, Friends and Family of Lesbians and Gays)? They would be a great support for you and your son. I also recommend the books *Beyond Acceptance* and *Always My Child.*

Your fears are valid regarding the unsafe sex and the experimental drug use. You have told him your concerns and the best part is that you raised a son so honest. Now you have to honor him with your trust and cross your fingers. If you push too hard you could alienate him.

I hope this helps you and your family.

Sincerely,
Joe Kort

Establishing Rules for Discussing Homosexuality Among Family Members

It is important to establish ground rules for discussing homosexuality among family members. The subject is charged for many reasons, as the examples in this chapter have shown. Emotions run deep, reactivity runs high, and individuals regress to primal coping mechanisms, relying solely on the reptilian brain, which operates only on survival. Family members will do or say whatever it takes to get relief.

Given all this, rules have to be established for the family to engage in healthy communication about the disclosure of being gay. Following are some you can teach your clients:

- Keep the dialogue about being gay or lesbian going, even if it makes family members uncomfortable. It is easy for the gay or lesbian family member to give up if the rest of the family does not want to talk about it or stops talking about it. This usually just means that people don't know what to say. You can prompt parents to keep talking to their child about the child's homosexuality with curiosity, asking things like, "What does gay mean to you?" or "When did you first discover you were gay?" or "If I said anything before I knew that was negative, I want you to know I am sorry." Whatever comes up for the family members, they need to be encouraged to keep talking.
- Take time-outs. Everyone needs to have permission to say when and if they are overwhelmed and unable to continue the conversation. Everyone needs to agree to take a time-out and agree when the conversation will continue. The time-out should never be more than 24 hours, or family members might have a tendency to avoid it for much longer and months could go by.
- Within the dialogue, feelings should be addressed and revealed only in nonreactive ways and through "I" statements such as "I have feelings about . . ." or "I am worried about . . ." In other words, if one or more person is having an overreaction, the conversation should stop immediately and only be resumed when reactivity can be contained. Emotional safety is the number one priority for all within these discussions. If someone no longer feels emotionally safe, they need to be able to express that and ask for the family member talking to state his or her thoughts in a different way or take a time out.
- Validate one another's points even if they are different from each other. It is easy to say that what someone is saying "doesn't make any sense" or is "completely ridiculous." Teach the family to refrain from making such statements and instead say, "What you have said makes sense *from your point of view.*" This is not agree-

ment, but it does not negate what the family member doing the validating is thinking. The family member will have a turn to share his or her side of things. The issue here is for all individuals to hear one another out and to be validated and accepted for what they think even if they disagree.

• Teach the family members how to stay emotionally connected and empathize with one another. For example, a gay son or daughter might say, "It must be scary to think about my going to gay bars in areas you don't think are safe." A parent might say, "I imagine you feel angry that my religious beliefs make it hard for me to accept your homosexuality."

These rules and guidelines are often very hard for families to follow on their own. Having a few family sessions can be enormously beneficial, with the therapist there to facilitate and point out overreactions, judgments, interruptions, and anything else that is standing in the way of effective communication.

I would like to end this chapter with a story from the Talmud:

A king had fallen out with his son. Very angry, the son left his father's castle and created his own kingdom, many miles away. Over time, the king missed his son and sent a messenger, asking him to return, but the son declined his father's invitation.

This time, the king sent the messenger back with a different message: "Son, come as far as you can, from your kingdom to mine. And I will meet you the rest of the way."

CHAPTER 9

Lesbian and Gay Sexuality

We can hide with sex, we can hide from sex, but we cannot be fully ourselves sexually and hide. Our sexual behavior is a core expression of who we are.

—Patrick Carnes, in *Sexual Anorexia: Overcoming Sexual Self-Hatred* (1997)

For over a year, I had been treating a heterosexual single client named Joyce. During a session following a romantic trip Joyce had taken with a new boyfriend, she reported that the vacation had gone well and that they had a great time sexually and romantically.

"And I also learned about shrimping," Joyce said excitedly.

"Did you like it?" I asked.

"Not at first," she said, scrunching her nose. "But I got used to it—especially the smell—and I had fun with it."

"What about the taste? I asked.

"It was delicious!" she exclaimed.

"*Delicious*? I've never heard someone use that adjective after they try it initially," I replied.

"I'll try anything once," she said happily, licking her lips. "It was hard to get used to using the net while doing it!"

At this point, I realized that we were talking about two different things. Joyce was a highly sexual woman. During our work together, she had a number of different male partners—even a woman for a while—and was experimental and open to just about anything sexually.

"Joyce, what are you talking about in terms of shrimping?"

"We went to Maine and went on the water in a boat with a net, catching shrimp to eat later in the evening. Why? What did you think I was talking about?"

"I thought you were talking about sucking and licking toes—that's also called 'shrimping'"!

We both laughed.

This comical misunderstanding illustrates how important it is that we clinicians be clear on the right questions to ask, know the sexual jargon and terminologies, and, most importantly, be willing to ask when we are confused or don't know the resources to give our clients.

Some straight clinicians erroneously expect gay and lesbian sex lives to resemble heterosexual ones: They assume, for example, that there is the same frequency in sexual contact and that gays' and lesbians' views on monogamy and penetration are identical to those of straight people. This heterocentric viewpoint is often what causes gay and lesbian clients to consult with me. They say, "My straight therapist just didn't get it."

Other straight clinicians may operate under the false assumption that gay men are more preoccupied with sex than straight men are, or that lesbians are less interested in sex than straight women. These kinds of misconceptions can derail therapy.

Gay and lesbian clients also often report sensing that their therapists don't want to talk about sexual issues with them. As one of my clients once said to me, "I was too afraid he [my past therapist] would not like me or understand me if I told him about my sex life."

This chapter will help you learn the terms and intricacies of gay and lesbian sex so that you can ask informed questions and treat your clients more effectively. Clinicians who can reassure their gay and lesbian clients that they are informed about the pertinent facts will find that their clients feel much safer in confiding in them.

It is important for me to note here that many of the claims I make in this chapter are generalizations. I in no way, of course, mean to stereotype men and women—straight or otherwise—nor do I mean to suggest that I know everything about gay and lesbian sex lives. But to present the types of problems you will see in your office, I make some sweeping statements. As you read this chapter, remember that there are always many exceptions to the rule.

Knowing Your Own Biases and Comfort Zones

Before you can listen to clients and be nonjudgmental about their sexual issues, you must be willing to explore your own feelings and beliefs about your personal sexual behavior. You need to know your own heterosexist biases about sex and sexuality. You may, for example, be tolerant of clients' homosexual identity as it relates to their self, family, friends, and partners but find that the details of their sexual life make you uncomfortable.

I don't believe that therapists are judgmental only about the sex lives of lesbian and gay clients. Indeed, most therapists are uncomfortable with the erotic lives of *any* of their clients—especially when the eroticism is directed at them by way of transference. It is normal to be uncomfortable listening to gay and lesbian clients, especially those of your own gender, talk about their sex lives. But because gays and lesbians have been insulted and stunted developmentally with regard to their sexuality, failing to acknowledge this area limits your ability to conduct full and effective therapy.

Clients always know when their therapists feel uncomfortable with a topic. I've had many clients tell me that when they tried to talk with their previous therapists about a sexual conflict or act they were met with resistance—the therapists wouldn't ask them to elaborate or even mirror back what they said, and would instead move on to an unrelated topic to escape their own discomfort or lack of knowledge.

Countertransference will inevitably enter the treatment room when your clients talk about their various sexual encounters, fantasies, experiences, and behaviors. As you read this chapter, monitor your own feelings, whether positive or negative. Let your judgments surface to consciousness so that you can either work on them or decide that addressing the erotic lives of your clients is not for you. The more uncomfortable you feel, the more you can understand your own values and honestly assess which clients you can work with and which would be better served by a different therapist.

The Case of Nancy, a Therapist

Nancy, a therapist, asked me for supervision regarding a lesbian client she was seeing. Jess, age 25, was in stage 5 of the coming out process (see Chapter 7 for the stages of coming out). She had begun meeting women online and at bars and was increasingly excited about her lesbian identity.

Jess had moved into a highly sexually charged phase. During sessions with Nancy, Jess would relate her sexual experiences and all that she was learning in great detail. When she asked if Nancy was comfortable hearing about it, Nancy replied, "Yes." But she really wasn't.

In supervision with me, Nancy admitted that she was more comfortable listening to her gay male clients' sexual exploits. She feared that Jess was acting out with her in the therapy—perhaps eroticizing her and "purposely" regaling her with details about her sex life to see if Nancy had lesbian tendencies. Even though she'd told Jess she was straight, Jess repeatedly asked if Nancy was certain she was heterosexual. Jess also related that she, herself, had believed she was heterosexual before realizing she was gay. Nancy became increasingly uncomfortable and believed that Jess enjoyed making her feel uncomfortable.

Jess continued to discuss her sexual feelings toward other women—including Nancy. To avoid Jess's "advances," Nancy talked about her husband more than she normally would and actually brought in a photo of him and their children to solidify her straight status.

Now Nancy was feeling guilty, worried that her countertransference would become obvious. She realized that she needed to better understand what was happening. She asked me, "Is it okay to tell Jess that I'm not comfortable hearing the details of her sex life? I don't want to shame her in any way but I do want the boundaries clear in the therapy room."

Nancy: Clinical Interpretation and Treatment

I immediately told Nancy it was normal for her to feel uncomfortable, given that she was a woman herself—and the object of Jess' erotic desire—and straight. But it was important to acknowledge her discomfort rather than try to be "politically correct" and pretend to adopt an attitude she didn't have. This was a relief to Nancy because she wanted to remain gay affirmative and keep working with lesbians.

Nancy and I also explored the normalcy of clients' romantic feelings for therapists. I asked her how she had felt when men expressed these feelings toward her. She said it had made her uncomfortable but that she felt more at ease working through the erotic transference with men than she did with Jess—who actually had never said she had *romantic* feelings for Nancy, just sexual ones. Nancy also admitted that with Jess, the erotic transference felt more aggressive.

I explained that for Jess and others who are in the midst of the coming out process, it is normal to have positive transferential feelings toward the therapist, including sexual and romantic ones. The aggressiveness Jess displayed (goading Nancy into thinking she might have suppressed lesbian tendencies) might be due to the fact that she was in stage 5—the "in your face" phase when many gays and lesbians think that everyone is (or should be) gay or lesbian.

I then asked, "Are you willing to explore your own sexual issues that might be interfering with your work with Jess?" Sobbing, Nancy revealed that when she was

13, an adult male neighbor had molested her while his girlfriend watched in obvious enjoyment. In her own therapy, Nancy had done a considerable amount of work around this and thought she was finished dealing with what the male neighbor had done. Now, however, she realized that she had never addressed her feelings about the woman who was there.

Jess's disclosure of her sex life triggered Nancy's memories of her perpetrator's girlfriend's erotic enjoyment of her abuse. Because it wasn't appropriate for Nancy to share her own sexual abuse issues with Jess, I recommended that she work this through in her own personal therapy and supervision and view it as an opportunity to finally resolve her own sexual abuse issues.

As a result of this conversation, some of Nancy's discomfort in working with Jess was reduced, but although she now realized why Jess was behaving in the ways she was, it still remained an issue. I advised her to talk openly with Jess about the possibility of an erotic transference to see Jess's reaction. Nancy could ask questions such as:

- "Jess, it's normal for clients to have sexual and romantic feelings for their therapists. I was wondering how you want me to feel about your expressing yours toward me?"
- "How do you think I feel about your having a sexual interest in me?"
- "How do you think I feel in return toward you?"
- "How do you want me to feel when you tell me that perhaps I am suppressing a homosexual orientation?"
- "If I *were* suppressing lesbian feelings, what would that mean to you?"

These are some standard questions that allow deeper work on clients' transference and help the client self-examine rather than focus on the therapist.

Nancy worried that these questions might embarrass Jess. Even if it were true that Jess had romantic feelings toward Nancy, Jess might lie to avoid the strain it might cause in their therapy. Nevertheless, I helped Nancy find the words to bring this out into the open, working it through to keep it safe for Jess to talk honestly about all of her sexuality.

I also advised Nancy to discuss with me her own discomfort over listening to lesbian sexuality. It was not appropriate for her to address her discomfort in detail with Jess. I suspected that Jess might be already picking up on it, as clients often do. It was normal for Nancy to feel uncomfortable, like any straight woman who was not familiar with the details of lesbian sex would. But if Nancy expressed some of her discomfort sensitively and admitted she was working on it in supervision to allow herself to listen to and help Jess, Jess might understand. Next, they could decide together if Jess should see another therapist—perhaps a lesbian—if Jess felt it was interfering with her therapy.

Many therapists don't agree with—and are uncomfortable with—any type of self-disclosure with their clients, arguing that a therapist's personal issues should remain outside the therapy room. I generally agree, but because gays and lesbians are hyper-vigilant regarding others' judgments, feelings, and discomfort, I thought it would be in Jess's best interest to hear Nancy express own her discomfort. This humanistic approach honors gay and lesbian clients' possible perceptions and minimizes their viewing the problem as being about them, something they have done their whole lives.

Ultimately Nancy did express her discomfort with Jess' sexual discussions and assured her that she was working on the issues that were surfacing outside the consulting room. Naturally Jess asked Nancy what those issues were. Nancy and I had anticipated this question, and I had coached Nancy not to respond to it. Knowing the reasons behind Nancy's discomfort would not be therapeutic for Jess. All Jess needed to know was that it was a source of discomfort and that her therapist was working on addressing it.

Nancy then asked Jess how she felt about hearing this. Jess sighed with relief, stating that she knew that Nancy was uncomfortable and glad she admitted it. Jess also expressed feeling honored that Nancy was taking time outside of their therapy to address the issues coming up. She said that this made her feel even more important to Nancy. Jess continued in her work with Nancy and through supervision Nancy was able to get past her countertransference.

It is unrealistic to think that as therapists we don't have judgments about things our clients tell us—we do. It is being *aware* of our judgments and leaving them out of the therapy room if or when they interfere with a client's progress that is the challenge. Other times, the challenge is to use our judgments for the benefit of our clients. We do this best when we understand our own judgments and ways of thinking and feeling.

The Case of Glenn

Glenn came to see me concerned about not finding Mr. Right. During the intake I asked him if he knew his HIV status (a standard question I ask all of my clients) and he said he was HIV positive. He had been living with HIV for the past 13 years.

Although he had some symptoms in the beginning, he'd been taking medication for 10 years and was symptom-free.

I asked Glenn if he felt uncomfortable disclosing his HIV status and questioned whether this might be part of the problem around his dating. He said he did not like to disclose, as each time he had to expect possible rejection. I empathized with how difficult that must be for him, but he said it was not a central issue for him. The way he worked around it was by not telling dating partners until they asked.

"Is that before you have sex with them?" I asked.

"Sometimes but not always," he replied.

Now I was concerned. "What about the men who don't know you are HIV positive—don't you feel an obligation to tell them?"

"No," he responded. "I play safe. I never do anything that is of risk with any partner. Besides, if they feel strongly about it they should ask. In my opinion every gay man should assume that whoever they are sexual with is HIV positive and play safe. Then no one has to disclose unless asked."

Now my negative countertransference toward Glenn was in full gear. Not being aware of the extent to which I was negatively judging him, I said, "Glenn, don't you think it is your obligation since *you* are HIV positive to let each man know before you have any kind of sex with him—even kissing?"

"No, Joe, I don't," he defensively responded. "It is painful for me to be rejected over and over again. As long as I always use condoms and never exchange bodily fluid, there is no reason to tell because the risk is low."

"But the risk is *not* nonexistent. Do you kiss the men and let them fellate you without ejaculating in their mouths?" I asked.

Angrily he retorted, "Joe, don't you know that even though HIV can be found in saliva and pre-cum, it is very unlikely to be contagious in those ways?"

"Yes, I know that, Glenn," I said. "It just seems like an ethical issue for the person infected."

"Why? I always tell the truth if I am asked. I never lie. Why does the responsibility rest with me only and not the man choosing to have sex with me?"

Glenn had a point. I had been thinking about the issue only in terms of my own view, which was that those with HIV have a responsibility to tell the unsuspecting sexual partner.

"You don't agree with what I am doing, do you, Joe?" he asked.

"Honestly, Glenn I don't. But I don't know really where I stand on this, as I've never had this conversation before. You've given me a lot to think about and I will do so," I replied.

Glenn: Clinical Interpretation and Treatment

Clearly I was having countertransference toward Glenn, which brought out his negative transference toward me in the form of defensiveness and anger. I had long had fears about becoming HIV positive during my single years. After I partnered, I felt safe from having to experience any of these dilemmas.

My conversation with Glenn exposed my bias toward the HIV-negative partner and against the HIV-positive one. I believed that HIV-positive people bore the larger share of the responsibility to tell potential sexual partners about their status. As a single man I always asked guys before having safe sex what their HIV status was. But not all gay men do.

I don't know what the ethical answer is. I imagine for each person it is different. However, I had to determine where I stood on this issue in order to work with Glenn and other clients who chose to take this stand. I had to be able to articulate where I stood and what I was willing and unwilling to say about this touchy subject when speaking with clients.

On the one hand I saw Glenn's point. Why should he have to tell if he wasn't going to be sexually unsafe? On the other hand, what about the men who trusted those with HIV to disclose and did not think it was polite to ask? I could see as I thought this through and talked with others supervising me that the words I chose to use in my discussions of this subject leaned in favor of the HIV-negative partner.

After some careful consideration, I decided how to manage my countertransference. I now tell all clients who are negative, gay or straight, to ask the person with whom they are engaging in sexual behavior about their HIV status—or to realize that they are taking a risk in not asking. I disagreed with Glenn's position about when to tell others about one's HIV status, and I make this position clear to clients who are HIV-positive and do not disclose. I want them to know where I am coming from as a therapist. I also explore with both positive- and negative-status individuals the psychological issues that would prevent them from telling or asking.

Clients who do not disclose their HIV-positive status and engage in *unsafe* sex must be informed that therapists have a legal obligation to report them. All therapists need to know their state's laws on reporting (guidelines vary from state to state). The best source of information on this topic is Anderson and Barret's (2001) *Ethics in HIV-Related Psychotherapy: Clinical Decision Making in Complex Cases.*

Educating Yourself: A Vital First Step

Before you can effectively address your lesbian and gay client's sexual lives, you must become familiar with same-sex sexual acts and the terms used to describe them. The glossary lists definitions of terms like *fisting, s/m, strap-on sex, docking, rimming,* and other terms that clinicians often do not know. Some of these sexual acts are specific to gay men and lesbians; most are done by both, though dealt with differently.

To communicate with gay and lesbian clients, you must be fluent in two idioms—the jargon that gays and lesbians use among themselves, and the standard clinical equivalents. Likewise, a working knowledge of gay culture is just as imperative as it would be when working with any other minority.

As you learn the sexual language used among gays and lesbians, you'll discover that they often deal with sexuality very differently than heterosexuals. For example, it's common for gay men to state in personal ads—and on a first date—what they like to do sexually and whether they are a "top" (the partner who anally penetrates) or a "bottom" (the partner who is penetrated). This is done to attract like-mined partners and to dissuade men who aren't a match.

In the master's class I teach for social workers, one female student was shocked to learn this. "If men did that in heterosexual personals," she said, "most women would find it a turnoff, and they wouldn't get many responses." But the gay male community is different. In fact, if a gay man *doesn't* put his sexual preferences (whether he is a "top," "bottom," or "versatile") in his profile, he's not likely to get many responses!

Why the labels? Straight relationships enjoy the traditional generalizations of sexual compatibility. But before two men meet, it's difficult for them to determine sexual compatibility. Of course, when it comes to each individual's sexual preference, there are no absolutes. Some men use these criteria merely as a guide, whereas others view them as deal-breakers before dating or sex.

Knowing sexual terms and behaviors is key to open, comfortable dialogue in the therapy room. It also helps prevent countertransference, as the following case illustrates.

The Case of Mark, a Therapist

Mark, a heterosexual male therapist, had helped a client, Luke, with the coming out process. Luke grew deeply attached to Mark and grateful for all the therapist had done to help him feel better about coming out to himself, his friends, and finally his family. Now, they agreed, it was time for Luke to start dating other gay men romantically. When Luke began having sexual hookups, Mark asked him how things were going and discovered that Luke was only receiving anal sex, not reciprocating.

Luke stated that he had tried penetrating his partners and had successfully entered men but never achieved orgasm. He told Mark he preferred receiving anal sex.

Assuming that all gay men "share" in giving and receiving intercourse, Mark warned Luke that this might prevent him from finding a partner. (I've heard many straight therapists say that they thought gay male couples "took turns" penetrating each other. The truth is that most gay men are generally either an anal penetrator or receiver, and they tend to want to know their partner's preference before entering into a hookup or relationship.)

Luke tried to take his therapist's advice, but he never enjoyed giving anal sex as much as receiving it.

Mark: Clinical Interpretation and Treatment

When Mark sought my supervision, I taught him the terms *top* and *bottom* and explained that gay men usually self-identify as either one or the other. Some men go both ways—calling themselves "versatile"—but this is not as common. Being the bottom is seen as inferior to being the top among gay men—to the point that gay porn stars never identify as a bottom, only as versatile. Inherent in this is the sexist belief that being the receiver is feminine. (As the joke goes, "At a gay male wedding, the father of the bottom pays!")

Mark then said to me, "I don't mean to offend you, but is that like one playing the woman and the other playing the man?"

"It's not about male/female role playing," I explained. "It's about just sexual preferences and erotic enjoyment." I also explained that some gay men never engage in anal intercourse, only oral sex and masturbation.

Now Mark was really confused. I had him read some books on gay sexuality, including Silverstein and Picano's (2004) *The Joy of Gay Sex*, and I encouraged him to admit to Luke that he hadn't understood enough about gay male sex. My concern was that he might have shamed Luke for not "acting like a man" in bed.

When Mark broached the subject, Luke revealed that he had indeed felt ashamed. He'd subsequently done some Internet research on gay sexuality and was considering switching to a gay male therapist who could "understand him." But he felt connected to Mark and wanted to keep working with him.

Mark's decision to seek supervision around his client's sexual issues saved his work with Luke. When I work with therapists, I try to debunk the erroneous beliefs they hold about gay and lesbian sexuality. On of the most common is the belief that genital penetration is the ultimate—if not the only—way to have sex and that any other practice is inferior. Many lesbians, for example, can fulfill each other sexually without penetration, and some gay male couples only perform oral sex or engage in mutual masturbation. In many therapeutic circles, it's believed that not having intercourse indicates a delayed, not fully developed sexuality—a bias from a heterosexist, patriarchal, sexist model. Many of your clients will also come in with this belief and will feel ashamed for not engaging in intercourse. It's your job as a therapist to normalize their sexual preferences.

Heterosexual Versus Lesbian and Gay Sexual Behaviors

As a gay affirmative therapist and educator, I have heard both male and female straight therapists ask things like:

- "If a lesbian needs to use a dildo, then why doesn't she just get a man?"
- "Why don't some lesbians want their dildos and sex toys to look like penises? Doesn't that reflect their hate for men?"
- "If a gay man is a top and receives oral sex but doesn't give it, then why not just be with a woman?"
- "Isn't it offensive and insulting to a potential partner if a person leads with sexuality, the way gay men do in dating?"
- "If lesbians aren't actively sexual with each other, then are they really lesbians?"
- "Why are gay men so promiscuous sexually?"

The answers to these questions might seem obvious, but they aren't to many clinicians. Many therapists still believe that homosexuality is defined *only* by sexual behavior and assume that if an individual is not being sexual he or she may not be gay. But heterosexuals who aren't being sexual with partners rarely endure questions about their sexual orientation, only about what's blocking their sexual intimacy.

Predictably, gay males and lesbians do behave sexually much like their heterosexual counterparts in terms of gender. To a degree, you can rely on what's known about men's sexual behavior and women's sexual behavior in general. Gay or straight, men are testosterone-driven, lead with sexual urges, and have more sexual partners than women. Men generally can be sexual without any flirting or even knowing their partners' names. They need no attachment, before or after. Of course, there are women like this too, but they are the minority. Both lesbians and straight women tend to be more relational. When being sexual, they usually value intimacy, attachment, and connection.

Whereas straight men are generally constrained by women's avoidance of quick anonymous sex without intimacy, gay men are not confined in this way. In other words, the gay male community enjoys easy access to promiscuity because of the absence of women to put on the brakes. This explains the more frequent sexual activity among gay men. It isn't that they are more sexual because they are gay; it's that they are male in a world without women. For better or for worse, the issue is about the differences between males and females, not gays and straights.

When addressing sexual issues in clients' lives, it is important to remember that you may experience negative reactions from gay and lesbian clients due to their hypersensitivity about the homophobia and misunderstandings you might carry as a straight clinician. If you understand that lesbian and gay sex has been judged as abnormal both historically and in psychotherapy up until very recently (see Chapter 1), you can anticipate their reactions and help validate and normalize them.

Often lesbians and gays will come to me after doing very good work with their straight therapists with the belief that their therapist could not understand or help them with their sexual issues. Sometimes this is assessment is unfair and untrue; the clients may simply not be giving their straight therapists a chance to show they *do* know a great deal—perhaps even more than the client does!

You can address this by asking your clients if they are concerned about talking about sexual issues with you. Invite them to tell you directly if they are holding back and give them permission to tell as much or as little as they want to. And finally, know your limitations. If you are uncomfortable with any parts of their sexual behavior and fantasies, refer them to someone who understands, is knowledgeable, and can help them.

Lesbian Sexuality

Believe it or not, some clinicians still hold the patriarchal belief that lesbians seek each other out of anger and resentment toward men who have frustrated or abused them. You will find some lesbian clients in your practice who feel this way, but they are certainly the minority in the lesbian community.

In general, less research is devoted women's health and sexuality than to that of men, and the same holds true for gay men and lesbians: A larger body of literature exists on the positives and negatives of gay men's sexuality. Before the 1990s, the material that *was* available on lesbians mostly consisted of misinformation and made sweeping, mostly negative, generalizations. The best book to date is sex-positive and informative: Felice Newman's (2004) *The Whole Lesbian Sex Book: A Passionate Guide for All of Us.*

Because therapists, like the lay public, are primarily misinformed, uninformed, or naïve about what lesbian sexuality is all about, many therapeutic mistakes are made with lesbian couples and individuals. Even your lesbian clients may believe the misinformation that exists on their sexuality. Gay affirmative therapy is intended to inform clinicians about what is healthy and what is not in the area of lesbian sexuality.

American heterosexual males eroticize lesbian sexuality. Countless times, I've heard straight men admit that their biggest fantasy is to get two (or more) lesbians in bed with them. The problem is that they confuse lesbian sex with an erotic performance by straight or bisexual women for the straight male's enjoyment. That's because pornography depicts "lesbians" as primarily heterosexual women performing sex acts on each other to arouse a male voyeur. Lesbian sex, however, has nothing to do with men. Genuine lesbians say that if they are going to be sexual with each other, they don't want a man in the room.

Many have assumed that sexual behavior might be secondary or even absent for lesbians because neither woman pushes for sexual activity. Women generally are taught not to be as sexual as men; some people believe they may be biologically less sexual. These assumptions are sweeping generalizations and are based on opinions, not research. The truth is that both gay and lesbian couples are more likely to equally share responsibility for initiation of sex, whereas in heterosexual relationships, males tend to apply more sexual pressure than women.

In a study by Joanne Loulan, women's sexual practices were found to involve hugging, licking, snuggling; kissing all over the body; touching, kissing, licking, and nursing on breasts; oral-genital sex; insertion of fingers or tongue in the vagina; and masturbation. Overall the study showed that 70% of lesbian sexuality tends to focus on oral-genital sex as a large component of the sexual relationship (Loulan, 1987).

Lesbians engage in sex roles of being tops and bottoms like gay males do, but they do not usually lead with that language in personal ads as gay men do. Many therapists erroneously think that lesbians rarely—if ever—engage in intercourse and only snuggle and kiss. The truth is that many have intercourse in a variety of ways, which you can ask about when you do your evaluation. It is important to ask clients about their sexual behavior rather than making assumptions about their preferences based on the scanty literature about lesbians.

When Sexual Abuse Is an Issue

There is a tendency to assume that lesbians are gay because they were sexually abused. As said repeatedly but never enough to help people remove this myth, sexual abuse cannot create a sexual orientation. However, even though this is a false assumption, it doesn't mean that issues of past sexual abuse don't come up in lesbian relationships. In fact, lesbian sex therapist and author Marny Hall reported that "lesbians report high levels of childhood sexual abuse" (Stewart, 2002, p. 14). Peggy is a good example of this.

The Case of Peggy

Peggy came to my office following a negative experience with her past therapist. She had sought therapy because she experienced sexual dysfunction each time her partner, Bonnie, gave her oral sex. Peggy was able to masturbate herself and tolerate Bonnie's digitally masturbating her. However, when it came time to receiving oral sex, she would lose her erotic feelings and shut down.

In addition, she did not want to give oral sex to Bonnie. She was not bothered by the fact that Bonnie was overweight or by the smell of her genitalia, which she stated was normal and not unpleasant.

When Peggy brought up this issue with her therapist, the therapist speculated aloud about whether Peggy was actually a heterosexual who was turned off to men because of past sexual abuse. The therapist was actually correct in guessing that Peggy was a sexual abuse survivor, but she had made this assumption without even asking Peggy about her past history or doing a thorough assessment. Peggy had, in fact, thought that her current sexual dysfunction might be related to her past abuse, and it was a direction she wanted to follow in therapy. But the therapist's assumption that Peggy was not a lesbian so angered Peggy that she terminated the therapy.

Crying, Peggy told me that her stepfather sexually molested her throughout her childhood until the age of 13. He would sneak into her room at night, get under her covers, lick her vagina for what seemed like an endless amount of time, and then leave. He would also take her to areas of the house that no one would enter, such as the basement cellar, lift her dress and pull down her panties, and lick her there. When she was very young—around the age of 4—he put her on top of the refrigerator and abused her there with cunnilingus. After the abuse, he would talk to her as if nothing happened, and she felt afraid to tell anyone.

When Peggy was 13 her stepfather began attempting to digitally manipulate her genitals and told her he was going to use his penis. She pulled away and stopped it immediately, ordering him to discontinue his assaults permanently and threatening to tell on him if he didn't. He never spoke to her again throughout the rest of her teens.

Peggy knew that this was in the way of her enjoying a good sex life with her partner. Although Bonnie was kind and considerate and did not force Peggy to do anything that made her uncomfortable, Peggy felt guilt and shame over not being able to have a more active sex life with Bonnie. Hearing her lesbian friends talk about the joys of getting and receiving cunnilingus caused her to feel even more shame and guilt. Peggy knew she was a lesbian and that she loved Bonnie. However, she worried that ultimately Bonnie would leave her if she did not deal with the abuse.

Peggy: Clinical Interpretation and Treatment

First I validated Peggy's anger and concern about her former therapist's premature judgments about her. If a heterosexual woman entered a therapy office struggling with sexual dysfunction with her male partner, a therapist usually would not suggest to the client that she might be lesbian. Instead, the therapist would probably try to get to the source of the sexual dysfunction, with the understanding that questions about the client's sexual orientation might be appropriate in future sessions if the exploration of the sexual dysfunction didn't seem to be yielding answers.

Next was the work of dealing with her partner, Bonnie. Was Bonnie truly okay with how things were? Was there a chance she would leave Peggy because of this? I asked Peggy to bring Bonnie in so that we could talk about this. Scared but hopeful, Peggy asked Bonnie and they both came in. Crying, they both stated how much they loved each other and how they enjoyed sexuality in other ways. Bonnie said that even if their sex life stayed the same, it was enough for her, as she loved Peggy that much. They took baths together, Peggy held Bonnie while she masturbated and vice-versa, and they enjoyed kissing and holding each other. Bonnie did say she would like Peggy to be able to give and receive oral sex at some point, but that her primary concern was for her to deal with her stepfather's sexual abuse of her.

The rest of my work with Peggy focused on having her talk through her sexual abuse by her father. I also was careful to ensure that my being male was not going to interfere with my work with her; she said that the fact that I was a gay male helped her work through feeling safe with a man who would not turn it into anything sexual.

Lesbian Bed Death: Myth or Reality?

The term *lesbian bed death* is said to have been coined by researcher Pepper Schwartz, who stated that lesbian couples have sex less frequently than heterosexual or gay male couples do (Blumstein & Schwartz, 1983). Conducted at a time when lesbian sexuality was first being discussed, examined, and researched, the studies claimed that in lesbian relationships both partners eventually stop asking for sex and allow their sex life to die out. According to Herbert (1996), "decreased sexual frequency of sexual interaction does not appear to affect sexual satisfaction among lesbian couples."

Today, the subject of lesbian bed death is very controversial, and standards according to which the studies were done have begun to be examined. Many lesbians themselves say that these studies on lesbian sexuality were done according to heterosexist standards. The lack of sex was based only on factors such as penetration and orgasm. Many lesbians do not restrict their idea of sex to intercourse or even orgasm. They report that a sensual bath, sensual massages, or romantic nights in front of the fire naked count for sex.

In all relationships—gay, lesbian, and straight—sexual desire tends to decrease after the romantic love and honeymoon period wears off, and often you will see a diminished interest in terms of frequency of sex and satisfaction. Although this is normative for most couples, research shows that the drop in erotic feelings does, in fact, happen sooner for lesbian couples than it does for gay and heterosexual couples (Hall, 1987). One reason for this may be the "dissolution of individual boundaries, a submergence of self in the larger arena of the relationship" (Hall, 1987, p. 138). This goes back to the enmeshed relationships lesbians create, wherein their individual boundaries are blurred and the "spark of differences that ignites eroticism disappears" (Hall, 1987, p. 138).

Author Esther Perel spoke of this very concept in her book, *Mating in Captivity*:

> Love enjoys knowing everything about you; desire needs mystery. Love likes to shrink the distance that exists between me and you, while desire is energized by it. If intimacy grows through repetition and familiarity, eroticism is numbed by repetition. It thrives on the mysterious, the novel, and the unexpected. Love is about having; desire is about wanting. An expression of longing, desire requires ongoing elusiveness. It is less concerned with where it has already been than passionate about where it can still go. But too often as couples settle into the comforts of love, they cease to fan the flame of desire. They forget that fire needs air. (Perel, 2006, p. 37)

Past sexual encounters, both positive and negative, can also contaminate sexual expression due to powerful associations, as seen in the case of Peggy. Traumatic sexual experiences such as childhood sexual abuse or rape can negatively affect sexual desire and behavior. Covert cultural sexual abuse can be another reason for lesbian bed death, as lesbians (more than gay men) tend to develop sexual anorexia from the messages of growing up gay. Being taught to despise and develop a distaste for the very thing you are sexually drawn is traumatic and gets played out among lesbians in this way.

Various writers and therapists have debunked Schwartz's theory (Hamadock, 1996; Iasenza, 1999). In her article "The Big Lie: Debunking Lesbian Bed Death," Suzanne Iasenza challenged the questions asked and the way in which the studies were implemented (Iasenza, 1999). She cited Pepper Schwartz's later work, *Peer Marriage,* which stated that heterosexual couples develop "peer" partnerships in which genital sex is not a primary part of their relationship (Schwartz, 1994), and argued that this would probably apply to lesbians and some gay males as well.

The reason to know and understand lesbian bed death is that it is feared by many lesbian couples. Also, there are many female couples who are together for many years and who no longer are sexual with each other. Whether or not that is a problem should be up to the couple and not come from an outside force.

One of the things Marny Hall does with her lesbian clients who suffer from lack of sexual desire and intimacy is give the homework assignment of sending them to the local sex emporium. "I ask them to browse, pick out some erotica that appeals to them. Over the years, I've found that couples often come home from these excursions with porn that features gay males. They claim that is it more of a turn-on than the lesbian books and videos" (Stewart, 2002, p. 14).

Some lesbians enjoy watching gay porn. In an article by Elizabeth Stewart in *In the Family Magazine* (Stewart, 2002), the author debunked the myth that lesbians enjoy porn with more of a storyline and emotional content: "One appeal of gay male porn they cited was that it doesn't get bogged down in plots, so there is less fast-forwarding to get to the 'good parts'" (p. 13). Stewart found that lesbians did not like the women-on-women sex scenes in heterosexual porn because to them the women seemed fake. What lesbians enjoyed about the gay porn was that the arousal of both men was "authentic, raw sexual energy" (p. 14). Although this survey was not scientific, many lesbians attest that this is true for them.

Gay Male Sexuality

Whereas lesbians tend to carry the torch for being less sexual, gay males carry the torch for being overly sexual. Gay men tend to establish their identities around sex and sexuality. This tendency may be intensified by the sexualized culture that exists among gay men.

Therapists treating gay male clients must remember that they have had to endure a lack of role models and images of men touching and expressing affection. Gay porn fills this lack, if only through sexuality. The gay man who lacks the courage to go to a gay bar finds porn the easiest, safest way to explore his sexuality. The closeted man knows that no one will judge him in a bookstore, X-rated theater, or especially on the Internet.

But using porn as one's initiation into gay manhood can feed into the feeling that being gay is forbidden and underground. Sneaking into a "dirty" bookstore can make one feel shameful, but also add to the excitement.

Many gay male couples feel shame that they are not having frequent sex with each other. The message—delivered both by the mainstream media and in the gay community—is that gay men are sexual and constantly on the prowl. However, this is not necessarily true. Nor is it the case that all gay men enjoy anal sex. Some will come into your office feeling shame about this or thinking that something must be wrong with them.

Bathhouses

Gay bathhouses (also called "the baths" or "the tubs") are places gay men go to have anonymous sex. Bathhouses may contain gym equipment, swimming pools, and steam rooms, but they are hardly used for that. Mostly, gay men pay an admission price to get a locker or a private room; they then walk around wearing towels around their waists and cruising each other. Some sex acts occur in the open, some in groups, and others in the private rooms. Men in the rooms keep the door ajar so onlookers can look inside. If mutual interest exists, the man enters the room and they engage in sexual acts. There is little to no talking.

Going to the baths requires few to none of the social skills that flirting or forming an attached relationship necessitates. Within the baths or other areas where cruising is common, few rituals are predictable and expected.

I have often likened the baths to a higher form of masturbation. Gay men act out what is going on in their imaginations, but no true intimacy is involved, and the activity is very self-absorbed on everyone's part. Even men who are there only to "please" other men sexually are really there to meet their own needs—which are to fulfill the needs of others.

Most interestingly from a cultural perspective, bathhouses are acknowledged and frequented in gay culture, yet there is a stigma attached to those who admit to or are seen as frequenting them. As openly acknowledged as going to bathhouses seems to be—even among straight people (singer Bette Midler admitted to having performed at bathhouses with Barry Manilow before they got their big starts)—it's impolite to talk about at parties, and when dating, many (if not most) gay men will never admit to going. I've heard both clients and friends tell me that they'd never date a man who goes to the baths, even though they may have gone themselves. Those who admit to going are generally judged as promiscuous and talked about in negative ways.

For this reason, most of your clients won't admit to going to bathhouses. But simply adding this to the list of questions you ask about their sexual history will help them relax and realize you're at least knowledgeable and willing to discuss it.

I encourage clinicians to withhold any negative judgments about the baths until they've gathered all the information. It may be a healthy legal outlet for some gay men—particularly older ones—to express their sexual needs.

Sexual Addiction and Compulsivity

Patrick Carnes has written extensively on the subject of sexual addiction. In fact, he coined the term *sexual addiction* in his landmark book *Out of the Shadows: Understanding Sexual Addiction* (Carnes, 2001), which illuminates for many men how to identify and get help for sexual behaviors that are out of control and causing them distress. *Cruise Control: Understanding Sex Addiction in Gay Men* by Robert Weiss (2005) is now available for gay men.

My own working definition of the term *addiction* is "any activity that interferes in a client's life in some way, but which he continues to partake of despite the negative consequences."

Sexual addiction is primarily a problem for males, both gay and straight. In recent years, however, a growing number of women are reporting experiencing it. Very few lesbians have been identified in treatment centers for sexual addiction.

I have already addressed how a lifetime of gay oppression has the same effect as sexual abuse. Given this, it makes sense that gays and lesbians suffer from problems similar to those of sexual abuse survivors. Many survivors of sexual abuse become adult sex addicts.

Many gay men have been taunted, bullied, and teased emotionally and physically. The gay child feels disengaged from the family, knowing he is different and a minority within his own family. Even if the family is close, the gay child will always keep his distance unconsciously or consciously in order to avoid being potentially ousted from the family. This disengagement from the family means no attunement to the developing identity of that gay child. Having to conform to heterosexuality in order to feel a sense of belonging within the family is a part of all gay children's growing up experience, but the negative effects can be profound.

Gays and lesbians experience a childhood of fear, risk, and danger of being discovered—all three of which heighten sexual arousal and desire. This is what gay men are capturing by going underground and having promiscuous sex with each other.

Another contributor to developing sexual compulsivity in the gay male culture is the availability of casual and anonymous sex. Unlike their straight male counterparts, gay men have many opportunities to find quick and easy anonymous sex. Gay men are vulnerable to sexual addiction not only from covert cultural sexual abuse but also from being rewarded for the "masculine" trait of being sexually predatory.

Yet another reason gay men are vulnerable to sexual addiction is that initiation into the gay community is still often sexual. There are few ways to enter the gay world without sexuality being involved, particularly when you are closeted. Our culture does not allow for too many avenues that provide discrimination-free places to experiment with meeting other gay men and women. The Internet, pornography, the bars, baths, and rest areas are so readily and immediately available that it makes sense that a gay teen or a closeted man's first exposure to gayness is through the doorway of sexuality.

When working with gay clients, I never minimize the lack of nonsexual ritual and initiation we have had to endure. As I mentioned earlier, our society lacks images of men, particularly gay men, touching and expressing affection. Gay porn reconciles this lack, if only through sexuality. The heterosexually married gay man who lacks the courage to go to a gay bar or support group finds porn the easiest, safest way to explore his homosexuality. The closeted man, who fears being hated and marginalized if he comes out publicly, can find some comfort, knowing that no one will judge him online, in a bookstore or in the privacy of his own home.

In the gay male community, sexual addiction is a touchy subject and rarely discussed. Gay men tend to see any criticism of their sexual behavior as yet another attempt to pathologize and judge them by heterosexual standards. Many become defensive when straight clinicians even ask about it. You need to know how to approach the subject sensitively and use language that assures gay male clients that you aren't trying to pathologize their sexuality. I advise clinicians to tell clients that it makes sense for them to worry that exploring a sexual addiction might feel like pathologizing gay sex because that is how it was viewed in the past. You can tell your clients that although their concern is valid, it's also vital to recognize that lives are ruined as a result of excessive sexual behavior.

The Case of Phil

Phil, a handsome 38-year-old, entered therapy with me to deal with the emptiness he felt regarding the absence of a partner in his life. After 5 years of being out of the closet, he believed he would have met a significant other by now.

Phil reported that before coming out, he used pornography and the Internet to fulfill his sexual desires. He had two sexual experiences with men but after each one he went back into the closet and felt tremendous shame.

Phil told me that during his first few years of being out of the closet, he experienced what he called "euphoria" and "a rush" in terms of how he was being sought after by gay men sexually and romantically. He had a youthful look and was well-built from working out, which along with his natural good looks brought him a lot of attention in the gay male community. But Phil was having a hard time giving up promiscuous sex. "All my friends go to circuit parties, rest areas, and baths. If I stopped, I'd have no social life. I just want to find a partner. I think that would help me not be so sexually driven."

When I asked him, "Don't you care about risking STDs?" his response was, "Well, that would be the price for having a high sex drive and missing out on all the years I was closeted."

Phil enjoyed the thrill of being hunted by the men and "taken." He said he did not believe any gay man was truly monogamous and believed he might be able to develop a new relationship and be sexual on the side as well. He decided that this was what gay life was and that relationships were something rare and short-term among gay men. Yet he still longed for a committed relationship.

I asked Phil about his childhood and he told me that he had been an effeminate boy. The last of six children, he recalled purposely not telling his "loving" Reform Jewish family that he was being bullied and abused in school. He did not want to "worry" his mother, who was overwhelmed with his other five siblings. He also thought his father would feel he deserved the abuse.

Phil was never interested in sports, but his father was. His brothers were "jocks," and Phil often felt left out of the things their father did with them. He felt unloved and often saw contempt in his father's eyes when Phil talked proudly of his music classes and instruments he played in band class. He devoted his childhood to trying to please his mother and became an overachiever to compensate for being gay—which he knew he was from a very young age. There was no sexual, physical, or spiritual abuse in his family.

Phil: Clinical Interpretation and Treatment

I saw Phil as suffering from the effects of covert cultural abuse. So deep was his desire to belong that he was willing to become infected to achieve it—as evidenced by his statement, "STDs would be the price to pay." Phil's covert cultural sexual abuse trauma included being treated in hostile ways and not being protected by his teachers or parents. His way of handling the trauma was to regulate his mood through sex. As a result, he become his own oppressor, searching for connection with other gay men through sex, which provided a pseudo-connection but potentially could cost him his life by infecting him with STDs including HIV.

Wanting to belong at any cost is a trauma response from the abuse gay men endure. As a clinician, I paid attention to the suffering that was underlying Phil's sexual acting out behaviors.

I told Phil that I did not believe that he did not care about the risk of STDs. Rather, he had learned not to care by emulating the indifference of his own caretakers and those who should have been looking out for him as a gay boy and teen. He had dissociated himself from the dangers he was putting himself in.

This interpretation angered Phil. He defended his parents as having "done the best they could." I replied that their best hadn't been good enough if he had to go to school worried that no one would protect him against bullies and not feeling as though he could tell them what was happening to him.

This was disturbing for Phil, who did not want to hold his parents accountable: "I don't like my father, but I also don't want to blame him or my mother. This is on me."

Any statement like this is a cry for help. I told Phil he was like a terrorist willing to die for his "cause"—in his case, protecting those who had left him in harm's way.

"But they did not know what was happening to me," Phil retorted.

"You should have been able to tell. And if they were tracking you more closely, they would have noticed something was wrong," I replied. "This is not about blame—it is about accountability and facts. The fact was that you did not tell and there was a reason you believed you couldn't."

That he didn't feel he could—or should—tell them was significant. His father should have been more interested in Phil's interests or included him in sports with the other boys. For his part, Phil should have felt secure enough to tell his mother what was happening and not worry about her feeling overwhelmed. After many months of our working together, he was able to see all of this.

Ultimately Phil agreed to attend Sex Addicts Anonymous. He began to connect to the danger he was exposing himself to. He realized that the highly sexualized life he was living was not about a high sex drive—it was about wanting to belong at any cost. He eventually met gay men who were not identified solely around their sexual escapades and began dating and learning intimacy skills.

Is it Sexual Addiction or Something Else?

Clinicians need to know how to differentiate sexual addiction from stage 5 of coming out, when gay men and lesbians date and experiment sexually. If stage 5 persists for too long (more than 2 to 3 years), sexual addiction may be an issue. Sexual abuse can also prompt victims to reenact their abuse, and you must learn to recognize this as well. In some cases there may be overlap, causing a dual diagnosis of sexual abuse and sexual addiction, as well as stage 5 behavior. And finally, heterosexually married gay men often are compulsive sexual, as they hide their orientation and try to keep it suppressed. Once they come out to their wives and integrate a gay identity, they no longer display sexually compulsive behavior.

Therapists can also explain to their clients that sexual addiction is not, in fact, about sex at all. It is about recreating unresolved childhood trauma involving emotional, physical or sexual abuse or neglect in the erotic. Compulsively sexual behavior is, by definition, behavior the client engages in despite not wanting to—just as trauma is something the child is forced into against his or her will. In other words, the acting out is a "return to the scene of the crime" and the psyche believes this time there can be resolution through sex.

Sometimes clients speak with pride about their sexual escapades and affairs. Others need to talk about it in detail in every session to reduce the shame and allow you to help them. It is easy for clinicians to have negative reactions and judgments about such behavior, but the job of the clinician is to listen to the suffering under the sexual acting out and help clients get in touch with it themselves.

Intake Questions

The best time to get a thorough history and current status of your client's sexual behaviors is during the intake process. An excellent resource for good questions to include in your intake and assessment forms is the book *The Art of Sex Coaching: Expanding Your Practice* (Britton, 2005).

If in response to these questions clients ask, "Why are you asking me this?" you can respond, "These are standard questions I ask all my clients." Hopefully this will be true or become true. Following are some helpful questions you can use with clients.

To both gay and lesbian individuals and couples:

- When did you first realize you had sexual feelings for the same gender?
- Is your sexual life satisfying to you? Are the frequency and the experiences satisfying to you?
- Do you ever feel bothered or disturbed by any sexual thoughts, feelings, or behaviors you have?
- Any history of sexual abuse?
- Do you practice monogamy or nonmonogamy? Define what monogamy [or nonmonogamy] looks like for you as a couple.
- Is there a sexual desire discrepancy between you, as there is in most couples? If so, how do you negotiate it as a couple?
- What have been your experiences with orgasm?
- Which (if either) is top and which is bottom, or are you versatile? Do you engage in penetration or not?
- Do you use pornography (video, magazines, Internet) separately or together?
- Do you use sex toys? If so, which ones? If not, explain why.
- Do you engage in vanilla sex or in kinky sex such as s/m and b/d?
- Do you have a fetish? If so, what?
- Do you use fantasy as part of your sexual expression?

To gay males:

- Do you know your HIV status? How do you protect yourself when having sexual contact with other men?
- Do you use condoms? Why or why not?
- Do you go to bathhouses, porn shops, or have sexual hookups from the Internet?

To lesbians:

- Does pre-/peri-/postmenopause affect your sex life and if so, how?
- Do hormonal changes affect your libido/sexual desire? If so, how?
- If you use porn, is it lesbian porn, heterosexual porn, or gay porn?
- Different people have different ideas about what constitutes sex. How do you personally define *sex*?

Questions to Assess Sexual Addiction

In 1997, Patrick Carnes and Robert Weiss developed the Gay and Bi-Sexual Addiction Screening Test (G-SAST) to help assess sexually compulsive or "addictive" behaviors (Weiss, 2005, pp. 25–29). Following is an adaptation of the test, which you can use with your gay male clients to determine whether or not they are struggling with sexual addiction.

Simply give clients one point for every "yes" answer. A score of 13 or higher indicates a possible sexual addiction that should be further explored in therapy.

❑ Yes   1. Was I ever sexually abused as child or as a teenager?

❑ Yes   2. Have I subscribed to, or regularly purchased, sexually explicit magazines or internet sites for cybersex?

❑ Yes   3. Do I regularly rent or buy sexually explicit videos or online porn?

❑ Yes   4. Did my parents have trouble with their own sexual or romantic behavior (for example, extramarital affairs, flirting with other family members)?

❑ Yes   5. Do I find myself preoccupied with sexual thoughts or planning sexual encounters?

❑ Yes   6. If I enjoy phone sex lines and online porn websites, has my use of them ever exceeded my ability to pay for these services?

❑ Yes   7. Do significant others, my friends, or family ever worry aloud or complain about my sexual behavior—as opposed to my sexual orientation?

❑ Yes   8. Do I have trouble stopping patterns of sexual behavior even when I know they're dangerous to my health?

❑ Yes   9. Do I spend time viewing pornography, enjoying phone sex, and logging onto cybersex chat rooms? Does that outweigh the time I spend on intimate, face-to-face, "live" contacts with romantic partners?

❑ Yes   10. When talking frankly and honestly with my friends or partners, do I hide or minimize the extent or nature of my sexual activities?

❑ Yes 11. Am I eager for social events with friends or family to be over, so that I can go out and get some action?

❑ Yes 12. Are bathhouses, sex clubs, or video arcades a regular—or preferred— part of my sexual activity?

❑ Yes 13. Do I think, or worry, that anonymous or casual sex has kept me from achieving long-term intimate relationships or other personal and creative goals?

❑ Yes 14. Once a new partner's sexual "novelty" has worn off, do I have trouble maintaining an intimate relationship?

❑ Yes 15. Have I ever cruised public restrooms, rest areas, or parks looking for sexual encounters with total strangers?

❑ Yes 16. Do my sexual hookups place me in danger of arrest for lewd conduct or public indecency?

❑ Yes 17. Have I ever been approached, warned, charged, or arrested by police or private "rent-a-cop" security personnel for engaging in sexual activity in a public place?

❑ Yes 18. Do I have reason to worry about contracting HIV and other STDs, but still keep engaging in risky, unsafe sexual behavior?

❑ Yes 19. Has any partner or friend of mine ever been hurt emotionally as a result of my sexual behavior (again, *not* my sexual orientation)? Have I ever found it simpler and easier to lie to someone I care about? Have I shown up late for a family reunion, wedding, or business appointment because a sexual liaison slowed me down?

❑ Yes 20. Does sex help me forget—or escape from—my problems and anxieties?

❑ Yes 21. After having sex, do I ever feel troubled, guilty, or ashamed?

❑ Yes 22. Have I made myself promises to change some form of my sexual activity—only to break them later, again and again?

❑ Yes 23. Does my sexual activity (again, *not* my orientation) interfere with professional or personal goals I've set for myself? After a late night of sexual activity, can I still do my best at my career? Has it damaged or ruined any relationship of value—friendship, romantic, or family?

❑ Yes 24. Have I ever paid for sex? (Not necessarily in cash!)

❑ Yes 25. Have I ever had sex with someone just because I was feeling horny and aroused at the time—but later felt ashamed or regretful, wishing the encounter never took place?

A Few Dos and Don'ts

When asking clients about their sexual practices, don't assume anything. This is a good rule to have with any of our clients, yet it can be difficult to do. Here are some of the dos and don'ts I recommend:

- Don't assume that there are sexual problems just because they are coming to see you.
- Don't assume penetration exists for gay or lesbian couples. Don't assume it doesn't, either.
- Don't use language just to impress your clients. Use informed language to show them they can trust you and tell you things you might already understand.
- Don't assume that because there is a lot of sexual talk, particularly among gay men, that it is pathological. Remember that gay men lead with sexual interests, especially in the context of dating.
- Don't assume everything they struggle with is related to covert cultural sexual abuse or homophobia when it might not be. It very well could be issues that affect straight individuals and couples as well.

CHAPTER 10

Working With Today's Lesbian and Gay Couples

What does a lesbian bring on a second date? A U-Haul!
What does a gay man bring on a second date? *What* second date?
—popular joke in the gay and lesbian community

This joke, often told within the gay and lesbian community, has much truth to it. But it also reflects the stereotypical behaviors of men and women in general. Women tend be more relational and men tend to be less so. In gay and lesbian relationships, there is a "doubling" of the qualities traditionally associated with that gender, making lesbian couples more likely to move quickly toward intimacy (Slater, 1995) and male couples likely to hold back romantically and not make themselves vulnerable to other males (Greenan & Tunnell, 2003).

Many therapists who work with gay and lesbian couples say that a "couple is a couple." These well-intended therapists are trying to say that they are not prejudiced toward these couples and would treat them like any other. But ignoring the impact of gender role traits among gay and lesbian couples does a disservice to them and ignores the specific issues these couples need to work on. Believing that a couple is just a couple is a covert form of homophobia and heterosexism because it diminishes or disregards the unique issues—positive and negative—that gay and lesbian couples face. At the same time, however, surprising similarities exist between heterosexual and gay and lesbian couples. It's as important to keep these in mind as it is to remember what makes each of these relationships unique.

It is also important to remember that although gay men and lesbians face many of the same prejudices and challenges, there are critical differences between gay male relationships and lesbian relationships. This chapter debunks some common myths about gay and lesbian relationships and explores the common differences and similarities between straight, gay, and lesbian couples.

Common Myths

There are several common myths about gay and lesbian relationships that many people—including therapists and even gays and lesbians themselves—buy into. Conducting therapy without challenging these ideas can lead to problems.

Male/Female Roles

Although some lesbian couples maintain strict "butch/femme" relationships, most gay and lesbian couples do not. It is a myth that one person plays the "male" role and the other the "female" role. All couples—straight and lesbian and gay—tend to think of one person having traditional "female" energy and the other "male" energy. Today's straight couples are abandoning the need to be in traditional male and female roles; they are realizing that each person should do what he or she does best without worrying if it's masculine or feminine. In this way, they are catching up to what gay and lesbian couples have been doing all along.

Isolation

Many people assume that all gay and lesbian couples live in isolation from friends and family. But studies have shown that this assumption is a misconception (Chernin & Johnson, 2003). These studies showed that gay and lesbian couples "develop caring, supportive networks of family and friends" (p. 117). That said, there are places—especially areas that are more conservative or religious and where gay communities are mostly invisible—where this may not be the case. It is up to the clinician to assess how isolated the couple is or is not.

Relationship Satisfaction

There are few, if any, differences reported in relationship satisfaction between heterosexual couples and lesbian and gay couples. Both heterosexual couples and lesbian and gay couples face a variety of common issues that can cause problems, including children, sex, money, communication, family of origin, conflict resolution, and balancing work with personal commitments. And like straight couples, lesbian and gay couples enter relationships with the initial infatuation stage of romantic love, go through the power struggle when the romance and honeymoon wear off, and then enter the final stage of real love.

What is unique to gay and lesbian couples is that that they are taught throughout their life that they will never be able to find a relationship and that if they do, it will not endure. As a result, when gay men or lesbians find romance, they tend to cling to it more than heterosexuals do. When these couples experience differences and conflicts, they may interpret it as confirmation that society is right and that gay and lesbian relationships are doomed to fail. Unfortunately, many people leave their relationships prematurely based on this misinformation.

In a society that sees most relationships—gay and straight alike—as disposable, lesbian and gay relationships are seen and treated as even *more* disposable. Lesbian and gay couples are not often asked about their relationships and if they are, the question is, "Are you still with that person?" The implication is that gay and lesbian relationships do not last. Lesbian and gay relationships *can* and *do* last, but as Berzon (2004, p. 16) has written, "there is a tradition of failure among these couplings" that is expected both by outsiders as well as the couples themselves.

What Makes Gay and Lesbian Couples Different From Heterosexual Couples

For 30 years, John Gottman, a well-known marital psychologist, has worked with heterosexual couples and, in the last decade, with gay and lesbian couples too. His work is research-based; he brings couples to a "love lab"—essentially, a pleasant bed-and-breakfast—and both videotapes them and monitors their heart rates and perspiration levels (measuring stress and anxiety) while they interact with one another.

In his work with Robert Levenson, Gottman showed that gay and lesbian couples have some advantages over their heterosexual counterparts (Gottman, 2004). To determine why relationships succeed or fail, Gottman and Levenson assessed 21 gay and 21 lesbian couples over 12 years, directly observing their expressions and tones of voice, conducting interviews and asking for self-reports, and videotaping the partners interacting. They compared these data to a "control" group of 42 straight couples. All the couples researched had been together at least 2 years.

Gottman and Levenson found that gay couples were comparable to heterosexual couples in the quality of relationships—reporting the same happiness and satisfaction. Interestingly, gay couples weren't as jealous as their straight counterparts. The study showed that two gay men can often admire another male and comment on how attractive he is with neither person taking it personally or feeling threatened. Both partners usually looked at the other man in appreciation rather than comparing him to themselves. Conversely, in my experience with heterosexual couples I've treated, women often feel as though their male partners, by commenting on another woman's good looks, have literally cheated on them.

Additionally, Gottman and Levenson found that same-gender couples were much better at talking openly and honestly about their sex lives. In an article by Mubarak Dahir in *The Windy City Times*, Gottman was quoted as saying that he had "no idea" what heterosexual couples were talking about when they discussed lovemaking (Dahir, 2001). (I believe this distinction arises because the gay community is forced into focusing primarily on the sexual aspect of their lives.) When two people of the same gender are a couple, they have the same orgasmic reactions, timing, and sensations. Heterosexual couples, being opposite-gendered, have less understanding of each other and function differently.

Gottman and Levenson also found that in the face of adversity, gay and lesbian couples were much more optimistic. When addressing conflicts between them, they used more humor and affection. In my own practice, I've noticed that lesbian couples generally hug each other before leaving my office at the end of a session. I've learned from that, and I encourage gay male couples to do the same. At the very least, one will crack a joke, and both will laugh—which can be just as effective. They leave in a connected way. I have not seen or been able to get heterosexual couples to do this after a heated session nearly as often.

Commonalities Between Lesbian and Gay Relationships

There are several commonalities between gay and lesbian relationships that set them apart from heterosexual relationships. Understanding these similarities will help you conduct more informed, effective therapy with your gay and lesbian couple clients.

Coming Out, Relationally

Both gay men and lesbians face new obstacles when they begin a relationship with someone of the same sex. It's easier to be gay and single than to be gay and partnered—particularly if you are not out or are in the early stages of the coming out process. When partnered, gay men and lesbians must take a stand on how they feel about going forward toward another level of coming out—a relational one. Whatever they might have done to keep their homosexuality less visible now becomes more problematic, involving hiding or removing one's partner from important social situations. If they choose to be honest and overt about their relationships, they face more obstacles partnered than single. Families, friends, and colleagues experience the existence of a partner as evidence of the person's lesbianism or gayness, and it may make them uncomfortable. Knowing in an abstract way that someone is gay or lesbian is one thing; seeing evidence of it—the partner—is another. It is another level of coming out for both the family and the gay or lesbian family member. Gays' and lesbians' willingness and bravery to face all of this usually comes from being in the later stages of coming out and feeling more solid and secure with their sexual identity.

Coping With Holidays

Each year as the various holidays start to approach I ask all of my couples what they plan to do. Most straight couples say they are going to one of the partner's parents' places, or are celebrating in their own home where families and friends will visit and blend together. Gay and lesbian couples, however, often have different scenarios. Often they decide to go separately to their own respective families (a consequence of internalized homophobia, addressed in the next section).

Straight therapists may miss this as an important issue. However, if a married heterosexual couple stated the same thing—that they planned to spend the holidays separately with their own families—it would be a red flag.

Although some of the problems associated with holidays are external, due to family reactions and feelings, others cut deeper and are internal, as was the case with Lisa and Paula.

The Case of Lisa and Paula

Lisa and Paula had been together for 13 years and were in couple's therapy with me. Their presenting problem was a growing distance between them over differences and conflicts they were unable to overcome. During our work together, as Thanksgiving was approaching, I asked them what they were doing for the holidays. Lisa told me she was going home to her family and Paula said she was going home to hers. I knew both had families locally and questioned why they were splitting up. They said this is what they usually did and that neither had a problem with it.

I questioned why they didn't do what most other couples do—take turns going to each other's families each year so they could spend the holidays together. Although some couples prefer to separate because they do not like the partner's family, this was not the case for Lisa or Paula. They were liked by each other's families and each enjoyed them as well.

However, although the couple was out to Lisa's family, they were not to Paula's family. In my early intake assessment I had asked them if Paula was out to her family and she told me she thought her family knew she was lesbian and they were a couple but they had never declared it openly. She said, "We use the 'don't ask, don't tell' method." The couple suspected Paula's family knew but Paula felt it did not need to be stated overtly.

So each year they went separately for the holidays. They spent nonholiday times with their families together but felt that going together on the holidays was being "in their face." In addition, both of the families expected to see them on each holiday and both women enjoyed helping their mothers cook and get things ready.

Then, however, Lisa spoke up and said it had bothered her that they went to their families separately. Her family always wanted Paula over for the holidays and wondered why Paula would not attend. Lisa had initially protested Paula's refusal to spend the holidays with her, but Paula was insistent, so she dropped it, deciding it was nothing to make a big deal about as Paula seemed so troubled by it.

My questioning brought this issue back to the surface. Paula became angry toward me for "raising an issue that was not a problem between them." But I disagreed. It was a covert form of internalized homophobia and I felt it needed to be addressed.

Paula started crying, saying that as the only daughter in an Italian Catholic family, she felt like a disappointment to her family, especially to her mother. She did not want to put her homosexuality in her mother's face. She knew it hurt Lisa but believed that Lisa could tolerate the hurt more than her mother could.

Lisa and Paula: Clinical Interpretation and Treatment

I educated both women about internalized homophobia among couples and explored whether this was an expression of that. Both denied that this was an issue and stated that it did not *harm* their relationship because they both agreed for it to be this way. I stated that I believed it *did* harm the relationship in subtle ways. I told them that the message they were giving to themselves as a couple and to their families was that they were not "really" a couple and that they could operate as singles at will and not be affected. I asked them to imagine their heterosexually married relatives doing the same.

Lisa defended Paula, telling her that it was okay that they went their different ways over the holiday. I stated that although it *might* be okay, I was not so sure. I kept pressing the issue a bit more, especially after learning that Lisa was not okay with this arrangement from the beginning.

I gently asked them—particularly Paula—if I could pursue this holiday issue with them as I was concerned it might be part of the distancing problem within the relationship. I stated that even if they separated only on holidays, their refusal to declare their relationship verbally and behaviorally would inevitably affect their relationship.

I then suggested to Paula that this might be more a question of individuation within her family. It turned out that Paula was still in a child role with her mother. I told Paula that I thought her loyalty was more toward her family of origin than toward her partner and explained how this would weaken the bonds of intimacy with Lisa. This angered Paula immensely and she accused me of making a bigger problem out of this than it was. I told her I was trying to prevent it from becoming a bigger problem than it could be for her relationship. Over time it would degrade their bonds and intimacy by neglecting times where couples re-romanticize and bond more deeply with family. I then turned to Lisa and addressed her codependency on the issue and identified how she enabled this detachment between them by not being consistent with her feelings about the holidays.

The issue that then came forward was that Paula *did* have internalized homophobia in terms of identifying herself overtly as a lesbian and in a lesbian relationship. This was connected to her developmental stage of identity and attachment issues with her mother. Paula knew her mother did not want to have to face her lesbianism in an overt way and remained quiet about it.

I educated both Lisa and Paula about the covert and negative ways in which their behavior harmed their relationship. Not identifying overtly as a couple minimizes the attachment to one's partner and keeps it from growing into a healthy adult relationship. For Paula, addressing this would mean bringing up the subject with her mother and tolerating her mother's disappointment and possible rejection—a developmental task of individuation that she had not completed. The reward would be going from child to adult and having a healthier relationship with her partner.

This delayed developmental task was Paula's to undertake. In the end, she did decide to sit down with her mother one-on-one and tell her that she was a lesbian and that she would be celebrating the holidays with Lisa from now on, which meant that they'd spend one year with one family, and the next year with the other family. They both cried. Paula's mother said she knew this day would come. She had wanted to initiate it herself but thought that Paula did not want to discuss it. She thought that because Paula did not bring it up, it must be taboo. Paula was shocked, as she thought the same with her mother.

As this case shows, initiating conversation about the holidays can be an effective way to tease out internalized homophobia within the couple.

Couples' Internalized Homophobia

In Chapter 2 I discussed how to identify internalized homophobia in gay and lesbian individuals; here, I will talk about how it manifests in couples. Missing the internalized homophobia among same-sex couples can cause prolonged time in therapy or, at worst, remove any chance of success in helping the couples at all.

Most couples don't enter therapy saying that they need to work on their own internalized homophobia as a couple. It is your job as the therapist to identify it, assess it, and help them address it. The following list, adapted from Kleinberg and Zorn (1998), outlines how internalized homophobia manifests, sometimes in subtle ways, in gay and lesbian couples.

- Couples don't identify as gay or lesbian even after they've been in a committed same-sex relationship for years.
- Couples hide their relationship even when it's objectively safe to be out.
- Partners avoid public displays of affection even when it's safe to do so.
- Couples believe that others would never accept them as a couple.
- Couples don't announce their anniversary to close straight friends because they believe anniversaries aren't as "important" for gay and lesbian couples.
- Partners avoid taking their partner to family gatherings.
- Partners use the term "I" instead of "we" when discussing events attended with the partner.
- Couples fail to recognize their partnership as a family.
- Partners criticize their partner for looking too effeminate or butch.
- Partners take on too much personal responsibility for relationship problems, stemming from the belief that gay and lesbian relationships cannot survive.

The previously discussed case of Paula and Lisa illustrates several of the issues outlined in this list. Pinpointing these forms of internalized homophobia was crucial to helping Paula and Lisa address their presenting problem of a distant relationship. It wasn't until Paula directly confronted her own hesitance to acknowledge her lesbianism that the couple's relationship began to improve.

What Couples Decide to Call Their Partner

For heterosexual couples, timelines and landmarks exist to mark the progress of their relationship, making it easy for them to know what to call their partner: During the dating period, the partner is called a boyfriend or girlfriend, during the engagement the partner is a fiancé or fiancée, and during marriage he or she becomes a husband or wife. Lesbians and gays, on the other hand, are left to create their own names for their partners. Terms such as *partner, lover, boyfriend, girlfriend, significant other, life partner,* and *spouse* will be used by your clients.

I have found that it is diagnostically and clinically valuable to hear how gay and lesbian partners refer to their significant other. You will be able to pick up on issues such as their internalized homophobia and their level of commitment or experienced commitment from their partner. Although it is important to use your clients' terminology when working with them, it is also important to know when to challenge them. For example, when I see couples who have been together for 2 or more years, have combined their income, are living together, are citing each other in their wills, and still are calling each other boyfriends or girlfriends, I challenge these terms, as they suggest that the relationship is not as deep as the one they have actually created.

Couples may not have thought about why they use the terms of endearment they do. In some cases, internalized homophobia may not be the issue; the couple may simply be comfortable with the word "boyfriend" or "girlfriend" and in the habit of using it. With no established markers such as marriage to push partners into using different terminology, couples may be less inclined to change their habitual ways of referring to each other.

It's up to the therapist to raise the couple's consciousness around this issue. It is also important to explore the concept of internalized homophobia with the couple and help them present themselves and their partner as a *family* unit.

The Case of Patrick and James

Patrick and James, ages 30 and 32 respectively, came to see me because even after 3 years together, James still didn't want to call Patrick his "partner" in front of his parents; he referred to him as a "friend." James was not out to his friends or family, nor was he out at work. Patrick was angry because he believed that James was either ashamed of him or did not care about the relationship enough to identify him as his partner. What made Patrick angriest was that at family gatherings, James's family would ask and talk openly about James's ex-partner, Marty, whom the family really liked. Marty, however, had never been identified as a partner either, so the family was not tuned in to being sensitive to the new partner, Patrick. When the family talked about Marty, they did it under the assumption that he was simply a friend of James.

"Have you met Marty yet?" James's parents asked Patrick at one family gathering. "He is the nicest guy." Then, turning to James, they said, "You seemed to have so much in common with him, and his family was so nice. Why don't you bring him around more than you have recently? Patrick would probably like him too."

James insisted the problem was that Patrick was being too sensitive, but the real problem was that James was not ready to come out to the degree Patrick wanted. James came from a conservative family and knew that they would have a problem with his being gay. He also knew it would cause problems at work, where he held a high-level corporate position. He did not want his job jeopardized by coming out.

Complicating things further was the fact that James brought his best girlfriend to office parties, introducing her as his girlfriend, and referring to her in place of Patrick when talking about his weekend activities. This infuriated Patrick and hurt him deeply. Both James and Patrick cried in my office about the pain they were in and how this was affecting the relationship.

"I am not asking that you come out at work and risk your fiscal success," Patrick said to James. "I am only talking about my being out as your partner at your family gatherings so people will stop talking about your ex. I mean, they don't talk about your sister's ex-husband in front of her new boyfriend!"

Patrick went on to say that he wanted to live together soon and have each other's families meet. He also wanted invitations they received to parties and other events to have both their names together, and for gifts to be given to them as a couple rather than to two individuals. Patrick's request made sense, but it seemed too overwhelming to James.

Patrick and James: Clinical Interpretation and Treatment

James was still in the early stage of coming out. I wasn't sure he'd ever achieve stage 6—some people remain in the earlier stages of coming out for years or even for most of their life. Patrick was out in every area of his life and wanted an open, out life with James. James had met many men and knew Patrick was the ideal partner for him, but he was highly resistant to being pushed out of his comfort zone by telling his family.

I pointed out the partners' different stages of being out and assured them that many gay couples experience this discrepancy. James needed to explore how willing he was to move into the next stage of coming out while Patrick needed to be patient and understand how difficult this was for James. James also had to consider whether his loyalty was going to be to his family or to Patrick. James became angry at me when I said this, accusing me of being a gay-pride flag-waver who was so out that I could not understand him and the difficulty of his situation.

I was ready for this negative transference, as I have had a lot of experience with this from gays and lesbians. Earlier in my practice, I would have looked at James's resistance as nothing more than internalized homophobia. However, I have learned over the years to consider many factors along with internalized homophobia, such as individual developmental issues, family of origin issues, and covert cultural sexual abuse issues.

I responded to James by saying that even if he was right about my being so out that I couldn't understand him—which he was not—he was in a position of losing Patrick if he chose to ignore Patrick's request. I identified and validated his fears about what would happen with his family. I educated him about covert cultural sexual abuse, explaining that I thought he was suppressing and postponing his trauma of growing up gay by not telling his family in order to avoid the anxiety and depression that could become activated from making Patrick a priority. There was a reason that James had spent a lifetime of not telling them, and we needed to discover what that reason was. I expressed curiosity about what James thought would happen if he came out to his family, and I wondered aloud about what could be so terrible that James would actually be willing to lose Patrick in order to avoid it.

James's resistance prompted the next part of their therapy, which was exploring James's identity development within his childhood. His family taught traditional values where "boys needed to be boys" and "girls needed to be girls." Thinking outside the box was not allowed. Once, when he was caught playing with his sister's dolls, he was shamed profusely by both his mother and father. For James, his identity imprint was inflexible, and he was at risk for losing not only his partner but also his sense of self if he did not examine this issue more closely.

I told Patrick that he could decide to leave the relationship and find someone else, but that if he loved James and chose to stay, he needed to understand and be curious about James's struggle. At the same time, James needed to look at how his position could cost him his relationship. I asked him to ask himself whether this was worth it.

Both Patrick and James were going to need to make compromises in terms of moving forward. I had James talk at length about his concerns in front of Patrick. His concerns at work were real. Although to outsiders his company claimed to be gay friendly, it was not. James had known and seen others be overlooked for opportunities and promotions simply for being gay. He could not change jobs or press the issue at work. Patrick asked if he would at least be willing to stop bringing his female friend to office parties, but James was not willing to do this at this time.

It took James 6 months to finally be able to choose his relationship (and himself) over his family of origin. His parents took the news very hard, as James had worried, and asked that he stay away from them for a while. Much to his surprise, James felt good about telling them, and although he was hurt by their distancing from him, he felt like he had gone from a boy to a man. The intimacy between him and Patrick deepened. After almost a year, James's family told him they were willing to see him again, but it was conditional—he couldn't bring Patrick with him. James declined, telling them it was with his "partner" or not at all. Ultimately, the family acquiesced and invited Patrick as well.

Partners in Different Stages of the Coming Out Process

Partners' being at different stages in the coming out process is a very common problem for gay and lesbian couples and is something heterosexual couples, obviously, never have to address. As the case of Patrick and James illustrates, this situation is stressful for *both* partners: The person who is fully out to family and friends may feel underappreciated, and the person who is not completely out may feel pressured and misunderstood.

As a therapist, it is important to assess the stage of each partner's outness and explore how discrepancies may be causing or fueling problems in the relationship. Clinicians need to help the couple navigate through this by highlighting their personal integrity as well as their relational integrity. You must educate the couple about the importance of pacing this according to the comfort of the partner who is struggling the most with his or her level of outness. It is essential for partners to be patient and express good will toward the other.

The different stages of outness can feel threatening to partners. The "lesser out" partner may feel forced by the other and experience a lack of sensitivity to their difficulty. The "more out" partner may feel their partner is being disloyal for not wanting to be more out and open to others, thereby limiting their freedom to be a couple in public and prevent them from going certain places together. In other words, it can look like one's partner is simply going too slow or fighting the coming out process for reasons that do not seem to make sense on the surface. Partners' empathy for one another can get lost in their attempt to remain a couple with these stage discrepancies. This is trauma work—even if it doesn't look like it. I recommend educating the couple about the effects of covert cultural sexual abuse on lesbians and gays, both as individuals and in their relationships. This may also help them both to understand on a deeper level what is happening.

Talking about each partner's childhood history in front of each partner and relating those experiences to their particular reasons for not being out is not only helpful for you as the clinician but also helps the clients better understand each other. Reframing is helpful here as well. For instance, if one partner wants to come out more and have more visibility as a couple, it can be reframed as an invitation to deepen the intimacy within the relationship rather than seen as a threat

Clinicians need to separately validate each partner in front of the couple during sessions. For instance, to the partner who is more out, you might say: "Waiting for James to come around must be frustrating and remind you of the time you were more closeted and how painful that was for you." To the more closeted partner, you might say, "It makes sense that you need some time and don't want to feel rushed— you probably feel anxious about losing the support of your family and friends, and then potentially losing your relationship with Patrick on top of that."

One thing to do next would be to help each partner validate where the other is in terms of being out and the comfort level around it. In other words, the more out partner might say, "It makes sense to me that you are not out given your fears—and the real possibility—of losing your friends and family." The more closeted partner might say, "It makes sense that you want me to be more out and open about our relationship and what you mean to me, as it hurts you to feel hidden and secretive." These kinds of validation help keep the partners more connected to each other and negotiate what to do.

Additionally, clinicians should educate clients about the realities of not being an "out" couple. This weighs heavily in a negative way on the couple. Ask them to imagine the stress that would be put on a marriage if a husband or wife refused to tell his or her family about the marriage. The bottom line is that if the couple wants to remain together, the more out partner may have to live with being closeted in the way the less out partner wants, and the more closeted partner may have to decide to come out more fully and risk rejection.

Couples cannot thrive if they remain at two different stages. It is like settling for a machine's operating on a lower performance level. I understand there are valid reasons to not be out to one's employer, family, and various friends. That said, the closetedness still affects the couple even on a subtle covert level and the couple needs to know this and prepare for this.

I explain this to couples, saying that although the relationship may endure, the level of satisfaction will be poor *in this area*. I do not believe it is healthy for the relationship and it will suffer even on a small scale in the long run. Every couple I have worked with and know who finally are as out as they can be have told me that, looking back, they see how their lives were negatively affected by being closeted, even if the reasons were valid.

The Case of Meghan

Sharon, a psychotherapist, came to me for supervision; she was concerned that she might not be working effectively with Meghan, one her clients. Sharon believed that Meghan's partner, Carla, was narcissistic and couldn't commit to the relationship. She was trying to direct Meghan away from the relationship.

For her part, Meghan was getting increasingly anxious and angry about Carla's behavior. Carla had been heterosexually married for 13 years and was a devoted mother of two children. Meghan and Carla had been friends for years; their sons played soccer together. Two years earlier, Carla confessed she was gay and in love with Meghan. They began an affair. Then, Carla decided she had to tell her husband and get a divorce so that she could move on to a more serious relationship with Meghan.

Meghan had dated many women; two relationships had ended because the other women cheated on her. Meghan knew that Carla was monogamous during her entire marriage (until they started their affair), which gave Meghan hope that Carla could be monogamous with her. She saw Carla as having the highest level of integrity.

Carla had recently begun going to the gym and working out. She felt good about how she looked in a way she never had before. When Carla's divorce became final she expressed interest in going to the lesbian bars. Meghan did not like socializing at bars and did not want to go, but Carla insisted and Meghan finally complied. When women at the bars approached Carla and began flirting with her, she flirted back.

When Meghan commented on this, Carla denied that she was flirting—she said she was just looking and having fun. She told Meghan she was being insecure and tried to reassure her that she was not interested in other women. But after a few months, Carla made friends with some of the women who frequented the bar, and she began going out regularly without Meghan. This created more conflict between them, and their fighting increased.

Supervision with Sharon for Meghan's Treatment

Carla was clearly in stage 5 of coming out—she was showing identity pride, enjoying her new body and the opportunity to flirt with other women. Meghan was shocked by this, as she'd never known Carla to be narcissistic or to consider herself a "player." This confused Sharon. She felt that Carla had come out 2 years earlier, when she confessed her love to Meghan. "She was out to herself before coming out to Meghan," Sharon told me. This was true, but the relationship accelerated Carla's coming out process, moving her from stage 3 to stage 5 (see Chapter 7 for the stages of coming out).

This rapid progression often occurs when gays or lesbians begin relationships. In fact, it is common knowledge among gays and lesbians that one should be wary of dating someone who is just coming out. There is an awareness that the person may not be stable precisely because he or she is caught up in a "gay adolescence" and needs to "play the field." This does not make the person a player or narcissistic; it simply means that the person behaves like a teenager for a time.

Sharon had to help Meghan decide if she could tolerate Carla's stage-5 behavior, knowing it was probably temporary. The risk was that it would last longer than Meghan could tolerate. The other risk was that during that time Carla could meet someone else and lose interest in Meghan. Even though Carla insisted she was not interested in anyone else, the inevitable stage 5 had its grip on her and there were no guarantees.

Eventually Meghan decided to stay attached to Carla and see where the relationship was headed. It was painful for her and she worried constantly that Carla would eventually end the relationship. Carla understood she was in stage 5 and that this worried Meghan, and she did all she could do to make Meghan believe she was attached and committed to her yet needed to feel some of her freedom to flirt and be social.

After 2 years of this, Carla settled down and no longer felt the surge of power of stage 5. She became tired of the bars and games of those she had been hanging around with. To Meghan's delight, they were able to nest and settle in and deepen their relationship as a couple. They made friends with other lesbian and gay couples, and although they occasionally went to the bars, it was not because Carla felt any urgency to go.

Differences Between Gay and Lesbian Couples

Just as heterosexual couples are different from same-sex couples in critical ways, gay male relationships are often different from lesbian relationships in important ways. Using your experience treating gay male couples as a template for treating lesbian couples—or vice versa—will compromise your ability to conduct effective therapy. As said in the beginning of this chapter, the "doubling" factor of traditional gender characteristics both complicates and helps these relationships. Therapists need to be aware of the most common characteristics that manifest in male and female couples.

Common Lesbian Relationship Dynamics

As the joke in the epigraph of this chapter plays on, lesbians tend to commit to relationships quickly and move toward a high degree of intimacy and dependency. They also are more inclined to remain friends with their former partners after they've ended the relationship.

Fusion, Merging, and Enmeshment

Much of the literature about lesbian couples focuses on the tendency toward merging, fusion, and enmeshment (Biaggio, Coan, & Adams, 2002; Slater, 1995). In many lesbian relationships, female traits are "doubled up": Both partners may have strong dependency needs, both may be focused primarily on the relationship (having been conditioned to strive toward intimacy), both may be less sexual and more domestic, both may lack differentiation ("You and I are one, and *I* am the one!"), both may place a premium on togetherness and emotional closeness, both may value romantic love and monogamy, and finally, both may give minimal importance to the partner's physical attractiveness (Biaggio et al., 2002).

Many lesbians say that the fusion between two women in lesbian relationships is the closest they can get to understanding how women relate outside the world of sexism and patriarchy. Indeed, some fusion may be a normative expression of what women want—a high level of closeness and intimacy that gay male and straight couples usually cannot experience (Biaggio et al., 2002).

But such a high degree of fusion can cause problems in a relationship. One problem of fusion can be that a partner's identity is overwhelmed by the other's. It is the concept of "you and I are one and I'm the one" or "you and I are one and you're the one"—depending on which partner is losing her identity. Another problem of fusion is the intolerance of differences between the two. Most couples have this struggle, where one partner insists that he or she is right and concludes that the other must therefore be wrong. However, this is magnified in fused lesbian couples, leading to strong feelings of anger and contempt. Fusion brings on a highly undifferentiated couple dynamic that can burn out and destroy the relationship. What starts as a healthy attempt at togetherness becomes a nightmare of enmeshment.

Working with these couples to help them differentiate can be challenging. I have often joked with lesbians that I need to get the "jaws of life" out to separate them and to help them see that two individuals can exist within a relationship and that both can be okay with that. Lesbian couples, like all couples, need to achieve a healthy balance of togetherness and separateness and understanding of "the other." I have found this work to be more difficult among lesbian couples.

The Case of Marilyn and Sheila

Together for 2 years, Marilyn, 40, and Sheila, 43, came to me complaining about their sex life. Marilyn was convinced that Sheila was not really "into" their relationship and would return to being with men.

Indeed, Sheila had a history of dating both genders. She had been heterosexually married but was now divorced; her two teenage children were living with her. Marilyn had been out since her adolescence and never dated men. Marilyn told me that when the couple started their relationship, she had been the one who "taught Sheila about lesbian sex." Sheila agreed, stating that she hadn't known the pleasures of receiving oral sex and being stimulated by a partner's fingers as well. However, Sheila still wanted penetration from dildos, and this often created friction between them.

Marilyn had been initiated into lesbian sex by an older, experienced lesbian who taught her that lesbian sexuality did *not* include using sex toys that resembled male genitalia. Marilyn believed that Sheila's interest in vibrators and dildos—particularly ones that resembled penises—was due to her "hanging onto her interest in men" and that she was rejecting lesbian sex. Sheila stated that she was not rejecting lesbian sex or Marilyn, but that she enjoyed that type of stimulation along with oral and digital sex.

For Marilyn, the last straw came when they purchased a strap-on; while Marilyn was wearing it, Sheila performed oral sex on the dildo as if it were a "real dick." Marilyn was enraged and hurt that Sheila might be fantasizing about being with a man rather than with her. She abruptly stopped the sex act, yelling and crying about how rejected she felt: "I don't get anything out of you doing that!" she said. "I don't feel a thing!"

Sheila stated that she had no interest in being with men again but did miss performing oral sex on them. Sucking a dildo as if it were real fulfilled her oral needs.

Marilyn continued to protest that this was not lesbian sex, explaining that lesbian sex is oral and manual. She also believed that if dildos were used, they shouldn't resemble penises. She stated that she'd been out longer than Sheila and accused Sheila of being naïve.

Marilyn and Sheila: Clinical Interpretation and Treatment

It became clear to me that Marilyn was engaging in maintaining an enmeshed and undifferentiated relationship. Marilyn was blocking Sheila from having her own independent sexual interests and autonomous expressions; she was trying to force Sheila into what Marilyn called "lesbian sex." To me, that seemed like way of controlling Sheila and making her more like herself.

I educated Marilyn that lesbian sex could indeed involve penile-shaped dildos if this is what they decided as a couple. Although a segment of the lesbian community intentionally chooses to stay away from anything male—especially in sex play—Sheila had the right to choose what worked for *her*. The question was why was Marilyn was so focused on rigid ways of being sexual with her partner.

I had both Marilyn and Sheila engage in basic safe dialogue, with one partner actively sending information about her point of view and the other actively listening and putting her own point of view aside momentarily. Called "intentional dialogue," this type of communication comes from the Imago Relationship Therapy (IRT) model, which I discuss at the end of this chapter. It blocks reactivity, interruption, and interpretation and allows for clear communication using the other's point of view. As Marilyn talked about this issue, it surfaced that she didn't feel involved emotionally and physically in the sex play because the dildo was not part of her body and she could not feel it. This revelation helped Sheila reframe Marilyn's resistance to using the dildo as a reflection of her desire to be connected to Sheila rather than as a rejection of her needs.

Another tenet of IRT is to have both partners talk about what childhood experiences the issue reminds them of. Marilyn said she felt that she was being ignored—which was a childhood issue for her. As a young girl, Marilyn assumed that her receiving love depended on how she dressed and behaved—and that was now showing up in the bedroom as well.

Once made aware of this, Marilyn was able to settle down and understand that Sheila's sexuality was a statement about *Sheila's* sexuality; it wasn't meant as a personal statement about Marilyn. Marilyn began working on her childhood issues around receiving love, and also on allowing her partner more sexual independence.

Former Partners

It is common for lesbians to remain friends with their partners after the relationship ends. Lesbians often become such good friends with their partners that the friendship endures even if the romance doesn't. Additionally, lesbians frequently bond with and create primary friendships with other lesbians. Some gay men are able to do this but it is much more commonplace for lesbians. I believe this is primarily due to gender; if men were more relational, perhaps gay male couples (and straight couples) would also be able to remain friends after the romantic love has gone. Slater (1995) postulated that "perhaps heterosexuals as a group limit this intimacy in order to avoid the jealousies, competitions, and likely threats to their couple relationships" (p. 138).

After the breakup of a lesbian relationship, there is often a period of distancing so that the ex-partners can grieve. After a while they pick up the friendship and even become friends with each other's new partners. Lesbian comics joke about this phenomenon as being part of being a lesbian. Kate Clinton, a popular lesbian comic, jokes about how she has a pushpin system on a wall in her home—when she finds out that woman A is no longer with her partner, woman B, and now she is with woman C, who is no longer with her partner, woman D (who is now with woman B), she says to her partner, "Honey, it's time to change the pushpins. A is not with B; she is with C now!" This joke always gets the mostly lesbian crowd roaring with laughter, as they immediately recognize themselves in it. However, for partners new to being out and still coming from a heterosexist mindset, this lesbian tradition may not be so funny, as the following case illustrates.

The Case of Christine

Christine, just recently out at the age of 33, told her therapist, Carol, she was uncomfortable with a new relationship she was having. When she went out with Bernie, her partner, Bernie would sit close to her friends, put her arm around them, and kiss them hello and goodbye. Some of these friends, including Bernie's best friend, were also Bernie's ex-partners, which bothered Christine even more.

Christine found this threatening and insulting. She compared it to her past heterosexual relationships, saying that her boyfriends were never affectionate with past girlfriends in front of her and would not have tolerated her doing this with other men, either. Carol, who was straight, agreed with her that it was disrespectful. This made Christine even angrier. She went back to Bernie and told her what her Carol had said, which prompted an argument. Bernie told her that it was commonplace for lesbians to be friends—even best friends—with ex-partners, and she gave Christine some books by lesbian authors to underscore her point. Christine went back to Carol with this information, suggesting that she read the material.

Several months later Bernie went out to dinner with her most recent ex-partner, with whom she had broken up 2 years ago. When Christine discovered this, she was devastated. She became angry with Bernie and told her that she would have to stop her relationships with her ex-partners if she wanted their relationship to continue. Bernie stated that her friendships with her former partners were deep and meaningful for her. She told Christine that although she loved her deeply and wanted to continue their relationship, if it came down to choosing between her or her former partners she would choose the latter.

"I know this is a typical lesbian thing but I don't think I can get used to it," Christine told Carol. She knew in her heart it was nothing personal—she had met other lesbians who were also friends with their ex-partners—yet she still couldn't get used to it.

Christine: Clinical Interpretation and Treatment

Carol called me for supervision, saying that she believed her countertransference was getting in the way of helping Christine. "If the guys I dated or my ex-husband had done anything like that, I would have felt insulted and provoked," she said. I told her that it made sense that she would feel this way because in the heterosexual community it is not the norm to become friends with an ex. However, for lesbians this is extremely common because of the strong relational bonds they form while together. Carol dealt with her feelings about her ex-boyfriends and ex-husband. "I would have liked to stay friends with a couple of them, actually, but they became jerks when I suggested it."

I told Carol to go back to the assessment she took of Christine and look into her childhood for signs about why she was having such a difficult time. It was likely that her distress was being caused by more than just the situation with Bernie's former partners.

When Carol asked Christine about her childhood, Christine reported that she was the oldest of five children and felt the most alienated. She did not feel liked by her mother, who fussed over Christine's more feminine sisters. Her father appreciated Christine's interest in sports but was more interested in his sons, who were just as athletic as Christine. Within minutes of beginning to tell Carol about her family, Christine was in tears.

This conversation helped Christine see that she was transferring her childhood feelings of abandonment onto Bernie. If Carol hadn't addressed her countertransference and educated herself about lesbian dynamics, she never would have identified the underlying source of Christine's pain. As she worked with Christine on her family of origin issues, Christine's reactivity about Bernie's friendships with former girlfriends gradually abated.

Common Gay Male Relationship Dynamics

The stereotypical gay man is thought to be sensitive, kind, emotive, expressive, and loving—more so than straight men. Women often say things like, "I wish my husband was as easy to talk with as gay men are." So it is natural for clinicians to think of gay men as more emotionally available and open. Although this may be true in terms of gay men's relationships with their family and with women in their lives, it does not tend to be the case in their romantic relationships with each other. Unlike lesbians, gay men often have difficulty showing strong emotions toward each other in committed relationships.

When two males enter into a relationship, they both bring their gender roles and socialization traits along with them. This translates into a lack—or even absence—of relational skills toward each other, as they have been socialized to disengage emotionally from other men.

Terrance Real (1997), author of *I Don't Want To Talk About It*, said it well when he wrote about how "boys are pressured to yield attributes of dependency, expressiveness and affiliation all of the self-concepts and skills that belong to the relational, emotive world" (p. 130). He went on to say that the price of traditional socialization for boys is "diminished connection to aspects of the self and diminished connection to others" (p. 137). Given all of this, male couples have to be taught how to develop interpersonal skills, dependency, intimacy, and expressiveness.

Males—both gay and straight—are socialized to be the breadwinners and taught to be sexual predators whose conquests are cause for pride and status. Strong emotions are discouraged. This makes it difficult for men to express anger, hurt, and vulnerability in healthy ways. Consequently, conflicts in gay relationships frequently involve money, jobs, sex, jealousy, and emotional closeness.

I often feel when working with male couples like the woman in a heterosexual relationship, who has to remind her husband about the relationship and to nurture it. Of course this is a sweeping generalization, but I find it to be true that men need to be coached on how to be in relationship whereas women have a head start in this area. Males don't necessarily know how to do naturally—or at all—with each other.

The Case of Will and Richard

Will and Richard had been together for 8 years. They came to me after Will's employer offered him a job out of state. Will wanted to take the job, as it offered a large salary and the opportunity to live in a warmer and more gay-friendly environment.

Over the past 5 years Will had been offered several promotions, and his status and income went up as well. Will had always made considerably more money than Richard did, which often left Richard feeling inferior and self-conscious, despite the fact that Will did not feel this way and never gave him the impression that it was a problem.

Richard had felt awkward about the salary discrepancy throughout their relationship. Even though Richard made a six-figure income, their friends often talked more about Will's job and status and assumed the couple's homes and cars were the result of Will's job and not Richard's. Richard felt hurt each time this happened, and he would remind his friends that his money was used to pay for much of what they owned, too.

Now the couple's relationship was at a turning point: Was Will going to take this job and move out of state? If Richard moved with him, he would have to give up his job. They talked about whether Richard should stay back in case Will's new job did not work out or if they should take the risk together as a couple.

I noticed while they talked about this in my office that they expressed little emotion and affect both toward each other and for themselves—it was as if they were going over a business deal. I commented on this, which prompted Will to cry. He turned to face Richard.

"I don't want you to feel pressured to come with me. I know you make a lot of money and enjoy your job too," Will stated.

Richard was more constrained emotionally and said, "Even though I have a good-paying job, I feel like my place is supposed to be going with you. But I want to have both. I love you and don't want to lose you or my job." After a pause, he continued, "It also bothers me that people will see me as 'the woman' in this relationship if I follow you. I know that sounds weird, but it's how I feel—especially because people are always viewing you as the breadwinner and not me, too."

"I'll let you decide whichever way you want to go with this, Richard," Will said.

Will and Richard: Clinical Interpretation and Treatment

I asked Will why he was not taking more of a stand with Richard about wanting him to come with him. I was concerned that perhaps unconsciously he did not want Richard to come. But this turned out not to be the case. "I don't want to pressure him," Will said. "I want him to come because he wants to, not because he has to."

"But Will, you have to let him know where you stand and that you really want him to come so he can make a decision with informed consent. If you don't, he may not realize how much you want him to come. If he feels pressured, that is his issue, not yours," I responded.

I asked Will to turn to Richard and tell him how he felt. Will did this, explaining to Richard that he really wanted him to join him and that he did not want to go alone. They wept together and held each other for the first time in the 6 visits I'd had with them. They were finally learning to open up more emotionally to themselves and each other. By having these difficult discussions about the pros and cons of all the options, they were pushing their relationship forward in a relationally mature way.

Monogamy Versus Nonmonogamy

Perhaps one of the most controversial issues for couples is whether they choose monogamy or nonmonogamy. (By nonmonogamy, I am not talking about cheating, affairs, secrets, and lies, but rather about a mutual decision on the part of the couple to have an open relationship.) This is especially an issue for gay male relationships. Male couples are more apt to have open sexual relationships than female couples. In fact, studies show that 75% of gay male couples become nonmonogamous after passing their 5-year mark (Nimmons, 2002; McWhirter & Mattison, 1984). Nonmonogamy is not, however, restricted only to male couples. As sociologist Helen Fisher (2004) has illustrated, as humans we are not wired for monogamy. It's a choice, as is nonmonogamy.

Many therapists assume that swingers and those in sexually open relationships have some kind of attachment disorder or problem that keeps them from enjoying full intimacy; monogamy is seen as the top of the hierarchy in terms of a good, healthy relationship. I used to believe this as well. But after more than 20 years as a therapist, I have seen all sorts of couples able make that arrangement work without creating problems in their relationships. Many have even become *closer* as a result of opening their relationship. Therapists must be careful not to advocate or condone monogamy or nonmonogamy; the question is what works for the couple, not what anyone else believes should or shouldn't work. That said, it's imperative to discuss the issue, as it is something your clients may face.

When you initiate the conversation about monogamy/nonmonogamy, make sure you understand how your clients define these terms. I once had a couple who told me during the initial consultation session that they were monogamous. Several months later, they mentioned that they'd recently had a three-way. When I asked if they had changed from monogamy, they assured me they hadn't.

I was confused. Hadn't I gotten the correct information in our initial consultation? "I thought you told me you were monogamous," I told them.

"We are," they said.

Now I was *really* confused! "But you just told me that you had a three-way."

"We did. But we only have three-ways together, and we always play together, never separately from each other." I asked what they meant by "play" and they said they only engage in sex with other people *together*—as a couple.

I slowly began to get it. Like many couples with open relationships, these men made a sharp distinction between *emotional* fidelity and *sexual* fidelity. In other words, they were emotionally monogamous but sexually open. For other couples, monogamy may mean having no sexual partners other than each other. Again, it's crucial to ask the couple to define their terms. You may discover that they don't have a mutual understanding, which is in itself diagnostic. You can then explore this issue with them.

I routinely ask couples, gay or straight, to explain their contract around sex and commitment. Do they have an assumed contract or explicit one? I don't jump to the conclusion that every couple or individual who comes in for therapy is in an open or closed relationship, nor do I assume that they have—or haven't—talked about it.

I have found from the trainings and talks I've conducted that those who have the most negative reactions to nonmonogamy are women and single gay men. Both tend to be very judgmental about the subject. I surmise that women tend to be more relational and, therefore, function more smoothly in a monogamous relationship. Over the years, I've found that gay men who are not partnered or find themselves in new relationships are the most judgmental of their nonmonogamous peers. They strive to maintain the ideal of monogamy because they've been taught they should want it. But after a couple has been together for a while, many agree to open their relationship to include others.

In some cases this may mean deciding to have three-ways; other times it might mean playing separately from each other. Some couples combine the two modes. I've also seen many gay male couples switch back and forth between monogamy and nonmonogamy; there don't seem to be any consistent patterns concerning when, how often, or how long they do so. Whatever the couple's agreement is, responsible nonmonogamous relationships do exist and to ignore or pathologize them with het-erosexist standards across the board does clients a disservice. Watching your own countertransference and checking your own biases is crucial.

Problems can arise, however, if secrecy is involved. Nonmonogamous relationships require extra dialogue, communication, and trust. That trust is broken if cheating occurs—if an agreed-upon contract changes without the partner telling the other. I tell clients, "If you and your partner choose to have responsible nonmonogamy"—or responsible monogamy—"it's imperative that you maintain effective communication. Healthy, open, and effective communication is like an antivirus program on a computer. Without it, you risk ruining your relationship." My questions for these couples include:

- Do you sexually play separately or together?
- Define "monogamy." What does monogamy mean to each of you?
- Is this really what you *both* want or is one of you acquiescing to keep the relationship together?
- How does it make the relationship work? Are there times when it doesn't work?

I do think, however, that there are times when couples with open relationships should be monogamous, if only temporarily. Following are a few situations in which it might be counterproductive for the relationship to be open.

- *If the partners enter therapy as a couple.* Clients who seek therapy as a couple typically have suffered some rupture in their connection, so I recommend that they remain monogamous until their issues are resolved. I always emphasize to them that nonmonogamy may *not* be the problem, but that therapy is about ruling out all possible causes of the distress. (Additionally, abstaining from outside sexual contact eliminates distractions.) Couples' reactions to this recommendation also tell me whether the subject should become an issue for treatment. For example, if they react negatively in a strong way and say something like, "We are not doing that—it is not the problem and don't try to make it one," then I might further explore the issue with them, making sure they understand that I am not biased toward monogamy.
- *If sexual addiction is an issue.* Sometimes both the partner who is sexually acting out and the coaddicted partner are struggling over what constitutes sexual acting out and what doesn't. Until they figure this out, I usually recommend that they maintain monogamy until the addiction is resolved.
- *If a couple is in the first 3 to 5 years of their relationship.* It takes that long for partners to bond to each other and establish a sense of safety, trust, and attachment. If, after the fifth year, they still want to try a nonmonogamous relationship, I recommend that they discuss it then.

Responsible Nonmonogamy

When both partners consent to a mutually open relationship, they are practicing responsible nonmonogamy. They are emotionally exclusive and sexually open. Here, each agrees to open the relationship in ways satisfactory to both. Some partners prefer not to know about their partner's sexual behavior outside the relationship; others insist on knowing. Rules are all-important here. I've heard gay male couples say, "We only do it on vacation" or "only with people we don't know." Working this out *in advance* is imperative.

Following are guidelines for establishing rules regarding nonmonogamy:

- *Play safely.* Outside their relationships, gay men should be very cautious about STDs, and they should use condoms. Assume that everyone else is HIV-positive and act accordingly. It's inappropriate and unrealistic to hope the person you're with is telling you the truth about his status—or about how recently he's been tested. Play safely, no matter what.
- *Maintain emotional fidelity.* Gay couples often report that what works best for them is to engage in encounters based on sexual attraction only, not on emotions or affection. In other words, it's about "no-strings sex and nothing more." They avoid getting to know their temporary partners on any deeper level. In this way, any sex brought into the relationship is simply behavioral in nature, not relational.
- *Maintain an open dialogue.* Effective dialogue is the best thing couples can do to ensure safety, respect, and trust.
- *Be aware of problems that can occur with nonmonogamy.* Jealousy is bound to arise at some point. I've heard partners, gay and straight, express their anxiety that their partner liked another person more, preferred sexual behavior from that other person, and so on. Resolving these problems, again, requires dialogue and safety between partners. It is our job as therapists to educate clients about these possible issues. Knowing the kinds of conflicts that an open relationship can present may help prevent some of them in the first place.

Treatment Approaches With Gay and Lesbian Couples: The Imago Relationship Model

I have found that imago relationship therapy (IRT; Hendrix, 2001) is an excellent tool in working with same-sex (and straight) couples. Most relationship models focus on differences between males and females. IRT, on the other hand, emphasizes the individual and not the gender, making this model perfect for gay and lesbian relationships.

Imago is the Latin word for "image." According to IRT, each of us assembles an imago from both the positive and negative traits of our mother, father, and any other primary caretaker we had growing up. The imago is the blueprint of the person we want in a committed, intimate relationship. Consciously or otherwise, we project this composite template onto prospective partners to see if they fit.

When working with straight couples, some therapists focus on how the wife might be projecting her issues about men onto her husband (particularly those related to her father) and how the husband might be projecting his issues about women onto his wife (particularly those related to his mother). However, IRT recognizes that it is the more dominant negative parent that is projected onto a partner and the gender is secondary.

It is the negative traits of the dominant parent—the one who affected the client most—that begin to interfere with the relationship. I teach my clients—both gay and straight—that they'll find themselves seeking to resolve issues from their childhood now, in their current relationship.

Another thing I like about IRT, especially when working with lesbian and gay couples, is that it turns conflicts that seem negative and hopeless into something promising, positive, and hopeful. Differences between partners on various issues can be very threatening to all couples, gay and straight alike, but particularly to the gay or lesbian couple.

Our society treats gays and lesbians badly for being "different" than the norm. This can make gays and lesbians resistant to change—they don't want to have to conform for anyone ever again. So when differences surface in gay and lesbian relationships and partners ask for change, they are met with a high level of sensitivity and suspiciousness. The partner's request can feel invalidating to the other partner, who hears, "You don't like me the way I am, just like no one liked me the way I was in my childhood." Additionally, when these differences and conflicts arise, it can feel like confirmation that society's attitude is correct and that gay and lesbian relationships are doomed to fail.

Validating a partner's reality, especially when it is different from your own, can feel threatening. To lesbian and gay couples the threat is more profound. IRT helps ease this by teaching the partners to validate and empathize with each other's realities. It is about respecting and honoring the differences and not invalidating either reality.

IRT helps couples see that behavior change requests help you grow as a couple and an individual. The concept in IRT is that we hire our partners to be our greatest teachers and then we go kicking and screaming into the classroom! The reframe here is that the behavior change request is for our own good as well as that of our partner. This helps clients be less reactive.

IRT also normalizes the tension and difficulty that all couples go through, calling it the "power struggle" and defining it as a necessary stage for growth of the individual and the relationship. This creates yet another anchor for lesbians and gays to stay in the relationship and work things out. Many gay relationships do not have children, marriage licenses, family support, and other factors that cause heterosexuals to pause and reconsider whether divorce is truly the right answer.

Finally, another aspect of IRT that is extremely helpful to lesbian and gay couples is turning to face each other rather than sitting side by side. Sitting face to face with the therapist off to the side remind couples that they are in charge and taking ownership of the relationship rather than passing that over to the therapist. It engages the couple to focus on each other as active partners without the therapist's being in charge.

Growing up gay and lesbian imprints the impulse to run from each other, turn away, and refrain from looking at one's desired love object. Making couples look into each other's eyes while doing their therapy work allows for safety and underscores the fact that looking and being with each other is normative and good.

Treatment Guidelines for Lesbian Relationships and Gay Relationships

The following lists outline treatment guidelines for lesbian and gay relationships, based on the separate issues typically involved in each.

For lesbian relationships:

- Help them view differences as valuable rather than threatening.
- Help them develop more autonomy as individuals within the relationship.
- Challenge their pseudo-mutuality as much as possible, helping them individuate and allow for differences.
- Teach them how to directly express their individual wants and needs in the relationship.
- Help them be more assertive in the relationship.
- Educate them about how to more fully enjoy the purely physical aspects of sex.
- Help them express anger in healthy, productive ways.

For gay male relationships:

- Teach them interdependence, as well as how to express a range of emotions.
- Teach them how to be more comfortable being vulnerable with each other.
- Emphasize cooperativeness over competitiveness.
- Emphasize emotional relatedness over physical attractiveness.
- Educate them about how to get greater enjoyment out of the emotional aspects of sex.
- Ensure that both partners have agreed to a contract about monogamy or lack thereof.

CHAPTER 11

The New Mixed Marriage:
One Lesbian or Gay Spouse and One Straight

Come on straight people . . . if you let us marry each other,
we will stop marrying you!

—Jason Stuart, gay comic

"Mixed marriage" usually refers to marriages between people of different races or religions. However, the mixed-*orientation* marriage—one gay spouse and one straight—has been around just as long and is becoming increasingly visible. The Straight Spouse Network (www.ssnetwk.org) claims that there are more than 2 million mixed-orientation couples, where one spouse is gay, lesbian, bisexual, or transgendered. As already addressed in previous chapters, most lesbians and gays seek self-esteem from outside validation. This is the main reason why they heterosexually marry, not because they are selfish or self-centered, as many people assume.

Of the many books and articles written for the heterosexuals in these couples, particularly well received is Amity Pierce Buxton's (2006) *The Other Side of the Closet: The Coming-Out Crisis for Straight Spouses*. As Buxton explained, not all gay-straight marriages follow the same path after the disclosure that one of the partners is gay or lesbian. She described three trajectories:

- A third of the couples break up quickly.
- A third stay together for 2 or 3 years to sort out alternatives but ultimately decide to separate.
- A third commit themselves to redefining the marriage so that they can stay together. Of these, about half determine after about 3 years that separation is

best for them, while the remaining half stay married with different arrangements for the marriage.

In a rush of countertransference, therapists often coach the lesbian or gay spouse to come out and the straight spouse to move on with his or her life and find another straight spouse. But as Buxton's statistics show, this isn't always the best option for the couple.

As homosexuality becomes more accepted by our society, more gays and lesbians will feel comfortable coming out from their heterosexual marriages. But often the people involved in these relationships lack the information they need to move forward with their lives. Both partners have their own coming-out process to undergo, but they can negotiate this process together as a couple. In fact, often they *need* to go through this process together. Therapists must remember this.

Clinicians must also remember that there are many men and women who know they are homosexual but choose not to self-identify as gay or lesbian. Many of these people heterosexually marry, as the following case illustrates.

The Case of Barry

Barry admitted to his clinician that he married at the recommendation of psychotherapists and doctors. During the 1970s, when he was in his twenties, he lived a gay lifestyle but found gay culture to be too sexual and promiscuous. He never could find a man with whom to settle down and have the ongoing monogamous relationship, including having children, he longed for.

After meeting a woman at work, Barry gave up trying to find a man to settle down with. He and his coworker fell in love, married, and had three children. Although Barry's wife knew of his sexual interest in men before they married, he assured her that he would not act on what he called his "sexual impulses" and denied having a true gay identity.

After 20 years of marriage, with the kids grown and out of the house, Barry was struggling with his sexual urges. He began experiencing depression and anxiety symptoms and went into therapy. He told the therapist that he had never acted on his sexual impulses in all the years of his marriage, but now, thanks to the Internet, these urges were more difficult to manage. It was easy to find pornography, which Barry often used to satisfy his sexual urges, and to initiate contact through chat rooms with men who wanted to have sex with other men.

Barry's therapist, who was gay affirmative and considered herself nonhomophobic, believed that Barry's use of pornography was akin to adultery and advised him to stop using it. She also urged Barry to consider coming out of the closet and leaving his marriage to pursue a gay lifestyle. However, Barry still did not see himself as gay and did not want to leave his wife. He loved her, believed they had a good life together, and did not see anything positive about living a gay life.

Ultimately, though, Barry did talk to his wife. Neither of them wanted to separate or divorce. Barry's therapist was not supportive of their decision to stay married and told him that it would inevitably lead to a life of depression for him and resentment on the part of both partners.

Barry: Clinical Interpretation and Treatment

Barry's case is more common than you might imagine. That's why clinicians need to know how to address the issue without inserting their personal biases, as Barry's therapist did when she urged the couple to separate. In this case, the therapist was acting on her own countertransference; she wasn't thinking of what was best for Barry.

Although Barry might have benefited from coming out as a gay man and finding a male partner had he tried it, from his point of view this would never work, and his clinician needed to honor this. Barry and his wife were already in their late fifties; deciding to stay together made the most sense for *them*. And in Barry's case he *was* out of the closet. He was simply choosing what to do with his sexuality now that he and his wife knew.

A more informed and attuned therapist would have helped Barry and his wife explore other options in addition to the possibility of leaving the marriage and moving on. For example, a more respectful and informed therapeutic intervention would have been to help Barry learn to avoid exposing himself to chat rooms that stimulated his homosexual urges and desire for contact. The therapist's negative stance on Barry's using pornography was also misguided. Barry's wife did not have a problem with his looking at pornography—she believed that as long as it helped him manage his sexual urges so that he didn't act on them with other men, she could live with that.

This is a good example of how a therapist's biases can derail effective therapy. In an attempt to be gay affirmative and nonhomophobic, the clinician, instead of following her clients' lead, pointed them in what was the wrong direction for their particular situation. Supporting clients who wish to stay married should *never*, however, involve using the methods of reparative therapy (discussed in Chapter 1).

Clinicians who treat mixed-orientation couples need to understand that a partner's coming out doesn't mean that the couple stops loving each other. In fact, I've found that uncovering one partner's homosexuality can actually strengthen a marriage—but only if both people in the marriage find the help they need. Most often, the person who has just come out is the one who seeks therapy, usually as a prelude to the couple's splitting up. But some mixed-orientation couples can make their marriages work, albeit in new ways, as I explain later.

Often the dilemma is centered not around sex but around love. Many of the heterosexually married gays and lesbians I've counseled have been married for 10 years or more. Most have children, have built good lives together, and feel a deep and abiding love for each other. Neither has fallen out of love. The prospect of separating and divorcing is devastating, not only for them but for their children as well.

With all couples—straight, same-sex, and mixed-orientation alike—the work is about *shared* responsibility. When the woman in a relationship is pregnant, *they* are pregnant. When one partner has an affair, they both share the burden of how it evolved and how to resolve it. When one partner has an addiction, they are an addicted couple. Given this, the therapist must explore the needs and desires of *both* the gay and the straight spouse in mixed-orientation marriages.

Therapist's Biases

There are several types of countertransference that may surface during work with clients in mixed-orientation marriages:

- Your feelings about affairs
- Your feelings about divorce—especially if children are involved
- Your homophobic feelings toward the gay or lesbian spouses
- Your interest in helping the straight spouses move on even if they don't want to or aren't ready to
- Your investment in keeping the straight spouse a victim and the gay spouse a perpetrator
- Your own unconscious homoerotic interests

As you read this chapter, pay close attention to your countertransference. The subject of mixed-orientation marriages is provocative for many people. Pay attention to what you dislike, or to your sense that you would have handled a particular case differently. Notice if you have overly strong reactions to what these couples do and what therapists—including me—have done to help them. This very well could be your negative countertransference. Better to clear it up here than in the room with your clients!

Why Do Gays and Lesbians Heterosexually Marry?

This is probably the most common question asked of gays and lesbians who heterosexually marry. Part of the answer, already discussed in other chapters of this book, is that our culture doesn't permit young people to explore anything but heterosexuality. Married gays and lesbians are a hidden population—even to themselves. Often they do not identify their homosexual interests as gay or lesbian. They are in the early stages of denial in the coming out process (see Chapter 7 for further discussion of the stages). Those with conscious homosexual urges and desires are urged to marry heterosexually in the hope that everything will "work itself out." This is particularly common among gay men, who are usually more conscious than women are of their homosexual tendencies. Lesbians are often genuinely unaware that they're attracted to other women in homosexual ways.

The following sections identify some other reasons why gays and lesbians may heterosexually marry.

Hetero-emotional, Homosexual

Some men and women are hetero-emotional but homosexual. They are not interested in anything more than sexual activity with members of the same gender. Some hetero-emotional gay men and women are married to the opposite gender but do not have sex with them. Yet they enjoy a life that's full of love and family, and they may or may not decide to be sexual with others outside the marriage.

In fact, a recent study shows that romantic love isn't limited by a person's sexual orientation. Lisa Diamond, a University of Utah psychology professor who studied the distinctions between romantic love and sexual desire writes that "it seems that individuals are capable of developing intense, enduring, preoccupying affections for one another regardless of either partner's sexual attractiveness or arousal (Diamond, 2004, p. 116). Diamond based her model on the notion of romantic love evolving from the attachment bond formed between infant and caregiver. After reviewing work by other love researchers and delving into accounts of love and friendship across cultures, Diamond distinguished love and sexual desire. In her model, sexual desire and romantic love are functionally independent, and romantic love is not intrinsically oriented to same-gender or other-gender partners.

In an article published in *Psychological Review*, Diamond stated: " . . . while the goal of sexual desire is sexual union for the purpose of reproduction, romantic love is governed by the attachment or pair-bonding system, with its goal of maintaining an enduring bond between two individuals" (2003, p. 174). And because romantic love, as she hypothesized, is an outgrowth of infant/caregiver attachment, there is no way to "code" romantic love for gender. Diamond also argued that the links between love and desire are bidirectional, because sexual desire can facilitate affectional bonding, and affectional bonding can facilitate sexual desire (Diamond, 2003).

According to Diamond's model, it's possible for someone who is heterosexual to fall in love with someone of the same gender, and for someone who is homosexual to fall in love with someone of a different gender. But gays and lesbians who fall in love heterosexually often cannot sustain a heterosexual lifestyle. In time, their defenses against their sexual identity begin to crumble and their true orientation, which is now in conflict with their chosen love attachment, surfaces. Many people suffer depression as a result of suppressing their sexuality. They also find that as their true sexuality surfaces they can no longer hide it or fight it, and they lose *sexual* interest in their opposite-gender partner.

Over the years, however, I've met and treated hetero-emotional, homosexual men and women who do decide to live heterosexually. When treating these men and women, I don't focus on trying to help them suppress their orientation; rather, I help them acknowledge it and move in the direction of their stated goal of choosing to live a heterosexual life—which sometimes includes *not* acting on their homosexual desires. They don't change their orientation; they simply choose how they want to live. Having weighed every consideration carefully, many live happy lives with their opposite-gender partner.

Family of Origin Conditioning

To better understand your gay and lesbian clients who marry heterosexually, you need to explore their family of origin issues. All gay men and lesbians who heterosexually marry have, along with social and personality traits, family of origin factors that led them to stay closeted and get married in the first place. Simply chalking it up only to a homophobic, heterosexist society is not enough of an explanation.

For example, gay men or lesbians may have been conditioned to be conflict-avoidant, obedient, conforming, appeasing, and people-pleasing. They may have been sexually or physically abused, or have suffered other forms of neglect and abuse, causing their defenses and adaptations to manifest by conforming to the "authority," just as children who are abused learn to adapt by conforming to what the perpetrator demands. Later, as adults, they reenact their early abuse by conforming to other figures or societal "authorities." Not all gay men and lesbians who suppress their homosexuality grow up to eventually marry, but covert cultural sexual abuse and other covert *and* overt factors can push them in that direction.

Some gay men and lesbians marry the opposite gender in order to be taken care of, to bond with a parental figure, as a cover or "beard" for their gay activities, or in the hope that straight sex will "cure" their desire for the same gender (or at least keep that desire strictly sexual). The latter is more common among men than among women.

Guilt and Shame

For many gay men and lesbians coming out of the closet, the journey is solely about themselves and their family of origin. They may feel shame and guilt about the disruption their coming out engenders, but they know that both they and their families must just get past it. For heterosexually married men and lesbians, however, the shame and guilt are compounded, and they inevitably feel 100% responsible for hurting their spouses and children. It takes them years to get through feeling that they've ruined everyone's lives, including their own. "How could I have done this to my spouse, to my kids?" is the mantra I hear in my office. "My spouse didn't know this about me when he married me! This isn't fair to him. It's all my fault, and I should suffer!" Everything negative that happens in their children's and straight spouse's lives is seen as related to their coming out.

Sexual Abuse

Some gays and lesbians are out of touch with their sexuality because of having been sexually abused as children or teenagers. This confuses their sexual identity. Also, as discussed in Chapter 4, covert cultural sexual abuse causes confusion over identity for most lesbians and gays even if overt sexual abuse does not occur. Because of the compulsory heterosexism that exists in society, it is the norm for these sexual abuse survivors to consider themselves heterosexual and attribute any homosexual feelings and thoughts to the sexual abuse. If a male is perpetrated by another male he might view his sexual feelings toward men as stemming from his abuse. If a woman is abused by a male perpetrator she might consider her feelings for women a result of her turning away from men. Many therapists support this theory, as do many books.

The research and clinical literature on sexual abuse show that those who have been sexually abused—whether heterosexual or not—have difficulty accessing and expressing their own genuine sexual orientation and desires. From a developmental perspective, the perpetrators of the sexual abuse contaminate their victims' arousal templates. So it makes sense that given their confusion, gays and lesbians choose heterosexuality, banking on the fact that it is inherently who they are.

Therapists need to explore the history of the gay or lesbian spouse to determine whether sexual abuse affected his or her choice to marry heterosexually, as well as help the gay spouse and straight spouse understand why the gay spouse chose heterosexuality.

Keeping A Straight Face

A gay client of mine once said that for him, married life was like "heterosexual prison." Sadly, he thought of himself as many inmates do: He had sex with his wife simply to relieve his sexual urges. He wasn't sexually attracted to her, yet he was not repulsed either. Out of love for her, he was able to be sexual and romantic with her. Other gay and lesbian clients I've had over the years agree that they live imprisoned within the structures and boundaries of heterosexism—and that, like the incarcerated, they do what they must to survive.

This explains why you will see in your practices among these couples that the gay or lesbian spouse loses complete interest in having sex with the straight spouse after coming out of "heterosexual prison." Like straight prisoners who engage in homosexual sex during incarceration, once released gays and lesbians no longer want to engage in heterosexual behaviors. This is the model to use when thinking of the gay spouses.

Many of these survival strategies are dysfunctional, causing long-term harm to both the gay or lesbian individual and the straight spouse, as well as to their children. The following sections describe several of these dysfunctional coping mechanisms.

Addictions

Some gay or lesbian spouses act out in addictive ways to avoid dealing with their gay identities: They drink too much, have promiscuous sex, do drugs, or overeat. Like any other time-consuming addiction, this is a way of burning off extra energy and avoiding introspection. Other addictions can be less obvious. People may distract themselves by spending too much time at work or committing themselves to sports or hobbies that suppress their unwanted impulses; they may also become flatly asexual as was addressed in Chapter 3.

Often these people have no one to confide in. They find it difficult to seek comfort in organized religion or through support groups like A.A. With no one to help them articulate their innermost feelings, they bottle up these inchoate feelings and fears, which slows the coming out process (Corley & Kort, 2006).

Infidelity

Most extramarital affairs, whether the couple is straight or gay, result from one or both partners' inability to achieve and keep intimacy. Although these factors affect many heterosexual marriages, the gay or lesbian spouse's predominant motive for "straying" is to find and reveal his or her true identity. Lesbians and gay men typically cheat or act out because they're repressing part of themselves. Therapists need to remind their clients that because society grants little to no permission to explore anything other than heterosexuality, it makes sense that homosexuals marry heterosexually and explore their homosexuality later. Of course, this exploration should have been allowed during their earlier adolescent and young adult years. The process is backward.

When the conflict does erupt years later, it is about their "identity," not about their ability to love and bond with their partner. Nor is it the result of marital problems.

Therapists need to understand this important distinction. They can help the gay or lesbian spouse understand that although he or she may be acting out of integrity by having an affair, the affair is often caused by unresolved identity issues—it isn't because the marriage is poor or because he or she is a bad person.

Typically, straight spouses feel as though *they* did something to cause their gay or lesbian spouse to seek affairs with the same gender. Therapists can also help straight spouses stop blaming themselves for their partner's wanderings and encourage them to avoid concluding that there was something wrong with the marriage itself.

Renaming Behaviors and Feelings

Some men who have sex with men and women who have sex with women do not see themselves as gay or lesbian or even bisexual. Men may tell themselves that their wives won't perform a certain sexual act they desire, such as oral stimulation, and then give themselves permission to find oral release from another man, never thinking of it as gay or as cheating on their wives because it was from a man. Women may have sex with other women and tell themselves that it is for their male partners who enjoy watching them with another woman. They won't label it as lesbianism at all.

Therapists need to know that there *are* men and women who are not gay and for whom the above situations are true. As discussed in Chapter 7, sexual behavior does not always reflect sexual orientation. Although some clients who engage in homosexual sexual behavior might be in denial about being gay or lesbian, others truly might just enjoy the behavior and not be. It's your job to find out which is the case, with the client leading the way and you helping them with the right questions.

It is also important to help the straight spouse understand that most gay and lesbian spouses really did not know that they were gay before getting married. Although popular wisdom has it that gay and lesbians always know, this is only partially correct. Gays and lesbians may say, "Looking back, I can see that what I was feeling was something gay or lesbian," but in the early stages they were truly not conscious of their gay identities.

Going on the Down Low

Going "on the down low"—a man's engaging in sex with other men and not telling his wife—is a consequence of not coming out to himself and to his marriage partner (King, 2004; Boykin, 2005). Psychological fallout from this uneasy dynamic includes depression and low self-esteem, plus many other dysfunctional behaviors I often see in my practice: suicide attempts, affairs (from cybersex to in-person meetings), and unprotected sex. This is because men on the down low don't admit to themselves that they are sexually interested in other men: If they were to use condoms, they would have to admit to themselves that they are "gay." They would also have to address their urges as meaningful rather than dismissing them as simply a sexual release. To stay in denial, these men have random, anonymous sex and suppress the knowledge of what this might mean even from themselves.

Closed Loop Groups

Some gay and bisexual men belong to closed loop groups—underground clubs frequented by heterosexually married men who want a boyfriend (also heterosexually married) on the side. The men remain "monogamous" to both their wives and their boyfriends. Each man knows of the other's secret life, but their wives don't. This is often an example of gay men wanting to have their cake and eat it too, believing they can keep a spouse *and* a boyfriend while not being up front about the latter. Accordingly, they change the definition of what they're doing from cheating to "not wanting to hurt her."

I don't support these arrangements for many reasons. My chief objection isn't moral but one of personal integrity—I believe we need to be congruent with ourselves from the inside out. An even bigger issue is that of the straight spouse's lack of awareness. If a couple mutually agrees to this arrangement openly and honestly—on the "up high"—then I completely support their decision.

Disclosure: From the Down Low to In The Know

Many people believe that *all* affairs or encounters should be disclosed, but therapists need to understand the need for selective disclosure. Just because a gay spouse has had sexual encounters and affairs with the same gender during the marriage doesn't mean that he or she has to tell the spouse about these experiences. Just as step 9 of A.A. declares, "Make amends whenever possible except when to do so would injure them or others."

When affairs or encounters *are* disclosed, it has to be done with discretion, by which I mean in a manner that causes the least possible harm to both partners and the children. Therapists need to help their clients achieve this. Success often depends on the personality and emotional stability of the spouse

Disclosing to a straight spouse that one is gay or lesbian can be difficult for many reasons. If children are involved, the first thing to address with clients, however, is the practical issue of state laws concerning visitation and custody of children. In many court systems, a gay spouse's affairs or homosexual partnering can be cause for limiting visitation or requiring supervised visits.

Here it is best for gay and lesbian clients to consider for themselves what feels right for them and for their children. If they know that telling could cause their straight spouse to try to keep the kids from them, they should not tell. Many of my clients do not like this option but I remind them it is for the children—it is not fair to them if the straight spouse, in his or her anger stage, forces supervised or limited visits.

If children are not involved, gay and lesbian spouses should carefully consider how much information about their extramarital affairs or sexual encounters their spouse really needs to know.

The Case of Betty

Betty, 32, was married and the mother of three children, ages 9, 6, and 3. She realized she was lesbian after she met Donna, a lesbian in her knitting group. They fell in love and began a secret relationship. Betty was in therapy and told the therapist about the situation. She finally realized she wanted to leave her husband and make a life with Donna. The therapist encouraged her to tell her husband the truth so they could have a healthy dialogue about how to move forward.

Betty's husband was outraged. He felt humiliated and betrayed by Betty's deception. He promised her that she would never see the kids again. He hired an attorney and outed Betty as a homosexual and adulterer. Betty became suicidal and was hospitalized. This only further injured her case in keeping her children.

In the end Betty was only allowed supervised afternoon visits with her children, and she had to come alone—she couldn't bring Donna. Betty's appeal for shared custody was denied. After 2 years fighting in court, Betty was granted rights to see her children without supervision and eventually was allowed overnight visitation. Even then, however, her partner was ordered not to be at home when the children slept over.

Betty: Case Interpretation and Treatment

Betty's therapist should have warned Betty about these legal ramifications before Betty revealed her sexual orientation to her husband. The legal system is often biased against the gay spouse. Withholding one's homosexuality during a divorce is a way to protect the children.

Many gay or lesbian parents can't imagine that their straight spouses would react vindictively, especially about the children. But spouses may react in unexpected ways out of anger and feelings of betrayal. Therapists should advise clients like Betty to contact the Straight Spouse Support group in their area or to find such a group online. This would have armed Betty with more information about how to proceed so that she could make a more informed decision. Therapists can also recommend to their clients that a gay or lesbian attorney informed about these types of problems be present in the courtroom when custody is discussed.

Straight Spouses Who Marry Gays and Lesbians

When I talk to straight spouses in mixed-orientation marriages, I often discover that personal issues played an important role in their deciding to get married. Although straight spouses may not have consciously known that their partners were gay, it usually wasn't an accident that they married people who couldn't completely commit or be as intimate and available to them as a straight spouse would have been (Kort, 2005a).

In some cases, a straight spouse is unconsciously drawn to a partner who might betray him or her. Perhaps this spouse suffered childhood traumas such as emotional boundary violations that remained unresolved; this could prompt the spouse to unconsciously seek a "familiar" partner who violates his or her trust all over again. Other times, straight spouses believe that they are attractive or skilled enough to "convert" an unavailable partner.

Some straight spouses marry gays or lesbians out of unconscious codependency and a desire to control or micromanage a "flawed" partner. A common partnering in this situation is a controlling women married to a gay man—especially a gay man who wants to be controlled. Often the gay man had problems in his family of origin: He may have been raised in a large or neglectful family that overlooked his emotional needs or lost a caregiver at an early age. The controlling wife, in turn, may have come from a disempowered role in her own family and feel a need to be in charge in order not to feel vulnerable.

Family of origin issues are always involved in any person's attraction to a mate. For example, suppose a woman grew up with a sexually abusive father. She may decide—consciously or not—to avoid future abuse by marrying a man whose sexual power is distant or who has problems with impotence. Or she may marry a gay man struggling to squelch his homosexual impulses. This can be a way of protecting herself from straight men's sexual aggression. Gay men make women like this feel safe, especially if sex is kept to a minimum.

Much less is written and known about the men who marry lesbians. I suspect they are attracted to lesbians for similar reasons that women are attracted to gay men—they unconsciously want to marry someone who is distant and cannot be fully available in the marriage emotionally and sexually. What I have seen in my practice over the years is that some men like that their wives occasionally enjoy sex with women. They find it erotic and do not equate it with lesbianism. To them, their wives are helping them with their erotic fantasies of watching and being sexual with two women.

Therapists must remember that straight spouses aren't without some accountability for the mixed-orientation union—there is usually a reason why they married someone who had limited emotional or sexual availability. Ignoring the psychological process that is at work for the straight spouse does both clients a disservice. It is also extremely important for the therapist to tell gay and lesbian spouses that that they are not 100% to blame for this situation. They need to consider why their partners married a gay spouse—consciously or unconsciously.

Straight Spouse Reactions to Disclosure

Often gay and lesbian spouses say they know how their straight spouses will react when in fact they don't. Some straight spouses manage to remain supportive and understanding, but many become angry and behave unpredictably, particularly around their own homophobia as well as in response to the threat of losing their spouse. Clients need to be prepared for the worst.

Many straight spouses react to the news that their partner is gay by going into the very closet their gay spouse is in the process of leaving. Once they acknowledge that they knew or suspected, on some level, that their spouse was gay, they have to deal with their own denial or, in some cases, their secret homophobia. Other straight spouses feel embarrassed, cheated, or fooled. They worry about being judged by others. They're not sure how to move forward—whom to tell, how to tell them, and when. Some straight spouses grow so enraged and bitter that they quickly divorce, never examining themselves and the situation from any point of view other than their own. They may try to turn their kids against their gay ex and refuse to reconcile.

Often straight spouses struggle with feeling that they weren't "man or woman enough" to keep the marriage together. They need to hear from a therapist that this isn't the issue—that the split-up has nothing to do with their performance as a spouse. They also need to understand that their gay partner's sexuality has absolutely nothing to do with *them*. They simply married a partner with sexual conflicts. An excellent resource for straight spouses is Amity Pierce Buxton's (1994) *The Other Side of the Closet*.

Some straight spouses want to stay married, even if they feel embittered and betrayed. Often this only perpetuates a bad situation. Women who cling to their negative feelings unwittingly betray their loyalty to the very men who have inflicted pain. Their motives for having stayed married—and now, their inability to move forward in life—reveal their underlying need to be attached to a man. Whether or not he can be there for her, she clings to her desire to remain part of a social unit. As one betrayed socialite defiantly declared, "I am *still* Mrs. Smith, and I intend to remain so!" Frozen in time, these women cultivate their humiliation because they enjoy the sympathy they receive as a "victim."

Some straight spouses, however, feel relieved. They may have blamed themselves for the problems in their marriage—especially sexual problems—only to now realize that they were not at fault. Others are happy to feel released from having a sexual relationship with their spouse and grateful to enjoy a continuing emotional relationship.

Straight spouses' reactions also depend on their feelings about the opposite gender in general. A woman who has negative impressions of men may use her husband as the nearest target. When one woman with whom I worked discovered that her mate was gay, she exclaimed, "This proves my point—men are pigs! Even when I tried to marry one who I didn't think was, he turns out to be one. Just like the rest—liars and cheats."

Unfortunately, society typically supports the "betrayed" ex-wife and blames gay men for marrying in the first place. In cases like this, the woman is rewarded for staying indignant and angry, thus keeping her a victim. A better strategy would be to approach a woman in this situation as someone who made a decision that didn't work out.

For men, learning their wives are lesbian can feel like a slight to their manhood. They are not only humiliated by their inability to fix the problem but also worry that others will see them as "less of a man" for having married a lesbian.

Coming Out as a Couple

Mixed-orientation couples come out in several typical ways. William Wedin, director of Bisexual Psychological Services in New York City, has identified four stages: humiliation, honeymoon, rage, and resolution (Ball, 2004). Just like the stages of the grieving process, these stages are not rigid or the same for everyone; individuals approach the crisis differently according to the context of their lives.

Stage 1. Humiliation

Both spouses may feel a significant amount of humiliation surrounding the coming out process. The gay or lesbian spouse feels humiliated about being gay. Straight spouses feel humiliated that they weren't "man or woman enough" to keep their mate interested. They may question whether they can trust anything that seemed real in the past regarding the marriage or their partner.

One wife said to her husband, "Is it because I repulse you and am fat?" Another husband asked his wife if she "used him" to have children. Others agonize over what they did wrong or why they did not see that their spouse was gay before this. During this stage, many report that they had no idea that their partner was gay.

Stage 2. The Honeymoon

Some gay spouses who come out are so grateful to their partners for still unconditionally loving and accepting them that they want to stay married. The more the straight spouse has genuine loving feelings and empathizes with what the gay spouse is going through, the more the gay spouse will be drawn to the straight spouse, due to the gay spouse's attachment need for closeness and comfort. Often, they also feel overwhelmed by the evidence that the straight spouse might want to stay. The emotional distress softens them for a period of time and both will have some hope for the marriage. Feelings of shame often diminish; both think that perhaps things will go back to the way they were before the disclosure.

Stage 3. Rage

Eventually, however, both partners realize that things will never be the same: The gay husband or wife can't retreat back into the closet, and the straight spouse can't deny the distance between them. Straight spouses often begin to interpret every negative feeling as a sign that their partner is unhappy with them, and gay spouses often respond to their partner's inquiries by being avoidant or overly emotional. The distance that was present in the marriage before the disclosure returns, and the straight spouse or both spouses turn to anger and rage as a distraction from the intense pain of the loss they feel.

Stage 4. Resolution

Once both partners understand that the coming out is about issues of identity, not dissatisfaction with the straight spouse or the marriage, mutual blame ends. The straight spouse can stop interpreting the sexual or romantic acting out as a personal affront, and the gay spouse can begin treating the straight spouse as a partner rather than as an adversary. They can then begin to deal with the impact on their relationship.

During this stage, each partner determines whether he or she wants to stay together or transition to another type of relationship. They take into account various factors such as children, social considerations, belief systems and personalities, and the degree of openness between them. If they stay together, they must negotiate and often compromise about how homosexuality will play a role in the marriage. Boundaries regarding sexual behaviors and coming out to others have to be determined. Decisions need to be made about what homosocial activities are acceptable to both, and what to tell children, extended family, and friends.

Does Coming Out Have to Mean Getting Out? Deciding Whether to Stay Married or Separate

Once the disclosure is made, the relationship undergoes rapid changes. Again, this is a rough transition; as a clinician, you need to smooth it. The first step is educating clients about their options. They can:

- Divorce and lead separate lives
- Wait to divorce until the kids leave home
- Decide on an in-house separation (usually a temporary solution)
- Divorce or separate but remain best friends
- Continue to live together as friends, or live close by
- Stay married but find new partners for the gay spouse and/or the straight spouse
- Practice responsible nonmonogamy (being sexually open to others but remaining emotionally monogamous to one's spouse)
- Allow the gay spouse to become "homosocial" (live as a gay person among the gay community but never have sex outside of the marriage)
- Stay together and renegotiate the terms of the marriage in other ways
- Choose not to act on sexual feelings and recommit to the marriage

It's very important to support couples who decide to stay together. Many therapists erroneously see divorce as the only option. To them, an arrangement to stay together constitutes an intimacy disorder. They evaluate the gay spouse as a person who needs to come out of the closet fully and lead a gay lifestyle. Other times the therapist will advise the gay partner to remain in the closet and be the spouse and parent he or she promised to be; in short, these therapists ask the gay spouse to rewrite history. Both of these approaches ignore society's heterosexism and homophobia and hold the gay spouse accountable as the only responsible party.

As a couples therapist, I take the position that it's not for the clinician to decide whether a couple should stay together. The final decision is theirs. Our job as therapists is simply to make our clients aware of their options and the possible ramifications of their decisions. The rest is up to them. We support them in what works for *them*, not us.

Before deciding on any course of action, a couple must clarify what is important to *each* of them personally and jointly. They can then begin to figure out what arrangement will work best for them. This can be, of course, an arduous process—such arrangements are often unorthodox, and there are precious few role models for what a healthy mixed-orientation relationship can be.

Staying Together

When mixed-orientation couples decide to stay together, they need to establish ground rules for what the new relationship will be. For example, they can practice responsible nonmonogamy, with clearly defined rules about what that means for both partners. Some couples allow the gay partner to explore gay porn, as Barry did.

Many see this as potentially addictive or even pathological, but I don't agree. I believe that couples should define healthy sexual and emotional fidelity *for themselves*. Part of this involves identifying healthy aspects of their old relationship—components they feel are worth preserving in their new marriage. The couple also needs to establish limits and boundaries. For example, they need to know when *un*healthy nonmonogamy may develop into affairs or lead one of them into sexual addiction.

Splitting Up

If the couple does decide to split up, it's important to explore how this will affect them and their family. As a therapist, you can help ease the hurt as much as possible, knowing that pain will inevitably be a part of the picture. Prepare gay spouses for the anger and misunderstanding that will come their way from straight spouses, children, family, and friends, and educate them on how to protect themselves against potential injury.

Many therapists—and nontherapists—dishonor gay men and lesbians who leave marriages and kids, and this fuels the gay spouse's guilt for marrying in the first place. The cultural and therapeutic mindset is that gay men or lesbians show more integrity by staying with their spouse and children than by leaving them, as they "made their choice" and should "live with it." But those who hold these views forget what brought the gay man or lesbian to heterosexually marry in the first place.

Many gay spouses never fully recover after a divorce. They say things like, "I never stopped loving him. The divorce was not about no longer loving or liking each other." They know inside that they are truly gay or lesbian, but they regret leaving a person they loved and splitting their families apart.

More men than women tell me that they never found a same-sex partner who was able to fulfill their emotional needs the way their ex-spouse did. In other words, they miss the relational part of their old relationship, an aspect that for most gay men—or men in general, for that matter—is often not very well developed.

Many gay women who come out in their heterosexual marriage are upset when the role of sex in their lesbian relationships diminishes. They, like their gay male counterparts, ask themselves why they left a relationship that was not sexually satisfying only to find themselves in another that is mostly sexless.

As therapists, we must help these clients understand that they need to work on the new relationship so that it includes both sex and relational closeness.

CHAPTER 12

Gay Affirmative Therapy Principles in Clinical Practice: Establishing a Differential Diagnosis

Nothing is ever settled until it is settled right.
—Rudyard Kipling

Many lesbians and gay men can appear to have mental health disorders when instead they are suffering the effects of suppressing their sexual identity or going through the coming out process. Depression and anxiety are basic components of suppressing one's sexual orientation and the coming out process. A lifetime of psychological splitting and compartmentalization may produce behaviors typical of personality disorders. The gay or lesbian child hears the message, "We will love you unconditionally as long as you are straight or pretend that you are." This promotes splitting, which "consists of compartmentalization of opposite and conflicting affect states; subjects may be aware of their contradictory, ambivalent attitudes but fail to recognize that they spring from their own internal conflicts" (Campbell, 2004, p. 622). Splitting, of course, is the essential ingredient in axis 1 personality disorders, but with gays and lesbians, this splitting is often caused not by a personality disorder but rather by an attempt to fit into a world that doesn't accept them for who they are.

Mental Health Disorders That Mimic the Effects of Covert Cultural Sexual Abuse

Long-term closetedness can lead a person to become overly rigid, judgmental, and difficult to work with (not just in therapy); have difficult friendships and tenuous romances; and have low self-esteem or grandiosity and narcissism that ultimately move from being a psychological defense to being part of the client's character. During the coming out process, particularly during stage 5, clients may appear bipolar, self-absorbed, narcissistic, and potentially a sex-addicted. However, once this stage of the coming out process ends, these clients no longer display any psychological problems.

Therapists need to differentiate between the stigma or stress of growing up gay and true psychopathology on the part of the client. Are clients reacting to the stigma of being gay and lesbian, the life of having been closeted, the difficulty of the coming out process? Or is psychopathology operating in addition to or separate from the stigma and stress of growing up gay? As author and psychotherapist Kristine Falco (1996) wrote:

> . . . misdiagnosis is occasionally possible in cases where a patient in a sexual identity crisis, or coming-out crisis, responds with mood swings, hyperactivity, and impulsive behaviors reminiscent of hypomania. Resolution of the sexual-affectional issue may alleviate symptoms and can help clarify the diagnosis. (p. 407)

As discussed in Chapter 6, developmental delays are often the real cause of apparent psychopathology and personality disorders.

Common mental health disorders that mimic the effects of covert cultural sexual abuse are:

- Borderline personality disorder
- Avoidant personality disorder
- Narcissistic personality disorder
- Depression disorders
- Anxiety disorders
- Bipolar/hypomanic disorders
- Addictions (chemical and behavioral)
- Obsessive-compulsive personality disorder

Common types of characterological-appearing overlays I have found in my practice and heard from those I have supervised are borderline-appearing personality traits, endogenous/chronic depression (dysthymia) and reactive depression (adjustment disorders), and narcissistic-appearing characterological overlay, which is often confused with narcissistic personality disorders in gay and lesbian clients. Although some clients are truly characterological, others may appear to be but are not—their symptoms are defenses and more neurotic than characterological.

According to Gonsiorek, if an overlay remains a part of a person's functioning for a prolonged period of time, it "may begin to set down increasingly deep roots and begin to dwarf the pre-existing personality structure" (1982, p. 19). He went on to say that "some victims may be scarred psychologically with the marks of social oppression of homosexuality as indelibly as some concentration camp victims retain their tattooed numbers" (p. 19).

Borderline Personality Disorder

The diagnosis of borderline personality disorder (BPD) is overused with lesbians, as it is for women in general (Falco, 1991). A quick look at the *DSM* criteria (1994) for a BPD diagnosis reveals a striking similarity between such symptoms and the behaviors typical of gays and lesbians, especially those in the coming out process. For example, gay and lesbian clients may exhibit the following (Ritter & Terndrup, 2002):

- Efforts to avoid real or imagined abandonment
- Unstable and intense relationships
- An unstable self-image or sense of self
- Impulsivity in areas that are potentially self-damaging
- Suicidal behavior, gestures, or threats
- Affect instability
- Feelings of emptiness
- Intense anger or difficulty controlling anger
- Transient, stress-related paranoid ideation

For gays and lesbians, these behaviors may be completely normative. It isn't surprising, for instance, that a lesbian who has spent her entire life suppressing her natural identity in an attempt to gain the acceptance of others might suffer from an unstable sense of self—or for a gay man who has felt invisible his whole life to suffer from feelings of emptiness. "Intense anger" is an appropriate reaction to years of oppression; paranoid ideation is completely understandable if one is at risk of losing one's job. You can see how all of these "symptoms" may not be indicative of BPD in gay and lesbian clients.

The Case of Shane and Fran

Shane, age 52, was the head physician of a local hospital. He contacted Rhonda for counseling with his wife, Fran. Shane was afraid Fran was going to divorce him, and he wanted to try to save the marriage.

Five years prior to Shane's making the appointment, Fran had found gay pornography on his computer, as well as chats of a sexual nature between Shane and other men. Fran confronted Shane, and he promised to stop looking at porn on the Internet and to discontinue all contact with gay men.

Three years later, however, Fran again found sexual emails on Shane's computer and he admitted to more sexual hookups with men. This time he said he was deeply depressed, which he believed drove him to return to the behaviors, and he entered individual therapy and began taking antidepressants, which helped his mood considerably. After 6 months, however, he stopped therapy, and soon thereafter, without telling Fran, he stopped his antidepressants as well. His depression returned.

A year and a half later, Fran found more gay porn and cell-phone text messages from men Shane had met up with. Fran demanded they enter couples therapy and threatened to leave the relationship. Shane threatened suicide if she left.

Shane and Fran entered therapy with Rhonda, a straight clinician, and liked her immediately. Shane commented on her professionalism and noted aloud that she had a Ph.D. Although Rhonda told Shane he could call her by her first name, he insisted on calling her "doctor." "You're the best and the only one I think can help me," Shane told her.

Shane admitted that he enjoyed looking at gay porn but said that it meant nothing other than a sexual release. "Sometimes I think I might be gay and other times I think I might be bisexual because I am so attracted sexually to you," Shane said to Fran. When Fran asked about his sexual hookups he said it was out of curiosity and nothing more. Fran felt betrayed and cheated and Shane was not able to validate or see *her* reality at all. He promised her he would stop again but Fran said she no longer trusted him. Shane responded by saying that she was overreacting, and he blamed his acting out on their constant arguing. "I had these fantasies throughout our whole marriage, but when you started up attacking me about my hours and the way I run my career, that pushed me toward acting out with other men."

During the therapy Shane would switch back and forth between blaming Fran and blaming himself for his homosexual acting out. He could not accept any form of sexual identity, as he felt nothing fit. He did not feel straight, as his sexual urges had always been toward men, and yet he enjoyed sex with his wife and looked forward to it.

Shane was unusually open about his past sexual escapades in front of Fran. "I am already busted, so I might as well confess everything," he said. He reported that he had met men through gay Internet sites, had safe sex, and engaged in nothing more in terms of relationships. He was truly confused by Fran's negative reaction. "If you would give me more sex with you, Fran I would not feel like I have to get it elsewhere. Be thankful that I don't get it from other women!"

Shane did reduce his work hours considerably during the couple's therapy and Fran was grateful. They began having sex again on a more frequent basis. However, Shane eventually started canceling appointments due to work hours. Rhonda offered him other times, none of which worked for him. One of the cancellations was less then 24 hours before the appointment, causing a missed appointment charge that Shane said he would not pay.

When the couple finally was able to come to another appointment, Shane challenged Rhonda's high fees and told her he had done some research and found therapists who would slide their fee scale for him. Fran colluded with Shane and said they wondered about Rhonda's commitment to them given what they called her "lack of flexibility."

Shane then asked Rhonda about her life and whether she was straight or gay. Rhonda's approach was to provide little information about herself, but she was willing to disclose that she was straight. Shane asked her personal questions about her marriage, to which she responded that it was not appropriate to answer but found it therapeutic to explore with him what he thought. This angered Shane and he told her, "I feel very exposed in here with you. Can't you just tell me some things to balance it out?" Rhonda declined, telling Shane it was not therapeutic. This made Shane angry and he told her that her approach was unfair.

Before the next session, Shane called Rhonda and left a message telling her in confidence that he had relapsed and met a man through the Internet and swallowed the man's ejaculate. He did not want Rhonda to mention it in the couple's session. Rhonda had made it clear to Shane and Fran that she was seeing them as a couple and that if one person told her something through a phone conversation, she would not keep it a secret. She called Shane back and told him this, which made him extremely angry.

In the next session, Rhonda urged Shane to admit to having unsafe sex. He did so, and then also disclosed that he'd had unsafe sex all along. "That explains the yeast infections I've gotten over these past years!" Fran screamed.

In the next appointment, Shane came in with personal information about where Rhonda lived, her age, and her husband's name, all of which he'd gotten from the

Internet. At this point Rhonda became fearful of Shane and sought supervision with me.

Shane and Fran: Clinical Interpretation and Treatment

Rhonda had diagnosed Shane as borderline personality disordered with depressed mood. She based this on his initial overidealization of her and then his negative transference toward her, his angry outbursts about her payment structure and schedule, and his intrusiveness in looking her information up on the Internet. She also noted the splitting he was trying to do between his wife and her around his sexual acting out and the attempted secrecy. In fact, the whole issue of his sexual identity seemed to support a BPD diagnosis in that he was unable to experience a consistent identity.

Rhonda saw Shane's workaholism and unsafe sex practices as confirming a BPD diagnosis because of their impulsivity. It did appear that Shane was characterological, but before confirming this I wanted to have Rhonda use some GAT interventions.

Rhonda said that Shane came from a strong Catholic family with rigid rules and that sexuality was never talked about. It was a matriarchal family: His mother and grandmother ruled with an iron first whereas his father was passive and spent most of his time out of the house either working or drinking.

In addition, there was an uncle who had molested a male cousin and who was referred to as the "uncle who queered the cousin." Shane had learned that this was homosexuality when, in fact, it was pedophilia.

As he had grown up with a strict mother, a rigid family style, and a homophobic message that gays are pedophiles, it was likely that Shane learned that to get his needs met, he had to go underground and do it secretly. Surely this would have provided the groundwork for him splitting part of his personality off.

Rhonda was focusing more on the marital problems because the couple insisted on dealing with "the here and now." I urged Rhonda to be stronger with them in the office in terms of keeping them focused on the underlying problems and not on the symptoms. If Shane were truly BPD, he would not be able to tolerate the insight and we would have support that he was characterological.

I asked Rhonda to translate Shane's sexual acting out behaviors as the initial stages of coming out and normalize his unsafe sexual practices as typical of stage 5 behaviors. Of course, we needed to keep in mind the fact that he hid them from Fran and put her at risk. I suggested that this might be due to his projecting his hostility toward his mother onto Fran. I thought his negative transference toward Rhonda was about his mother, too, and urged her to explore this with him.

Rhonda did all of this and Shane, caught off guard, started crying. He began admitting to having had more than just sexual contact with men. In fact, he dated and had fallen in love with a man, but the relationship had not worked out. However, he did not want to lose Fran and was willing to do whatever it took to keep the marriage.

I talked with Rhonda about interpreting his anger and depression as signs that he was keeping his sexuality closeted. I had Rhonda interpret Shane's overworking as his way of not facing his sexual desires. Rhonda started translating Shane's behaviors from the normative framework of a developing gay identity and over time Shane accepted this. However, he and Fran had to now face what would happen to their marriage.

As they ventured into the marital work with Shane coming out as a gay man, he went to gay support groups, no longer had an issue with Rhonda's fees, and stopped canceling appointments. His anger subsided and he was able to do the real work of facing his identity and his marriage.

Avoidant Personality Disorder

In the first three stages of coming out, many lesbians and gays display traits of an avoidant personality disorder. They may be reluctant to venture into the gay community and simultaneously withdraw from the straight community. The more they recognize they are gay or lesbian, the less likely they are to want to socialize with their straight friends out of fear of being discovered.

The fear of developing close relationships may be conscious or unconscious, but either way it becomes a way of life. What these clients are really doing is keeping the covert cultural sexual abuse at bay so they can avoid dealing with the trauma. With the help of GAT and group experiences, they can overcome this avoidant style. If the avoidance persists despite such treatment, it would be appropriate to start exploring personality dynamics and mood-related disorders.

Narcissistic Personality Disorder

It has long been a stereotype that gay men and lesbians are self-centered, narcissistic, and pleasure-seeking. Historically, it was believed that homosexuality was a form of sexual perversion in which the individual takes himself as a sexual object. Psychoanalysts saw a close connection between homosexuality and narcissism stemming from the view that homosexuality is a more primitive condition than heterosexuality, with impoverished object relations. The diagnosis of narcissistic personality disorder

(NPD) was commonly used among psychotherapists for gay men and some lesbians. It was concluded that one's narcissistic tendencies caused a homosexual acting out, as lesbians and gay men looked for the ideal self in a member of their own gender.

Some historic studies exploring personality disorders in gay male subjects primarily administered the psychological projective tests such as the Rorschach Ink Blots (Reiss, 1980). These studies showed that gay men were more prone to narcissism (Exner, 1969; Raychaudhuri & Mukerji, 1971).

GAT understands that the narcissism found in these projective tests are a defense rather than a personality disorder. A study done by Alexander and Nunno found that the narcissistic responses were a result of the gay men having high levels of introspection and turning inward (Alexander & Nunno, 1996). Alexander believes, and I agree, that a gay man's outward, inflated sense of self masks an underlying rage and depression associated with an inadequate and fragmented sense of self that stems from a lifelong self-hatred (Alexander, 1997).

It makes sense, then, that seeing these traits in a therapy room, a clinician would make an assessment of narcissism. Narcissism usually requires constant admiration and attention from others in order to undo feelings of inferiority. To mask shame—a negative view of the self—narcissism is used as a defense to represent a positive view of self. This is exactly what clinicians will see in their clients.

However, clinicians need to be aware of the underlying feelings of shame, guilt, and depression in gays and lesbians, which are often masked—a behavior called "the narcissism defense"—by demonstrating the very opposite feelings and behaviors in interpersonal relations. The narcissism defense is used to keep others from getting too close and from doing additional harm to an already fragile sense of self. From a gay affirmative approach, narcissism is seen as a healthy defense—a natural process of growing up gay and a vital part of healthy adaptation, which helped them get through childhood.

Depression Disorders

Sometimes what can look like a chronic depression can simply be the result of being treated as invisible throughout your life. Once clients progress through the stages of coming out, the depression lifts.

Sometimes, however, clients remain depressed even after they have come out of the closet, gotten involved in lesbian and gay social situations, and begun to feel positive about their identity. In these cases, a clinician might be tempted to give a diagnosis of dysthymia or major depression. However, before making such diagnoses, clinicians must address the client's loss of heterosexual privilege and the grief surrounding it. There may also be tremendous losses from telling long-term friends and family members. In some cases, changes in how family or friends relate to the client contribute to the depression.

If such factors are addressed and clients remain depressed for more than 6 to 8 months afterward, a diagnosis of depression should be considered. An excellent resource on depression for gays and lesbians is the book *Queer Blues: The Lesbian and Gay Guide to Overcoming Depression* (Hardin & Hall, 2001).

Anxiety Disorders

As I have already discussed, lesbian and gay children typically grow up in a state of constant hypervigilance, worrying that they will be discovered and humiliated. It is a severe threat to one's psychological and sometimes physical well-being to keep such a secret and then to reveal it to others. Adult clients may find it difficult to control or stop their worrying. Ruminating about what will happen when they come out is common, as is excessive worry, feeling on edge, and muscle tension and sleep disturbance. All of this will usually abate after clients successfully pass their identity crisis and accept their gay or lesbian orientation.

Bipolar/Hypomanic Disorders

Research shows that there is no difference among gays or lesbians and heterosexuals in terms of frequency of bipolar disorders (National Institute of Mental Heath, 1987). The coming out process—especially stage 5—can look hypomanic or bipolar. Clients may do many things that resemble the symptoms of hypomania and then plummet into depression when things don't work out as they hoped.

The Case of Jonathon

Jonathon was a 38-year-old married man with two children ages 7 and 9. His wife was pregnant with their third child. Jonathon reported that his marriage was happy and he did not want to leave his wife even though he had secretive sexual fantasies about men. "They're just sexual kinks that I can take care of online," he said.

One night, however, Jonathon was online in a chat room and started a conversation with Dave, who lived in another state. They stayed up until 6 A.M. talking. The next night, the same thing happened. This continued for weeks, and Jonathon, once the quintessential devoted father and loyal husband, began missing work and neglecting his responsibilities as a parent and spouse.

Realizing that he was developing romantic feelings for Dave, Jonathon decided to arrange to meet him. He told his wife it was a business trip and left her to care for their children alone. The relationship soon became more serious, and Jonathon fell in love, spending countless nights online, on the phone, and traveling to visit Dave—all during his wife's pregnancy. Convinced he was having an affair, his wife confronted him, but Jonathon denied everything.

Jonathon ran up credit card bills, missed payments on other bills, and was completely focused on nothing but Dave. He started using party drugs and traveling to attend circuit parties across the country. He was scarcely available for his wife's doctor appointments around her pregnancy.

When his wife complained and expressed her anger, Jonathon told her that "everything had always been about her" throughout their marriage and that "now it was time for him." He denied that his behaviors were affecting her or the family in the ways she said they were. As he put it, he was just finally creating a "slice of life" for himself.

Eventually Dave told Jonathon that he had met someone else. Jonathon was devastated. Angry with Dave for "leading him on and then dumping him," Jonathon fell into a deep despair. His wife was about to have their baby and he was never more depressed.

Jonathon now realized how much he had put at risk. His job was in jeopardy because of his absences; his marriage and his relationship with his children had suffered immeasurably. He found himself hopeless and helpless and crashed into a deep depression.

Jonathon: Clinical Interpretation and Treatment

Jonathon's therapist was not aware that Jonathon had been looking at online gay porn, and she was under the impression that he had never previously experienced sexual feelings for men: He had told her that he met Dave through work and that it was "a fluke" that he felt this way for another man. She diagnosed him as having undergone a hypomanic episode, explaining that he met all the criteria: inflated self-esteem and grandiosity while not thinking about the effects on his wife and children, decreased need for sleep, and excessive involvement in pleasurable activities with a high potential for negative consequences.

The problem with this diagnosis was that Jonathon never had experienced an episode like this before, nor had anyone his family. Jonathon was not hypomanic; he was in stage 5 of coming out and had fallen into romantic love.

Like with any new relationship, Jonathon had a different experience with Dave.

For years Jonathon had experienced online sexual hookups that were meaningless in terms of emotion. Each man served as a physical release and nothing more. Dave, on the other hand, brought out an emotional side that Jonathon did not know he had. The more contact he had with Dave, the more he wanted to see him. Just like anyone who falls into romantic love, Jonathon needed less sleep, became consumed with the object of his affection, and felt euphoric due to the internal chemicals of phenylethylamine and dopamine, making him appear to have an inflated self-esteem.

While this was happening, Jonathon was also coming out. So in addition to experiencing all the "symptoms" of romantic love, he entered his gay adolescence and abandoned all responsibilities. From this perspective, it made sense that Jonathon behaved in the way he did. Dave's breaking off the relationship jolted Jonathon back to reality, and he finally realized what had happened to his life.

Addictions (Chemical and Behavioral)

As discussed in earlier chapters, clients going through a gay or lesbian adolescence may seem to exhibit addictive behavior. They often act out with drugs and alcohol and sexually experiment with numerous partners. When we watch young adults on a college campus, we might easily be able to diagnose them as alcoholics, drug addicts, and promiscuous sex addicts. Their behaviors and lives appear this way. But when they leave college and start settling down, their profiles begin to look very different. The same is true for lesbian and gays—the difference being that they experience this period when they come out, which may not happen until well into adulthood.

If addictive behaviors persist one year after the client has gone through all of the coming out process, a diagnosis may be appropriate. Some lesbians and gays do go on to become addicts trapped in the disease and unable to pull themselves out, as I discuss later in this chapter.

Obsessive-Compulsive Personality Disorder

Some of your gay and lesbian clients may be obsessed with orderliness, perfectionism, and control. They may be overly conscientious and inflexible about matters of morality, ethics, and values. Those who are struggling with whether or not to come out may be able to cite verse after verse of religious doctrine. All of this is typical of obsessive-compulsive personality disorder (OCD). The reality, however, is that many of these clients engage in these behaviors as a way to keep their sexual identity suppressed, and all of the symptoms fall away after they come out of the closet.

Establishing a Differential Diagnosis

Establishing a differential diagnosis is essential in working with any client, but it is especially important when working with gays and lesbians. Although the effects of covert cultural sexual abuse may mimic mental health disorder symptoms in many cases, there *are* times when gay and lesbian clients do suffer from a true mental health disorder that is independent from the trauma of covert cultural sexual abuse.

In working with lesbians and gays you must determine whether the symptoms are the result of covert cultural sexual abuse or indicate a true mental health disorder. If you always assume that the symptoms are the result of the trauma of growing up gay and only later consider other possibilities, you may not effectively help the client. Conversely, if you begin by only considering mental health disorders and pursue GAT later, you will probably miss important issues that need to be addressed. Striking a balance can be difficult; excellent data-gathering and history-taking skills are essential.

When clients are unresponsive to gay affirmative interventions, it is important to examine other factors that may be stalling therapy. This was the case with Ben.

The Case of Ben

Ben, a 35-year-old gay male, came to me after a breakup. Ben told me he was deeply in love with this man and could not understand what had made his partner leave him. Their relationship had lasted a total of 3 months. In fact, Ben had never sustained a relationship beyond 6 months, which bothered him. He was frustrated with the gay community and told me that he wished he were born straight, as women would be more interested in him and what he had to offer than gay men seemed to be. He was referring to his professional and financial success.

Ben was likeable and charismatic. He told me that in relationships he was generous—perhaps to a fault. He said he "wined and dined" the men he dated and enjoyed being able to provide for any man he could meet. He also told me he did the same for friends and even some strangers. He took pride in his generosity.

As I took a background history, Ben explained that his parents were Mormons and unaccepting of homosexuality. He remembered his father telling the family, "No son of mine is ever going to be a queer," after seeing Ben playing with Barbie dolls. When Ben came out at the age of 19, his father kicked him out of the house. His mother sent him money, however, as Ben was in school and could not support himself.

When Ben was 24, his father reconciled with him and their relationship became closer, even though his father still did not accept his homosexuality. They agreed to disagree. Ben never brought up his homosexuality and they never asked.

Ben's mother continued to send him money, which now paid the mortgage on his house. When I asked him why she continued to give him money and he continued to accept it despite the fact that he had a well-paying job, Ben said, "That is the least she can do for having married my father, with all he has done to me in my life as a gay man."

Ben frequently began his sessions with me by asking if his clothes and haircuts looked expensive. "This is what people wear and how they look in New York," he explained. He told me he shopped at the finest places, getting everything tailored to his body. He worked out five times a week and often talked about how he had to resize his clothes because he was growing out of them from bulking up. When people made fun of his clothes he saw them as being envious.

Ben's family did not take an interest in his work, his financial success, or his physical build. Instead, his mother would tell him he looked "overweight" and physically unusual and his brothers would tease him about his "girly" designer hair-cuts and shoes. Ben cried as he told me that this type of abuse occurred throughout his entire life.

Ben: Clinical Interpretation and Treatment

It was difficult for me to determine whether Ben was truly narcissistic, was reacting to family of origin dynamics, or was suffering from the trauma of covert cultural sexual abuse. He seemed to have inflated self-esteem, a grandiose sense of importance, and a sense of entitlement. He required excessive admiration by me and thought that others envied—or should envy—him. In working with Ben I kept the NPD diagnosis in mind but saw his need for constant affirmation and admiration as the result of the rejection he experienced by his family. I used the trauma framework of covert cultural sexual abuse regarding the rejection he experienced in childhood about his atypical gender expression as well as the spiritual abuse by the Mormon religion in which he was raised.

I decided that group therapy might help Ben explore and heal his relational wounds, and I discussed this with him. I knew I was taking a risk because if he did suffer from true NPD, he would not last very well in group therapy. Ben agreed to attend the group therapy, telling me he wanted to stop repeating the relationship patterns he had.

Ben came to the group sessions dressed in provocative clothing that showed off his muscular arms, legs, and torso. Even during the winter months, he wore shorts and tank-tops. He talked about how he was able to find a "bargain" and shared the cost of the clothes, which were high-priced even with the discount. He asked for time in group each week and if he did not get it, he would complain the following week that the group was "too big in terms of the number of gay men" and that the time was not divided right by me as the facilitator.

Despite Ben's grandiosity, the group liked him and related well to him initially. They gently gave him feedback about his consistent need for attention and "showi-ness." Their interest was to help him drop his false sense of self and "get real" in the group. He told them they must be jealous of how much he had achieved. This was not the case, of course, and the group members told him how attractive he looked and how they enjoyed his sense of fashion. What they did not like was his leading with that. Ben also talked openly about how his mother made his house payments and the group confronted him on his sense of entitlement. Ben felt increasingly rejected by the members of the group, just as he had felt in his family.

After several weeks, Ben started missing some group sessions. When asked why he was not coming, he said he had to travel to New York to purchase the latest clothing by the fashion designers. When the group and I challenged his reasons for missing sessions, he interpreted it again as jealousy.

One night Ben came to group and informed everyone that he felt it was time to move on and receive a "different style of therapy." He said that neither the group nor I were meeting his needs and that he was leaving to see a "better trained" therapist.

The group responded angrily to this. Some called Ben a "bitchy queen" and said they expected more from him. Others felt dismissed and used by him. As the facilita-tor, I used these responses as a way for the other gay men to address what Ben was bringing up for them. I asked them to explore that instead of attacking Ben. Ben, however, interpreted my attempt to protect him as a desire to take the focus off of him. When I tried to explain that I wanted him to hear their responses but in a non-attacking way, he became angry and stormed out of the group before it ended.

I never heard from Ben again, despite my attempts to contact him. In retrospect, I realize that he truly had a narcissistic personality disorder. Had I worked with him longer in individual therapy, I would have probably seen more of this and not placed him in group therapy. However, the group therapy highlighted his narcissism in a way that might not have been as evident in individual therapy.

The Case of Lynn

Lynn sought therapy after a breakup with her partner, Andrea, of 7 years. Lynn was 30 and Andrea was her first love. According to Lynn, the breakup had "come out of nowhere." They were living together, planning on having children, and supported by each other's families. Lynn never suspected that Andrea was considering leaving.

One day Andrea came home and told Lynn she had fallen in love with another woman. Lynn was devastated. She begged Andrea to go to couple's therapy but Andrea refused. In less than a week Andrea moved her belongings out and moved in with her new love. Lynn sank into a deep depression and went into individual therapy with a straight therapist.

During her therapy, Lynn began taking antidepressants and engaged in weekly sessions. Over the next 8 months she cycled between getting better and then relapsing back into her depression whenever she received a call or email from Andrea. She was suffering from sleep problems and weight loss. She would regularly drive by Andrea's new home with the hope of getting whatever glimpse of Andrea she could.

Lynn's depression was triggered whenever she was reminded of Andrea—whenever a piece of mail was not forwarded to Andrea or when one of her friends mentioned something about Andrea and her new partner. Lynn asked her friends to stop talking about Andrea, and she asked Andrea to stop contacting her, but she still found herself reminded of her and would regress back into depression.

As Lynn started dating again she found numerous dysfunctional women and blamed the lesbian community for being so "messed up." She lamented lesbians' "serial monogamy" and inability to commit. She talked about how single lesbians made moves on partnered lesbians and didn't value other's relationships.

Lynn's therapist explored the possibility of covert cultural sexual abuse and PTSD expressed through internalized homophobia, which Lynn insisted she did not have. She explored Lynn's growing up years around being lesbian, but Lynn reported no dysfunction within her family. She said she felt loved and close to both of her parents. When she came out to her family, they were accepting and loving and just wanted her to be happy. When she partnered with Andrea, her mother embraced their relationship and developed a close relationship with her.

Sadly, Lynn's mother had died from an aggressive return of breast cancer a year before the breakup with Andrea. Lynn was devastated but at least had Andrea at her side. Now she had lost Andrea, too, and the therapist worked with her around the grief of losing the two most important people in her life.

After 2 years, however, Lynn still was not improving. Her therapist now began to wonder whether Lynn's inability to move on from the breakup was due to growing up lesbian, even though Lynn had said her family had always been supportive. She began using a trauma-based framework in her treatment. But this didn't work either, so she sought supervision with me.

Lynn: Clinical Interpretation and Treatment

When the therapist talked about Lynn's mother's death, I asked for more information about Lynn's relationship with her mother. The therapist explained that they truly were close and that Lynn felt loved, supported, and affirmed by her mother throughout her life.

Lynn's mother had been diagnosed with breast cancer when Lynn was 5. It was treated and stayed in remission throughout Lynn's childhood, but the family nonetheless remained fearful that it would return.

I asked the therapist to talk more about this with Lynn. When she did, Lynn said that she had been frightened most of her life that her mother would die. This turned out to be the real issue: Lynn was struggling with symptoms of PTSD not from growing up lesbian or losing her partner but rather from the anticipated loss of her mother throughout her entire childhood. When the therapist started talking about this with Lynn, everything clicked and seemed to make sense to her. It explained why Lynn could not let go of Andrea and held on longer than expected. It helped her understand that she was reenacting what she did with her mother—which was stay close and not let her mother out of her sight for fear of losing her.

Lynn gradually began to improve. Each time she had an episode of depression triggered by learning something about Andrea, she recognized it as related to her past and was able to talk herself through it.

To make accurate diagnoses you need to look at the whole picture and rule out as much as possible. As you help clients through their problems and symptoms, the bigger picture will become clearer and you will be more able to assess whether your clients have a mental health disorder or whether they just appeared to have one because of their situation as gay or lesbian.

Dual Diagnosis

In general, GAT explores the trauma, shame, alienation, isolation, and neglect that gays and lesbians grow up with. Important as this is, therapists need to recognize that gay and lesbian clients who seek treatment may have other issues as well. Because of the historical pattern of pathologizing homosexuality (discussed in Chapter 1), GAT has tended to minimize assessing and diagnosing *any* pathology and has deemphasized emotional disorders that are not related to growing up lesbian and gay.

There can sometimes be too much emphasis, however, on the trauma of growing up gay and the coming out process, leading therapists to overlook or mistreat problems that are not directly related to the client's sexual orientation. GAT clinicians must remember that lesbians and gays suffer from the same mental health disorders that straight clients do.

Some clients have emotional and personality disorders that, I believe, result from a lifetime of closeted dissociation, adapting to the sexual/romantic orientation that others expect. Others have personality disorders that would have been present regardless of the client's sexual orientation. In some cases, the suppression of one's sexual identity also suppresses other problems, which do not surface until the identity does.

In cases of true dual diagnosis, treatment in addition to GAT may be needed. This is sometimes the case even when the mental health disorder has been triggered by the trauma of growing up gay, as patterns of behavior can become entrenched over the years and extend to areas of clients' lives that have little to do with their sexual identity. For example, a client whose depression was triggered in response to a hostile school environment may find that his depression returns every September long after he has finished school and begun his adult professional life. For this client, antidepressant medication in addition to GAT may be the best solution.

The same is often true in cases of chemical dependency. While clients are in the closet, they are vulnerable to developing chemical dependencies or patterns of chemical abuse. In the early stages of coming out, they may keep their gay identities suppressed by drinking too much or using marijuana. During the socialization process, most gays and lesbians frequent bars where they are vulnerable to drinking too much to avoid their anxiety.

Sometimes chemical abuse is simply a stage and naturally tapers off with the passing of stage 5. Other times, however, it may develop into alcoholism and has to be treated as such.

The Case of Esther

Esther, a 45-year-old single woman, came to me with the recognition she was lesbian and wanted to come out. She had never married or acted on any of her feelings toward women. She was now ready to come out and live as a lesbian.

Esther's childhood was riddled with shame from both her parents and her brothers. Teased for not being "feminine" enough, she was a tomboy at heart. She always thought it was from having four older brothers and trying to keep up. Her father and mother wanted her to be more feminine and forced her to wear dresses and have her hair done at the beauty shop with her mother. She rebelled against this as a little girl until one day she saw the contempt and anger in her mother's eyes. She remembered this vividly, and from that day forward she decided conform to whatever her mother wanted to get the love she so desperately needed from her. She wore the dresses her mother picked out for her, started using makeup, and stopped playing sports. She told me that at points she even fooled herself into thinking that this was who she was—a girly girl just like her mother wanted.

After finishing a Ph.D. in education, Esther decided to become a nun. She was in the convent for 5 years and during this time recognized that this was not the life for her. She left on bad terms with the church and returned to live at home with her parents at the age of 35. She became a teacher in a local school district and was much happier in that profession.

During college and her time in the convent, Esther began drinking. Even after she returned home, her drinking increased to the point that she was experiencing blackouts and passing out. She received her first drunken driving charge at the age of 40 and went to classes mandated by the court. Drinking was "all she had left" to make her own choices around, Esther told me. She said her drinking had subsided, that she was able to control it, and that she no longer experienced blackouts.

During therapy we explored Esther's childhood, and she was able to address the covert cultural sexual abuse she suffered at the hands of her mother. She recognized that the reason she became a nun was to keep her lesbianism at bay and suppress her sexual urges. During therapy with me she began going to lesbian bars and events and enjoyed her experiences. Over the next year she came out to her family and friends. Although her mother was disappointed, she ultimately accepted Esther as a lesbian.

Esther denied that she was alcoholic and explained that she had started drinking heavily again from being at lesbian events. She told me that the lesbian community also drank heavily, particularly those who played baseball with her during the summer.

I asked Esther about her family patterns surrounding chemical use. She reported no family history of drinking or drug abuse. She said she drank heavily during college but was able to stop for long periods of time. She also said she was able to recreationally drink when "she wanted to" but admitted that she could drink a fifth of vodka in a night with her friends.

Esther refused to go for chemical dependency treatment, believing her drinking was a stage of the coming out process and that after she stabilized and settled down as a lesbian her drinking would subside. I was not so sure and challenged her thinking, but this made her angry, so I agreed to work with her and see how it went.

The following year Esther received another drunken driving charge. Now she finally had to face the fact that although the drinking was initially about suppressing her lesbian tendencies and masking her core self, she now had a real problem. Esther was an alcoholic.

Esther: Clinical Interpretation and Treatment

Mandated by the court, Esther went for treatment at an intensive outpatient program at a local chemical dependency center. We agreed she would finish chemical dependency therapy there and then return to therapy with me. The staff advised her to stay closeted—that the other patients would not take kindly to having a lesbian in their group. Their intention was to protect her but instead Esther was insulted. She did come out in the group and she received much criticism from the other patients, just as the staff had warned her. The staff did not protect her, and Esther called me, sobbing, to ask what she should do.

I advised her to confront the staff and to sign a release for me to talk to them but she was determined not to return. She feared she would relapse if she complied with my advice. I recommended that she return to therapy with me and also attend gay and lesbian A.A. meetings. I gave her a list of A.A. locations and she followed through on going.

During the next year Esther was able to stay sober and go to meetings. Recognizing that suppressing her lesbianism had contributed to her alcoholism, Esther hoped that resolving this would prevent her from becoming a problem drinker again, and she started drinking once again. Within 3 months she was back to abusing alcohol.

This time, however, Esther had begun dating a woman who was also in A.A., and the woman told her that if she did not stop, she would leave her. Faced with the loss of this relationship, Esther finally accepted that regardless of how her drinking began, she truly was an alcoholic and could not return to social drinking.

Working With Lesbians and Gays

In this book I have tried to illustrate the various presenting problems and concerns typical of gay and lesbian clients. Although I have tried to be as thorough as possible, there are many issues and treatment approaches I did not cover. Ethnic and minority issues, for example, may intersect with gay and lesbian identity issues in myriad ways that are beyond the scope of this book. I also did not speak about the issues of bisexuality or transgendered individuals. This is not because I don't believe they exist, because they do. I rather wanted keep the focus on lesbians and gays to prevent the book from becoming unwieldy in length. There are many good books on bisexuality and transgender issues, and I encourage readers to refer to them.

What I hope to have conveyed in this book is the importance of not assuming that gays and lesbians suffer problems simply *because* they are lesbian or gay but to rather consider these issues as stemming from the trauma involved in being invisible, neglected, and ignored in a predominately heterosexist world. Many of the issues facing gays and lesbians are connected in some way to covert cultural sexual abuse and the trauma of growing up gay. That said, there are also many clients who suffered covert cultural sexual abuse but did not experience it as the type of trauma I have addressed throughout this book. These clients are much like those individuals who were sexually, physically, and verbally abused but seem to have the resilience to get past it and not have it contaminate their lives.

The most important thing we can do as clinicians is learn as much as we can about the clients we are sitting across from. You now have the framework and tools to conduct GAT. Deciding whether GAT is enough or if there are other issues that need to be addressed is something you will have to feel out on your own with each client.

Clients will help you know what direction to pursue as you continue checking in with them. It is important that they feel they can be honest with you even if it means telling you your style or approach is not for them. This may mean you need to refine your skills or it may mean you are not the right therapist. My goal in writing this book is to let you, the straight therapist, know that you *can* be enough for your lesbian and gay clients, as long as you remain educated about the particular issues they face.

Glossary

> SOPHIA (*to Blanche*): Jean is a lesbian.
> BLANCHE: I've never known one personally,
> but isn't Danny Thomas one?
> DOROTHY: Not *Lebanese*, Blanche. Lesbian!
> — Transcript from an Emmy-winning
> episode of *The Golden Girls*

What if your lesbian client comes in and says the following:

I'm looking for a relationship with a lipstick lesbian, not a chapstick one. I don't want some militant dyke who's all butch and is attracted to me for political reasons! I'm not into that butch/femme thing. I just want a normal relationship with an effeminate woman like me.

I once dated this woman I met at Womynfest who turned out to be a granola dyke. On our first date she was packing, and I was horrified. I told her I was not into that. But I was actually very sexually attracted to her, and that was a plus because in my last relationship, we experienced lesbian bed death, and I don't want to go there again. Unfortunately, though, I found out later that she was married to a man, using him as her beard, so I broke up with her.

My best friend—my ex, that is—tells me I'm too picky about the type of women I look for in a partner. But what does she know? She lived for a while as an ex-gay. That whole reparative therapy stuff is awful, and it's what caused our breakup. I'm looking through the entire LGBTQ community for the perfect woman, who is not questioning, isn't from Dykes on Bikes, isn't a separatist, and isn't doing an Anne Heche on me.

Or what if one of your gay male clients says:

I went barebacking last night with a leather daddy I've seen at the tubs. I got sick of the circuit party I was at so I went to a leather bar. I did some Tina along with some Special K and he did some poppers. The guy's lover was there, but they have an open relationship, so my tricking sex with his BF wasn't an issue. The leather daddy was not a bit Nellie and he was a great top. I have been with too many queeny guys who just want to bottom.

I told my fag hag friend Michelle about this, but she just doesn't understand. Michelle is not a friend of Dorothy, but I consider her family even though she's a breeder. Michelle is more like a drag queen than anything else. She has the best gaydar and has helped find me boyfriends as a result.

When working with gay and lesbian clients, it's imperative to get the terms correct. Just as when working with any minority—religious, ethnic, or otherwise—making sure your vocabulary is medically accurate and politically correct creates a safe, supportive space for your clients.

The gay male and lesbian communities use different terminologies and jargon in each community. Of course, some overlap exists between gays and lesbians, but each group has its own unique slang, "code" words, and euphemisms, and in cases of overlap, the terms may have different connotations for each community.

Over the years, other minority groups have changed how they want to be referred to in an attempt to change how they're treated. For example, African-Americans went from being called "Negro" and "colored" to "black" and "people of color" and finally to the current politically correct term *African-American*. Today, the word *queer*, once a pejorative term, is often used in a positive way. Dozens of books and articles are published with *queer* in their titles, and the term has come into common, affirmative usage by lesbians and gays as well.

It is always best to ask how your client self-identifies and use the same terms he or she uses, even if you feel uncomfortable with them on a personal level. For example, I don't personally like to use the term *homosexual*. But when my clients identify themselves as "homosexual" and dislike the terms *gay* or *lesbian*, then that's the word I use. The word *gay* is affirmative and refers to a life of being out and open about one's sexual/romantic orientation. However, many people in the beginning stages of coming out feel uncomfortable with the term. Similarly, some lesbians prefer to be called "gay" rather than "lesbian," whereas others find the term offensive when used to describe women.

It is also important to understand, as a straight therapist, that some "reclaimed" terms used by gays and lesbians to refer to themselves are considered offensive when used by straight people. For example, some lesbians call themselves "dykes" and some gay men call themselves "fags," but these same lesbians and gay men would take offense if a straight person called them that. (In fact, there is some disagreement in the gay and lesbian community itself about these terms, with some gays and lesbians finding them offensive regardless of whether it's another gay person using them.) In these cases, straight therapists should *not* use the same terminology the client uses, just as a Caucasian person should never use the "n-word" to refer to African-Americans, even if some African-Americans use the word themselves. If you are unsure about whether your using a term might be considered offensive, it is best to not use it until you have established a rapport and can ask the client how he or she feels about your using it.

I don't pretend to know everything that exists in the gay and lesbian community, or cover it all within this book. But I can give you, a straight practitioner, a good start. When clients enter your office, you'll be up to running speed, equipped with the basic information you need you to know. I've heard numerous clients say they didn't want to teach their straight therapists about the gay and lesbian community—or were tired of having to do so. All they need to hear are errors in your language to assume you are uninformed or misinformed, patronizing, or—even worse—that you'll try to change them.

As you grow familiar with these terms, check in with your own countertransference. What are your feelings about these words and their connotation? Then consider how you will feel responding to a lesbian or gay client using these words. Better you use this chapter for checking your own judgments and feelings than waiting to do so in "real-time" sessions with clients.

Mainstream Terminology

The following terms are used by the mainstream population to describe things pertinent not only to gays and lesbians but also to heterosexuals.

Homoerotic—Usually, sexual arousal or desire for a member of the same gender on a subtle level. Also can be used to describe the enjoyment of watching or participating in same-gender sexual activity.

Sexual Behavior—The acts that one regularly performs when aroused.

Sexual Fantasy—Imagining or play-acting various sexual acts and behaviors, either to facilitate masturbation or to "jump-start" arousal with a partner.

Sexual Orientation—The innate, main focus of one's sexuality, often with the understanding that a sexual "orientation" is also affectionate, spiritual, emotional, relational, and psychological. It is enduring, lasting, and unchanging.

Sexual Preference—What makes up one's arousal template and brings one sexual stimulation and fulfillment; not necessarily limited to orientation, but often includes preferred sex acts and a personal affinity for certain body or personality types. See also *sexual preference* in the glossary section on derogatory and offensive terms.

Terms of "Enqueerment"

These terms are used within the lesbian and gay community and by heterosexuals who are gay affirmative.

Allies—Heterosexuals who confront heterosexism, homophobia, and heterosexual privilege in themselves and others out of a concern for the well-being of lesbian, gay, bisexual, and transgender people.

Ex-Gay—Someone who does not want to be homosexual and believes he or she has "changed" his or her sexual and romantic orientation to heterosexuality; a popular term in reparative therapies.

Ex-Ex-Gay—Those who have been through the reparative therapies, realized the sham of "sexual reorientation," have accepted their homosexuality, and now self-identify affirmatively.

GLBTQ—An umbrella acronym to include everyone within the community (gay, lesbian, bisexual, transgender, questioning). Also can be LGBTQ.

Pridefest—A yearly local gathering of gays and lesbians where businesses and organizations can share information. Often, but not always, held the same weekend as a gay pride march.

Queer—Originally a verbally abusive word to put down gays and lesbians, now a largely political term to describe gay, lesbian, biattractional, and transgendered persons. It is an umbrella term for the gay community and has been growing in popularity. Usually it is used solely in a political context to refer to people who strive to subvert the heterosexual paradigm; for example, you might refer to an activist or very open gay man or lesbian as "queer," or you might use it to describe the community as a whole (the "queer community"), but you probably wouldn't use it to describe an individual who is still closeted. Unlike the terms *dyke* and *fag*, *queer* is generally considered acceptable for use by gay friendly heterosexuals (although not all lesbians and gay men may feel this way).

Self-Identification

I once had a client who stopped me during our fourth session and said, "Joe, I am bi, not gay. You keep calling me gay." I apologized. Frustrated, he said, "I even checked the bisexual box on your intake form. Did you read it?" My lapse with this client reminded me how easy it is to overlook the individual client's language—even on such an important topic as self-identification.

Biattractional or Bisexual—A term used to describe someone who forms emotional, romantic, or erotic attraction to members of either gender, or who has the potential to form it. Many of these individuals prefer to call themselves simply "bi," as it reflects their romantic interests in members of the same gender whereas bisexual emphasizes the sexual aspect.

Bi-Curious—A term used to describe heterosexual individuals who wonder what it's like to be sexual with a member of the same gender.

Gay—An affirmative word to describe men who form their primary romantic and sexual relationships exclusively with other men including affectional, psychological, spiritual, and erotic attraction to their own gender. Some women prefer to be identified as gay as well.

Hetero-Emotional—Emotionally attracted to the opposite gender but sexually attracted to the same gender.

Heterosexual—Having an enduring affectional, psychological, spiritual, and romantic, erotic attraction to the opposite gender exclusively.

Homo-Emotional—Emotionally attracted to the same gender but sexually attracted to the opposite gender.

Homosexual—A mostly outdated and offensive term historically referring to a lesbian or gay male. Because of the clinical history of the word's being used in the "disease" model of homosexuality, it has become offensive, just as *Negro* and *colored* have for African-Americans. Though still in use as a clinical and technical term (and used by reparative therapists and religious organizations), it's not generally used by lesbians or gay men, except those in the early stages of coming out.

Lesbian—An affirmative word for women who form their primary romantic and sexual relationships with other women and have an enduring affectional, psychological, spiritual, and erotic attraction to someone of their own sex. The word derives from the Greek island of Lesbos, where the poet Sappho lived, circa 600 BCE, and wrote many love poems to other women. It's not clear when the word *lesbian* was first used to describe women who love other women, but it can be traced back to the 1800s and came into popular use during the feminist era of the 1960s and '70s. Some lesbians prefer to be identified as "gay" rather than "lesbian."

MSM—An umbrella term for gay, straight, or bisexual men who have sex with other men. It does not involve romance and often is used to describe men on the "down low."

Questioning—Being undecided or confused about one's sexual and romantic orientation; often used by gays and lesbians in the early stages of coming out. Also used by some bisexuals who are beginning to explore bisexuality.

Transgendered—An umbrella term for those who cross-dress (transvestites) or are going through gender reassignment (surgical transsexuals). Also sometimes used to define people who are simply expanding the societally imposed definitions of female and male genders. This is more an issue of identity, not homosexuality. Transsexuals and transvestites may be heterosexual, homosexual, or bisexual.

Many transsexuals do not identify as transgendered at all. Their statement is: "I have not *become* a man or women—I was *always* one, just in the wrong body. Now my outside matches my inside, and I am still attracted to the same gender as before."

WSW—An umbrella term for lesbian, straight, or bisexual women who have sex with other women. It can involve romance or just sexual behavior.

Terms of Endearment

Heterosexual couples describe themselves in standard and simple terms—"husband and wife," "boyfriend and girlfriend," and "fiancé and fiancée." Betty Berzon wrote of the terms *husband* and *wife* by recognizing that much is conveyed in these words and you are informed immediately as to who they are and what they mean to each other for the rest of their lives (Berzon, 2004). There's no standard governing which word is best for each individual or couple. It will be unique to the individual and couple you treat.

Boyfriend or Girlfriend—A term that many gay and lesbian couples use even when they've been together for many years.

Husband or Wife—Terms being used now that gay civil unions are allowed in some areas. Some couples use these terms regardless of whether there are legal sanctions or whether they've had a formal wedding ceremony—religious or otherwise. Other couples may reject these terms on the grounds that they feed into a heterosexist marriage model.

Life Partner—A term used by people who feel that *partner* is too ambiguous and that the addition of the word *life* better reflects the relational part of their relationship.

Lover—A term more commonly used in the 1960s, '70s, and '80s by both gays and lesbians. Many now feel it refers only to the sexual side of the relationship.

LTR—Acronym for long-term relationship.

Partner—A term that originated when gays and lesbians began legalizing their relationships, creating wills and power of attorney. The then-popular word, *lover,* did not work for legal documents. Now *partner* has become common outside of legalese as well.

Significant Other—This term, commonly used by unmarried heterosexual couples living together, has been adopted by many lesbian and gay couples who want to recognize the true nature of their unmarried relationship.

Terminology Specific to Gay Men

Gay men organize their lives around sexual expression more than lesbians tend to do. Thus, the words and expressions specific to gay men often involve sexuality.

From the 1960s to the 1980s, before the Internet, gays used nonverbal signals to indicate their sexual preferences. For example, a man wearing a tattoo, band, earring, or other jewelry on his right side was a bottom. If these things were on the left, the man was a top. Gay men also wore handkerchiefs whose colors signified certain sexual practices. Wearing these colors in the left or right hip pocket would alert potential partners if the wearer was a top or bottom. The system finally grew so complex that some enterprising soul issued an informative poster, often seen in gay bars, headlined "The Ultimate Hankie Code"! These nonverbal signs are rarely used today due to gay men's ability to communicate in less pressured environments, such as Internet chat rooms.

Barebacking—Having anal sex without a condom. Gay men state that there are benefits to barebacking, which include increased sensation to the penis, a greater feeling of closeness to their partner, and more spontaneity. The sex seems "unplanned." The danger, of course, is an increased risk of STD infection.

Bathhouses/Baths/Tubs—Environments where gay men go to have sexual contact with one another. Socialization is minimal to nonexistent. Gay men "cruise" each other, enjoy sexual contact and release, and then leave. The bathhouse usually rents lockers and rooms. A swimming pool and weights may also be available. Men walk the halls wearing towels or nothing. Group sex or one-on-one hookups can occur anywhere, but usually in a room or steam room. Often gay pornography is shown on multiple televisions.

Though gay men commonly frequent bathhouses, a stigma exists against it. Gay men who go to the baths are looked down upon and judged harshly for being promiscuous by other gay men, even those who have frequented the baths.

Bear—A gay man who is "beefy," if not overweight, and usually (though not always) hairy as well.

Bottom—A term often used to describe the partner who is penetrated during anal sex, but can also describe the passive partner in a relationship. There is much negative social stigma attached to be being a bottom, which is why many gay men do not admit it. It's often equated with effeminacy, even though it inherently has nothing to do with mannerisms or gender expression.

Bug-Chasing—Purposely seeking to be infected with HIV. There are so-called bug-chasing or gift-giving parties where men go with the intention of getting infected or infecting others.

Bug Juice—A term used by bug chasers to talk about HIV-infected sperm.

Circuit Parties—Highly organized parties attended by thousands of gay men from all over the world. A block of events is scheduled throughout the weekend, with numerous parties and one main party on Saturday night. These parties feature many "recreational" drugs along with promiscuous barebacking sex, but they can otherwise be an entertaining way for gay men to literally dance all night and have fun.

Closed Loop Groups—Underground clubs frequented by heterosexually married men who want a boyfriend (also heterosexually married) on the side. The men remain "monogamous" to both their wives and their boyfriends. Each man knows of the other's secret life, but their wives don't.

Cruising—Seeking contact in a public place such as a park, rest area, bathroom, or bathhouse to hook up with another gay man for sex and nothing more. This promiscuous behavior, very businesslike and genitally focused, is the opposite of flirting; it is not relational and there is no emotion involved. Today, most cruising is done online.

Many younger gay men consider cruising to be something of the past that older gay men and closeted gay men on the downlow did, which is predominately true.

Drag Queen—A gay man who likes to dress in women's clothing, often in public or as part of a theatrical performance.

Gift-Giving—See *bug-chasing*.

Leather Daddy—An older gay man who wears leather and often, though not always, practices bondage/dominance (B/D) or sadomasochism (S/M). Leather daddies like to take care of their "boys." This is all about role playing and leather drag.

Nellie—A gay man who is thought to be innately effeminate.

Otter—Gay men within the "bear" community who are who are slim and hairy. They are attracted to bears and bears are attracted to them.

Queeny—A gay man who is judged to be innately effeminate; can also be used to describe behavior that is catty and stereotypically female in a negative sense.

Rent Boy—A man over 18 who is paid for sex by other men; otherwise known as a hustler, male prostitute, or sex worker.

Rice Queen—A gay man interested primarily, if not exclusively, in Asian men.

Rimming—A common sexual practice, also known as analingus, wherein a partner gives or receives oral stimulation to the anus. Although some straight men do this to women (as popularized on the show *Sex and the City*), it's more common among gay men.

Size Queen—A gay man primarily attracted to genitally well-endowed men.

Tea Dance—Gay male parties that involve drinking and dancing and usually begin at 4 P.M.; considered preparties before the bigger parties at the clubs later in the evening. The term is derived from what historically were called "tearooms"—restrooms where men met for hookups (Humphreys, 1970).

Top—A term often used to describe the penetrating partner during anal sex. Usually the top is also the one who is orally fellated and may not reciprocate. Can also describe the dominant partner in a gay relationship. This dynamic is agreed upon in the relationship and not imposed, as in many heterosexual relationships.

Versatile—Men who enjoy being either a top or a bottom. In a gay relationships, versatile men enjoy shared dominance. They're comfortable being dominant, passive, or both. Some versatile men let the nature of each relationship dictate which role (or roles) they assume.

Terminology Specific to Lesbians

Many of these terms have to do with relational issues or self-identification.

Bottom—The partner who passively allows her partner to direct the sexual acts, which usually consist of the bottom being pleasured; often (though not always) the "femme" in "butch/femme" relationships. In terms of power dynamics, the "top" is generally considered to be in control because she directs the sex; however, the bottom can also be seen as in control because she is the one being pleasured (like a gay male top being orally fellated).

Butch—A woman masculine in her dress and behavior; usually is sexually and romantically attracted to "femmes."

Butch/Femme—Role-playing that replicates the "old" pattern of heterosexual behavior, with one partner being masculine and the other feminine.

Chapstick Lesbian—One who is unaffected, natural, and forgoes makeup and dressing in feminine clothes.

Doing an Anne Heche—Beginning as a heterosexual, later experimenting with a single lesbian, and then switching back to men (as did the actress Anne Heche).

Drag King—A lesbian who likes to dress in male clothing.

Dykes on Bikes—A group of lesbians who enjoy riding motorcycles and often appear in gay pride marches.

Femme—A feminine woman; usually is sexually and romantically attracted to "butches."

Granola Dyke—A lesbian of the Birkenstocks-wearing, tofu-eating, folk-music-loving, "earthy crunchy" hippie variety. Often she has unshaven legs and armpits and prefers the more natural look.

Herstory—The experiences and accomplishments of women as seen from a historical perspective; also, the composite of experiences making up a woman's life.

Lesbian Bed Death—A controversial expression describing the slow decline of sexual interaction between lesbian partners in a couple. See Chapter 9.

Lipstick Lesbian—A feminine woman who wears makeup and enjoys the stereotypically feminine role. She can be attracted to other lipstick lesbians or more masculine lesbians.

Packing—Wearing a strap-on dildo either for sex or hidden under her clothes while out in public. Usually she is considered the "butch" in the relationship.

Power Dyke—A lesbian who has gained a position of power professionally or politically, either in the LGBT community or the world at large.

Sapphist—A lesbian of culture and refinement.

Separatism—An ideological stance in which women minimize interactions with men and with women who relate to men. In the early years of the feminist movement, some lesbians chose to avoid interacting with males in order to distance themselves from male-dominated society. The idea was that women could never truly understand themselves as powerful beings if they were immersed in the dominant, sexist culture. They believed that even well-meaning men were sexist and influenced by the patriarchy. Avoiding all men was impossible, but they chose to have all of their significant relationships with women. From lesbian separatism the idea of women-only spaces came into being at concerts, conferences, and festivals.

Stone Butch—A lesbian who gets pleasure from pleasing her partner but does not like to be touched sexually.

Top—The partner who assertively directs the sexual acts, which mostly consist of pleasuring the bottom; often (though not always) the "butch" in "butch/femme" relationships.

Womyn—A variation of the word *woman* that is purposely misspelled by feminists and lesbians who find it offensive to have the suffix "man" in *woman*. Not all feminists/lesbians like this term, but it's been claimed as a subtle empowerment tool by both groups. Some lesbians go through a developmental stage during their identify formation of being anti-male and use this spelling to correct the sexism and patriarchy they have suffered.

Womynfest—An all-women's festival, primarily lesbian, that began 30 years ago and is held each summer in Michigan.

Other Expressions

Beard—A gay man or lesbian's straight spouse.

Closeted—A term used to describe lesbians, gays, or bisexuals who hides their identity.

Fag-Hag—A straight woman who prefers to socialize primarily with gay men. This term was popularized by the television show *Will & Grace*, in which the title character Grace creates a life around her gay friend Will. Often such women suffer low self-esteem and have issues with heterosexual men.

Fisting—Slowly inserting the hand and forearm into the anus or vagina by keeping the fingers straight and close together and then typically (though not always) clenching into a fist.

Gaydar—The ability to intuit whether a person is gay or lesbian; a take-off on the word *radar*.

Gay Friendly—A term used to describe nongays who arc allies and supporters of gays and lesbians.

On the Down Low (or "On the DL")—A term used to describe men who do not self-identify as gay but who enjoy homoerotic and homosexual sex and secretively seek it out.

Out of the Closet (or just "Out")—Being open or public about one's orientation. Some people are "out" in some settings (for example, with friends) but not in others (at work or with family).

Passing—Pretending to be straight by presenting physically, behaviorally, and verbally as if one were heterosexual.

Straight-Acting—A term popularly used by gay men to refer to masculine, gay, "macho, macho men"; sometimes used by lesbians as well to describe effeminate lesbians. Actually it is an internalized homophobic word that equates male heterosexuality with masculinity and being gay with effeminacy.

Straight But Not Narrow—A term used to describe gay friendly heterosexuals who are supportive of gays and lesbians.

Code Words and Symbols

Over the years, gays and lesbians coined words and expressions to let them speak openly in public settings where they weren't out.

Family—Someone who is part of the gay or lesbian community, though usually closeted. Often a gay person will say "he's family" about someone he knows to be gay.

Friend of Dorothy—A take-off on "Friends of Bill," a euphemism that members of Alcoholics Anonymous use to "pass" in the presence of ordinary social drinkers. "Friend of Dorothy" is usually used by gay men as a way of identifying themselves or someone else as gay. On the daily calendar of cruise ships (both gay and straight) "Friends of Dorothy" is used to identify a gay A.A. meeting.

Black Triangle—Lesbians began wearing black triangles in remembrance of lesbians killed by the Nazis during World War II. The Nazis not only targeted Jews but also rounded up millions of homosexuals, gypsies, prostitutes, and "antisocials." Although they assigned lesbians no specific color patch, some believe that lesbians were grouped with other "antisocials," who wore a black triangle. Lesbians today sometimes wear black-triangle buttons or jewelry as a symbol of pride and as a covert way to identify themselves.

Pink Triangle—The Nazis forced men of homosexual orientation to wear pink triangles on their clothing. Gay men today have reclaimed the pink triangle, along with other former badges of shame such as the term *queer*, and turned it into as a symbol of strength and solidarity.

Rainbow Flag—In 1978, Gilbert Baker of San Francisco designed a flag with six stripes, each in a different color of the rainbow, as a symbol of gay and lesbian community and pride. It quickly replaced the pink-triangle symbol, which until then had been the most popular symbol of gay pride. You'll now see it used in gay pride marches, on bumper stickers and decals, as well as in storefronts to indicate that a business is gay-owned or gay friendly.

Drug Terms

The following drugs are popular at gay male circuit parties and bathhouses. Although some lesbians also use such drugs, especially while clubbing with gay male friends, they don't play a role in the lesbian community.

Crank/Crystal Meth/Ice/Tina—Considered a "party drug," crystal methamphetamine is one of the fastest-growing drugs in the gay community. It provides a quick sexual arousal and the ability to stay up and aroused all night or even for days. Long-term, it inhibits penile erection, causing users to go from tops to bottoms, requiring Viagra or other erectile medications, and risking HIV infection through unsafe sex due to impaired judgment. Crystal meth is highly addictive and harder to kick than most other drugs, even crack cocaine.

Ecstasy—A party drug widely used at circuit parties. Originally prescribed for physical and mental pain relief and as an adjunct to psychotherapy, it quickly became a street drug that was abused at rave parties and by gay men. It is now illegal.

Poppers—Amyl nitrite, an inhaled stimulant commonly used by gay men to enhance sexual arousal. Once a party drug used at tea dances and gay clubs, it is now used only as a sex drug in the bedroom and while cruising. Thought to contribute to HIV infection in 1989, it was banned for sale at all locations such as porn shops and bathhouses. However, urban gay male culture continued selling it, and it is widely available on the Internet, where websites use coded words such as "leather cleaner" or "liquid incense" to market it. Although it does not cause HIV infection, it does impair reasoning, putting users at risk for unsafe sexual practices.

Poppers in their present form are little brown bottles containing a liquid mixture of volatile nitrites. When inhaled during arousal and before orgasm, poppers seem to enhance and prolong the sensation. Poppers facilitate anal intercourse by relaxing the muscles in the rectum and deadening any sense of discomfort.

Tweaker—Someone who is heavily under the influence of crystal meth. The expression is: "He is tweaked" or "He is tweaking."

Derogatory and Offensive Words

When I was a boy, degrading, humiliating names like "faggot" and "queer" were hurled at me repeatedly. Today, younger kids and teenagers still use "gay" to degrade and humiliate others. You can hear "That is so gay!" in school corridors and in the malls. Like slang expressions such as "I was gypped" (derived from gypsies being thieves), these slurs have become so commonplace that people use them without even knowing where they originated or how they might offend.

Alternative Lifestyle—For gays and lesbians, *heterosexuality* is the alternative lifestyle. Use of the term *alternative lifestyle* to refer to gays and lesbians implies that being gay is a choice.

Breeder—What some gays and lesbians derogatively call heterosexuals.

Dyke—A term sometimes reclaimed and used with positive connotations in the gay and lesbian community to describe lesbians but considered offensive when used by heterosexuals.

Fag—Commonly believed to be derived from the word *faggot*, a term sometimes reclaimed and used with positive connotations in the gay and lesbian community to describe gay men but considered offensive when used by heterosexuals.

Gay or Lesbian Lifestyle—Most gays and lesbians say they have a "life," not a "lifestyle." As a gay comic once said, "It is like my dog. He doesn't have a lifestyle—he just has a life!" Like the term *sexual preference*, *lifestyle* implies that being gay is a choice.

Sexual Preference—An offensive term when used to describe a person's sexual orientation, as it implies that homosexuality is consciously chosen or "preferred" rather than innate. Used correctly, *sexual preference* refers to what makes up one's arousal template and brings one sexual stimulation and fulfillment. For example, one's sexual preferences might include oral stimulation but not penetration.

References

Aarons, L. (1996). *Prayers for Bobby: A mother's coming to terms with the suicide of her gay son.* New York: HarperCollins.

Ainsworth, M., Blehar, M., Waters, E., & Wall, S. (1978). *Patterns of attachment: A psychological study of the strange situation.* Hillsdale, NJ: Erlbaum.

Alexander, C. J., & Nunno, V. (1996). Narcissism and egocentricity in gay men. In C. J. Alexander (Ed.), *Gay and lesbian mental health: A sourcebook for practitioners* (pp. 1–13). New York: Haworth Press.

American Psychiatric Association. (1968). *Diagnostic and Statistical Manual of Mental Disorders* (2nd ed.). Washington, DC: Author.

American Psychiatric Association. (1980). *Diagnostic and Statistical Manual of Mental Disorders* (3rd ed.). Washington, DC: Author.

American Psychiatric Association. (1987). *Diagnostic and Statistical Manual of Mental Disorders* (3rd ed., rev.). Washington, DC: Author.

American Psychiatric Association. (1994). *Diagnostic and Statistical Manual of Mental Disorders* (4th ed.). Washington, DC: Author.

Amico, J. (2003). Healing from spiritual abuse: Assisting gay and lesbian clients. *Addiction Professional, 1*(9), 18–20.

Anderson, J. R., & Barret, R. L. (2001). *Ethics in HIV-related psychotherapy: Clinical decision making in complex cases.* Washington, DC: American Psychological Association.

Baker, J. M. (2002). *How homophobia hurts children.* Binghamton, NY: Haworth.

Ball, A. L. (2004, December). When gay men happen to straight women. *O, The Oprah Magazine,* 236–265.

Barron, N. (1998). Living into my body. In D. Atkins (Ed.), *Looking queer: Body image and identity in lesbian, bisexual, gay and transgender communities* (pp. 5–15). Binghamton, NY: Harrington Park.

Bartholomew, K., & Horowitz, L. (1991). Attachment styles among young adults. *Journal of Personality and Social Psychology, 61*, 226–244.

Bass, E. & Davis, L. (1988). *The courage to heal: A guide for women survivors of child sexual abuse.* New York: Harper & Row.

Berzon, B. (2001). *Positively Gay,* 3rd Edition, Revised and Updated. Berkeley, CA: Celestial Arts.

Berzon, B. (2004). *Permanent partners: Building gay and lesbian relationships that last* (Rev. ed.). New York: Plume.

Besen, W. R. (2003). *Anything but straight: Unmasking the scandals and lies behind the ex-gay myth.* Binghamton, NY: Harrington Park.

Biaggio, M., Coan, S., & Adams, W. (2002). Couple's therapy for lesbians: Understanding merger and the impact of homophobia. *The Journal of Lesbian Studies, 6*(1), 129–138.

Bieber I., Dain, H. J., Dince, P. R., Drellich, M. G., Grand, H. G., Gundlach, R. H., Kremer, M. W., et al. (1962). *Homosexuality: A psychoanalytic study.* New York: Basic.

Blumstein, P., & Schwartz, P. (1983). *American couples.* New York: William Morrow.

Bowlby, J. (1988). *A secure base: Parent-child attachment and healthy human development.* London: Routledge.

Boykin, K. (2005). *Beyond the down low: Sex, lies, and denial in black America.* New York: Carroll & Graf.

Britton, P. (2005). *The art of sex coaching: Expanding your practice.* New York: Norton.

Brown, L. S. (1989). Lesbians, gay men and their families: Common clinical issues. *Journal of Gay and Lesbian Psychotherapy, 1*(1), 65–77.

Buloff, B., & Osterman, M. (1995). Queer reflections: Mirroring and the lesbian experience of self. In S. Iasenza & J. M. Glassgold (Eds.), *Lesbians and psychoanalysis: Revolutions in theory and practice* (pp. 93–106). New York: Free Press.

Buxton, A. P. (1994). *The other side of the closet: The coming-out crisis for straight spouses.* New York: John Wiley and Sons.

Buxton, A. P. (2006). Counseling heterosexual spouses of bisexual men and women and bisexual heterosexual couples: Affirmative approaches. In R. Fox (Ed.), *Affirmative psychotherapy with bisexual women and bisexual men* (pp. 106–135). Binghamton, NY: Harrington Park.

Campbell, R. J. (1988). *Campbell's psychiatric dictionary* (8th ed.). New York: Oxford University Press.

Carnes, P. (1997). *Sexual anorexia: Overcoming sexual self-hatred*. Center City, MN: Hazelden.

Carnes, P. (2001). *Out of the shadows: Understanding sexual addiction* (3rd ed.). Center City, MN: Hazelden.

Cass, V. (1979). Homosexual identity formation: A theoretical model. *Journal of Homosexuality, 4*(3), 219–235.

Chernin, J. N., & Johnson, M. R. (2003). *Affirmative psychotherapy and counseling for lesbians and gay men*. Thousand Oaks, CA: Sage.

Clark, D. (2004). *Loving Someone Gay,* 4th Edition, Revised and Updated. Berkeley, CA: Celestial Arts.

Coleman, E. (1981/1982). Developmental stages of the coming out process. *Journal of Homosexuality, 7*(2-3), 31–43.

Corley, D., & Kort, J. (2006, September). The sex addicted mixed-orientation marriage: Examining attachment styles, internalized homophobia and viability of marriage after disclosure. *Journal of Sexual Addiction & Compulsivity, 13*(2–3), 167–193.

Dahir, M. (2001, February 21). A gay thing, *Windy City Times.*

Diamond, L. (2003). What does sexual orientation orient? *Psychological Review, 110*(1), 173–192.

Diamond, L. M. (2004). Emerging perspectives on distinctions between romantic love and sexual desire. *Current Directions in Psychological Science, 13*, 116–119.

Downey, J. I., & Friedman, R. C. (2002). *Sexual orientation and psychoanalysis: Sexual science and clinical practice*. New York: Columbia University Press.

Drescher, J. (1996). Psychoanalytic subjectivity and male homosexuality. In R. P. Cabaj & T. S. Stein (Eds.), *Textbook of homosexuality and mental health* (pp. 173–187). Washington DC: American Psychiatric Press.

Drescher, J. (1998). *Psychoanalytic therapy and the gay man*. Hillsdale, NJ: The Analytic Press.

Drescher, J., & Merlino, J. P. (2007). *American psychiatry and homosexuality: An oral history*. Binghamton, NY: Harrington Park.

Duberman, M. (1991). *Cures: A gay man's odyssey*. New York: Dutton.

Duberman, M. (1993). *Stonewall*. New York: Plume.

Erickson, J. M. (1997). *The life cycle completed*. New York: Norton.

Exner, J. E., Jr. (1969). Rorschach responses as an index of narcissism. *Journal of Projective Techniques and Personality Assessment, 33*, 324–330.

Falco, K. (1991). *Psychotherapy with lesbian clients: Theory into practice*. New York: Brunner/Mazel.

Falco, K. (1996). Psychotherapy with women who love women. In R. Cabaj & T. Stein (Eds.), *Textbook of homosexuality and mental health* (pp. 397–412). Washington, DC: American Psychiatric Association.

Fisher, H. (2004). *Why we love.* New York: Henry Holt.

Friedman, R. C., & Downey, J. I. (2002). *Sexual orientation and psychoanalysis: Sexual science and clinical practice.* New York: Columbia University Press.

Gartner, R. B. (1999). *Betrayed as boys: Psychodynamic treatment of sexually abused men.* New York: Guilford Press.

Gartner, R. B. (2005). *Beyond betrayal: Taking charge of your life after boyhood sexual abuse.* Hoboken, NJ: John Wiley and Sons, Inc.

Gonsiorek, J.C. (1982). The use of diagnostic concepts in working with gay and lesbian populations. *Journal of Homosexuality, 7*(2-3), 9–20.

Gottman, J. (2004). What we've learned: What makes same-sex relationships succeed or fail? Retrieved June 20, 2007, from www.gottman.com.

Gould, D. (1995). A critical examination of the notion of pathology in psychoanalysis. In J. Glassgold & S. Iasenza (Eds.), *Lesbians and psychoanalysis: Revolutions in theory and practice* (pp. 3 17). New York: Free Press.

Green, R. (1987). *The sissy boy syndrome and the development of homosexuality.* New Haven, CT: Yale University Press.

Greenan, D. E., & Tunnell, G. (2003). *Couple therapy with gay men.* New York: Guilford.

Hall, M. (1987). Sex therapy with lesbian couples: A four stage approach. In E. Coleman (Ed.), *Psychotherapy with homosexual men and women: Integrated identity approaches for clinical practice* (pp. 137–156). Binghamton, NY: Haworth.

Hamadock, S. (1996). Reinventing your erotic relationship: A couples group approach to lesbian bed death. *In the Family Magazine, 2*(2), 6.

Hanley-Hackenbruck, P. (1989). Psychotherapy and the coming out process. *Journal of Gay and Lesbian Psychotherapy, 1*(1), 21–39.

Hardin, K. N., & Hall, M. (2001). *Queer blues: The lesbian and gay guide to overcoming depression.* Oakland, CA: New Harbinger.

Helminiak, D. A. (2000). *What the Bible really says about homosexuality: Millennium edition updated and expanded.* San Francisco: Alamo Square Distributors.

Hendrix, H. (2001). *Getting the love you want: A guide for couples.* New York: Owl Books.

Herbert, S. (1996). Lesbian sexuality. In R. P. Cabaj & T. S. Stein (Eds.), *Textbook of homosexuality and mental health* (pp. 23–742). Washington, DC: American Psychiatric Press.

Herek, G. M. (2006a). *Facts about homosexuality and mental health* [On-line]. Available: http://psychology.ucdavis.edu/rainbow/html/facts_mental_health.html.

Herek, G. M. (2006b). *Facts about homosexuality and child molestation* [On-line]. Available: http://psychology.ucdavis.edu/rainbow/html/facts_molestation.html.

Herman, J. L. (1992). *Trauma and recovery*. New York: HarperCollins.

Hooker, E. A. (1957). The adjustment of the male overt homosexual. *Journal of Projective Techniques, 21,* 18–31.

Humphreys, L. (1970). *Tearoom trade: Impersonal sex in public places*. New York: Aldine de Gruyter.

Hunter, M. (1990). *Abused boys: The neglected victims of sexual abuse*. Lexington, MA: Lexington Books.

Iasenza, S. (1999). The big lie: Debunking lesbian bed death. *In the Family Magazine, 4*(4), 8.

Isay, R. (1994). *Being homosexual: Gay men and their development*. Northvale, NJ: Jason Aronson.

Isay, R. (1996). *Becoming gay: The journey to self-acceptance*. New York: Pantheon.

Jones, E. (1957). *Sigmund Freud: Life and work* (Vol. 3). London: Hogarth.

Kaufman, G., & Raphael, L. (1996). *Coming out of shame: Transforming gay and lesbian lives*. New York: Doubleday.

King, J. L. (2004). *On the down low: A journey into the lives of "straight" black men who sleep with men*. New York: Broadway Books.

Kinsey, A. C., Pomeroy, W. B., & Martin, C. E. (1948). *Sexual behavior in the human male*. Philadelphia: Saunders.

Kinsey, A. C., Pomeroy, W. B., Martin, C. E., & Gebhard, P. H. (1953). *Sexual behavior in the human female*. Philadelphia: Saunders.

Kleinberg, S., & Zorn, P. (1998). Multiple mirroring with lesbian and gay couples: From Peoria to P-town. In W. Luquet & M. T. Hannah (Eds.), *Healing in the relational paradigm: The imago relationship therapy casebook* (2nd ed., pp. 135–150). Washington, DC: Brunner-Routledge.

Kort, J. (2002, Summer). Gay men and their porn. *In the Family, 8*(1), 8–12.

Kort, J. (2003). *10 smart things gay men can do to improve their lives*. New York: Alyson Books.

Kort, J. (2004, May/June). Queer eye for the straight therapist. *Psychotherapy Networker,* pp. 56–61.

Kort, J. (2005a, September/October). The new mixed marriage: Working with a couple when one partner is gay. *Psychotherapy Networker,* pp. 83–89.

Kort, J. (2005b). Covert cultural sexual abuse of gay male teenagers contributing to etiology of sexual addiction. *Journal of Sexual Addiction and Compulsivity, 11*(4), pp. 287–300.

Kort, J. (2006). *10 smart things gay men can do to find real love*. New York: Alyson Books.

Krakauer, I. D., & Rose, S. M. (2002). The impact of group membership on lesbians' physical appearance. *The Journal of Lesbian Studies, 6*(1), 31–43.

Kubler-Ross, E. (2003). *On death and dying.* New York: Scribner.

Laird, J. (1998). Invisible ties: Lesbians and their families of origin. In C. J. Patterson & A. R. D'Augelli (Eds.), *Lesbian, gay, and bisexual identities in families: Psychological perspectives* (pp. 197–228). New York: Oxford University Press.

Levine, P. (1997). *Waking the tiger: Healing trauma.* Berkeley, CA: North Atlantic Books.

Lew, M. (2004). *Victims no longer: The classic guide for men recovering from sexual child abuse* (2nd ed.). New York: Perennial Currents.

Lewes, K. (1988). *The psychoanalytic theory of male homosexuality.* New York: Jason Aronson.

Lorde, A. (1984). *Sister outsider.* Freedom, CA: Crossing Press.

Loulan, J. (1987). *Lesbian passion,* Minneapolis, MN: Spinsters Ink.

Maltz, W. (2001). *Sexual healing journey: A guide for survivors of sexual abuse* (Rev. ed.). New York: HarperCollins.

Maniaci, T., & Rzeznik, F. (Directors). (2004). *One nation under God* [DVD]. New York: First Run Features.

Massachusetts Youth Risk Behavior Survey Results. (1999). Malden, MA: Massachusetts Department of Education.

Malyon, A. K. (1982). Psychotherapeutic implications of internalized homophobia in gay men. In JC Gonsiorek (Ed.), *Homosexuality and psychotherapy: A practitioner's handbook of affirmative models* (pp. 59–70). New York: Haworth Press.

McNaught, B. (1993). *Homophobia in the workplace* [Video]. Available from: www.brian-mcnaught.com.

McNaught, B. (1997). *Now that I'm out, what do I do?* New York: St. Martin's Press.

McWhirter, D. P., & Mattison, A. M. (1984). *The male couple: How relationships develop.* Upper Saddle River, NJ: Prentice Hall.

Mohr, J. J., & Fassinger, R. E. (1998). *Individual differences in lesbian/gay identity: An attachment perspective.* Manuscript submitted for publication.

Money, J. (1988). *Gay, straight and in between.* New York: Oxford University Press.

Morrow, S. L. (2000). First do no harm: Therapist issues in psychotherapy with lesbian, gay, and bisexual clients. In R. M. Perez, K. A. DeBord, & K. Bieschke (Eds.), *Handbook of counseling and psychotherapy with lesbian, gay, and bisexual clients* (pp. 137–156). Washington, DC: American Psychological Association.

Myers, A., Taub, J., Morris, J. F., & Rothblum, E. D. (1998). Beauty mandates and the appearance obsession: Are lesbians better off? In D. Atkins (Ed.), *Looking queer: Body image and identity in lesbian, bisexual, gay and transgender communities* (pp. 17–25). Binghamtom, NY: Harrington Park.

National Institute of Mental Health. (1987). *National lesbian health care survey.* (Contract N. 86MO19832201D). Washington, DC: DHHS Publication.

Neisen, J. H. (1993). Healing from cultural victimization: Recovery from shame due to heterosexism. *Journal of Gay and Lesbian Psychotherapy, 2*(1), 49–63.

Newman, F. (2004). *The whole lesbian sex book: A passionate guide for all of us* (2nd ed.). San Francisco: Cleis.

Nicolosi, J. (1997). *Reparative therapy of male homosexuality: A new clinical approach.* Northvale, NJ: Jason Aronson.

Nicolosi, J., & Nicolosi, L. A. (2002). *A parent's guide to preventing homosexuality.* Downers Grove, IL: InterVarsity Press.

Nimmons, D. (2002). *The soul beneath the skin: The unseen hearts and habits of gay men.* New York: St. Martin's.

Perel, E. (2006). *Mating in captivity: Reconciling the erotic and the domestic.* New York: Harper Collins.

Raychaudhuri, M., & Mukerji, K. (1971). Homosexual and narcissistic reflections in the Rorschach: An examination of Exner's diagnostic Rorschach signs. *Rorschachiana Japonica, 12*:119–126.

Real, T. (1997). *I don't want to talk about it: Overcoming the secret legacy of male depression.* New York: Scribner.

Reiss, B. F. (1980). Psychological tests in homosexuality. In J. Marmor (Ed.), *Homosexual behavior: A modern reappraisal* (pp. 296–311). New York: Basic Books.

Rich, A. (1980, Summer). Compulsory heterosexuality and lesbian existance. *Signs, 5,* 631–660.

Ritter, K. Y., & Terndrup, A. I. (2002). *Handbook of affirmative psychotherapy with lesbians and gay men.* New York: Guilford.

Rothblum, E. D. (1994). Lesbians and physical appearance: Which model applies? In B. Greene & G. M. Herek (Eds.), *Lesbian and gay psychology: Vol. 1. Theory, research, and clinical applications, psychological perspectives on lesbian and gay issues* (pp. 85–97). Thousand Oaks, CA: Sage.

Salter, A. C. (2004). *Predators, pedophiles, rapists and other sex offenders.* New York: Basic.

Savin-Williams, R. (2005). *The new gay teenager.* Cambridge, MA: Harvard University Press.

Schwartz, P. (1994). *Peer marriage: How love between equals works.* New York: Free Press.

Siegel, D. (1999). *The developing mind: How relationships and the brain interact to shape who we are.* New York: Guilford.

Signorile, M. (1996). *Outing yourself.* New York: Fireside.

Silverstein, C. (1991). Psychotherapy and psychotherapists: A history. In C. Silverstein (Ed.), *Gays, lesbians, and their therapists* (pp. 1–14). New York: Norton.

Silverstein, C., & Picano, F. (2004). *The joy of gay sex: Revised and expanded* (3rd ed.). New York: HarperCollins.

Slater, S. (1995). *The lesbian family life cycle.* New York: Free Press.

Socarides, C. (1968). *The overt homosexual.* New York: Grune and Stratton.

Solomon, M., & Siegel, D. (2003). *Healing trauma: Attachment, mind, body, and brain.* New York: Norton.

Stewart, E. F. (2002, Summer). Hot man on man action (and the lesbians who love watching it). *In the Family Magazine,* 13–14.

van der Kolk, B. (1996). The complexity of adaptation to trauma: Self-regulation, stimulus discrimination, and characterological development. In B. van der Kolk, A. C. McFarlane, & L. Weisaeth (Eds.), *Traumatic stress: The effects of overwhelming experience on mind, body and society* (pp. 182–213). New York: Guilford.

van der Kolk, B. (1988). The trauma spectrum: The interaction of biological and social events in the genesis of the trauma response. *Journal of Traumatic Stress, 1*(3), 286.

Weinberg, G. (1983). *Society and the healthy homosexual.* New York: St. Martins.

Weiss, R. (2005). *Cruise control: Understanding sex addiction in gay men.* New York: Alyson Books.

Wilson, G., & Rahman, Q. (2005). *Born gay: The psychobiology of sex orientation.* London: Peter Owen.

Wright, D. (2000). Illusions of intimacy. In J. Cassese (Ed.), *Gay men and childhood sexual trauma: Integrating the shattered self* (pp. 117–126). Binghamton, New York: Harrington Park.

Yarhouse, M. (1998). When clients seek treatment for same-sex attraction: Ethical issues in the "right to choose" debate. *Psychotherapy: Theory/Research/Practice/Training, 35*(2), 248–259.

Zur, O. (2007). *Boundaries in psychotherapy: Ethical and clinical explorations.* Washington DC: American Psychological Association.

Index